DOV FEDLER

Misadventures in Movie-making

JOANNE FEDLER

Copyright 2021 by Dov Fedler

First published by Tafelberg, South Africa, 2020
Second edition by Joanne Fedler Media, Australia, 2021

All rights reserved.
No part of this book may be reproduced or transmitted in any form or by an electronic or mechanical means, including photocopying and recording or by any other information storage or retrieval system without the prior written permission of the author.

Cover design by publicide
Book design by Nazli Jacobs
Edited by Karin Schimke

ISBN: 978-1-925842-29-6 (paperback)

ISBN: 978-1-925842-30-2 (ebook)

For my brother, Mot.

A note to my reader

When writing memoir, there are two rules to keep in mind: first, a writer must remember the reader.

The reader. The reader. The reader.

Second, writing is always about the story.

The story. The story. The story.

A memoir should track the truth. Except, it must also be true to the story.

This means there are times when a writer may have to embellish, obfuscate, conflate and conjure to keep the thing alive. A good falsehood should be buried close to what really happened. It's called 'poetic license', as long as no good truths were harmed in the making of the story.

In making meaning of our memories, we sometimes want to remember how we should have been and not the way we were.

And if you lie close to the truth, an amazing thing occurs. The dead rise, not in sombre shrouds but amazing Technicolored dreamcloths in celebration of a new life, a greater truth – one that serves the reader and the story.

I did write and direct a movie. Many of the people and interactions in here happened more or less as I've told them.

But in this kosher feast, you may find some little porkpies.

Yet it is all Beth Din approved.

I swear I have told the truth, the whole truth and nothing but the truth – for the sake of my reader and the story – so help me . . .

Foreword

It all happened in this one. The big float called the Twentieth Century drifts by as I cheer it on.

All too soon, it is gone. This was my time. It had Einstein, Freud, Louis Armstrong, Frank Sinatra, Elvis, the Beatles, Dylan, and Superman. It had everything. What a time to be alive.

It was the age of the cartoonist and the movie. First, there was Saul Steinberg, Ronald Searle, then Mort Drucker, Will Eisner, Jules Feiffer, Shuster and Siegel. It was up and away with *Mad* magazine, Blondie, Peanuts, Popeye and Krazy Kat.

Forget about the two wars and the Bomb. Hitler was only a bad bedtime story like the bogeyman. None of the horrors came near me. They hurt my mother, but then the people she mourned were only sepia photographs in a worn album, not quite real.

I had all the luck – right time, right place. I was born when the Second World War was already in progress. My parents were ravaged by the first. But come, no sad reflections here. I am not going to rain on my own parade.

I turn in my excitement to share with it with someone: 'Did you see that? Did you catch Bogart and Bergman, Kurosawa and Kubrick, Andy Warhol and *The Big Lebowski*?' But my crowd has dispersed, gone with the wind to their old-age homes, their faded recollections, but mostly to their resting places.

Beside me is a young woman who is fifty years behind me. Can it be so much? Everyone who commissions me for cartoon work is that young. Her job is in communications for a big bank. Her credentials are impressive. She does not lift her head or eyes from the rectangular, flat object she holds, a modern-day prayer book. Her thumbs move restlessly across it.

'How was that, and how about Gershwin and "Rhapsody in Blue"?'
She lifts her head briefly. 'Sorry, I was texting. Rhapsody in what?'
'Blue – Gershwin?'
'Never heard of them, but I can always Google it.'
I stare at her nonplussed. 'How did you miss "Rhapsody in Blue"?'
'Before my time.'

I ponder this for a moment. When I arrived, Gershwin was already gone. Yet in my head, he is ever alive, and I am filled with remembrance of things passed. Dare I mention Proust? *The Great Gatsby*? To have missed Gershwin is to have missed Mozart.

I turn my face to the road that has become a highway. Updates and tweets flash by. A sign reads, 'Beware – Information Overload'.

My memories lie like roadkill on the verge as Google thunders by and memories are just dust. My mind is only human. I can only grasp and digest so much. The gap keeps widening and stretches out of reach.

Nostalgia, as some genius noted, is not what it used to be. Gershwin is forgotten. I am out of place, out of pace with the quick march to the instant answer. Memory has always been my compass. I have found my way by what came before.

It has to be preserved, so I remembered.

How then shall I communicate with the woman thrumming her Android?

I have a story yet to tell, so I offer some notes at the beginning of each chapter and at the end of my tale, short answers to enquiries about who and what the hell I am talking about. Pause, if you will, for a moment and hear my white noise.

As the Great Millennial Parade begins to pass trailing tweets, selfies and emojis, I see a new generation following over the horizon who will not have heard of Justin Bieber.

Fame is a fleeting thing. Names are quickly forgotten. Here too you will find many that resonated so loud and long that we thought it was a summons from eternity .

So, dear reader, I recommend you the ever-present Google from whom you will come to know all.

DOV FEDLER
October 2019
Johannesburg, South Africa

CHAPTER 1

Zulu

(1964)

The film that made a star of Michael Caine. It was filmed in KwaZulu, recording an encounter between Zulu impis in battle with a British legion defending a fort. Mangosuthu Buthelezi, the politician and Zulu leader who founded the Inkatha Freedom Party, appears as a warrior.

What is the isiZulu for 'furtive'?

This is not some idle curiosity, like something I could satisfy with a quick visit to Google. It is 1983 and, as yet, there is no easy access to information to bail me out. The Androids have yet to invade. I need more than just a word to proceed. In this moment, I need to be fully conversant in and with the Zulu language.

I have come this morning, fully prepared to begin filming and directing a comedy movie called *Timer Joe Part 3* that I have written. I come armed with a tower of notes. My notes have notes that begat more notes. My producer stands beside me as I am about to address the cast for the first time. He is as relaxed as I am nervous.

'Good morning, everyone,' I begin.

He cuts in there to feed me a vital piece of information. 'They only speak Zulu.'

I have the first scene all mapped out. I even have storyboards to show both my camera crew and cast. This first take to get things started is dead simple. All it requires is for an actor to walk across the frame, looking furtive. It shouldn't take more than a minute to film, is my guess.

My camera crew is just two people, the man behind the lens and a Man Friday whose job is to hold and move stuff. That my cameraman, Hennie Basson, is in fact a major shareholder and driver in this venture is as yet unknown to me. My understanding is that *Timer Joe* is the singular property and brainchild of one Moe Mankowitz, my producer.

When I first met Moe some two years earlier at my studio, that was the understanding with which he left me. I am naïve enough to believe that making Hollywood-style movies for local black people is his vision alone. I will learn later that the apartheid government subsidised such movies as a transparent display of their fairness to one and all. It is the wagon on a great trek to profit, and those making the movies and cashing the subsidies need not be black. Hennie Basson sits up front, whipping it up.

My great trek to understanding is a long one yet.

Right now, I am caught in a freeze-frame *Matrix* moment, trapped in translation. I haven't a clue how to continue. The cast stands silent. They have no 'good morning' for me.

'How are we supposed to do this?' I turn to my producer.

CHAPTER 2

Wing and a Prayer
(1944)

*Don Ameche leads his men to defeat the Japanese
at a heavy cost.*

'We wait.' Moe's gum allows him to chew out. Even now, a waft of Wrigley's instantly transports me to Bree Street in 1983. Proust had his Madeleine. I have Moe Mankowitz's chewing gum stuck to my soul. Moe's speech sounds like wet dough slapping on a kitchen table.

In *The Color of Money*, Paul Newman describes Tom Cruise as a character. Cruise mistakenly takes it to mean that he possesses character. As the movie progresses, Cruise goes on to learn the difference. Moe is working on becoming a character. He thinks he is both Paul Newman and Tom Cruise, but he also thinks he is Martin Scorsese, or Samuel Goldwyn. He's caught between playing a matinée idol and a mogul. Moe is always on camera, in the movie of his mind.

My actor is on his mark, ready for this first take.

'What are we waiting for?'

Moe does not answer but looks down Bree Street where it meets Nugget. We are at the bottom end of town where the slicker shopping options metastasise into smaller industrial enterprises and little shops servicing working-class black people. The cafés sell Russians and chips, and lots of one-litre Cokes. There are shops that sell Basotho blankets. This part of town has taken on the mantle of Crown Mines, the concession stores I remember from my childhood.

Seemingly from nowhere, a minibus weaves across the width of Bree, heralded by a rage of bleating hooters.

The vehicle pulls up dead in front of us and brakes hard. The driver has done this all with just his left arm. His right one dangles bored from the window. Passengers emerge like miners rescued from a pit. It must have been some ride. The vehicle seems to sigh with relief as the last person steps out, and it takes off, as though from a pit stop at Kyalami. In a heartbeat, further down Bree, the hooters resume their conscientious objection.

A young Nelson Mandela lookalike – the Joe Louis haircut, the brush moustache, the razor parting of the hair almost in the middle – wearing a lavender-tinged grey suit steps forward. His tie is a rainbow. He is not just a face in the crowd. I remember him from the audition the other day, when he wore an aquamarine suit and another, different, explosive tie. The remaining passengers assemble behind him like a squad of cadets. On the left is a very large woman with arms like traffic cones, wearing bright-orange batwing spectacles with lenses that Hubble would be proud to boast. There are other women, all grandmothers by the looks of them, the kind of cosy matrons who might sing at their chores in kitchens. But who are they?

The Half-Nelson steps forward and shakes hands with Moe.

'Sorry, we are late.'

He moves, like the Duke of Kent at Wimbledon, down our short line of three to shake hands. Hennie Basson, our cameraman, is first on my left.

'Howzit?' he greets each one of us as he goes for the brother handshake. Oh, shit. I'm in trouble. How does it go? A touching of palms, a clutching of thumbs and then what is it? Repeat or retreat? How many times is it touch and clutch? I try to watch how Moe does it, but he has no idea. It looks a like they're playing pat-a-cake, pat-a-cake. Finally, it is my turn to muddle through. I am grateful when it is over but there are more to come. Now the whole team comes down the line to handwrestle. The Half-Nelson slots himself in between Hennie and Moe as they parade past. There are eight more handshakes to get through.

'Who are these people?' I whisper to Moe.

'His investors,' he replies.

'Investors in what?'

'In his business. His *stokvel*.'

'What is his business?

'This and that.'

'What are they doing here? What are they buying?'

'A piece of the movie.'

'But that is your business?'

'I guess,' he shrugs.

Moe is a master of the cryptic. Conversation interferes too much with his Wrigley's commitment, a lot like President Gerald Ford, of whom it was said, in the mid- and late 1970s, that he could not tie his shoelace and chew gum at the same time. Fake news has been with us a while. Moe too is no *schmoe*.

Stokvel? I am aware of the concept. My understanding is that working people pool their money to buy essentials in bulk from places like Makro. But buying into movies? As producers? That is an enterprise surprise.

I struggle to process the information in order to see them as bankers as, one by one, they come to shake hands. The arm-cone lady leads. There are only three men in the group. They look like weary, reluctant husbands dragged along on a shopping expedition. The women are as large as the men are skinny, like worn leather, their heads salted like pretzels. The women are demure, barely murmur and are reticent on the handshake thing. It is, after all, a 'my brother', not 'my sister', ritual, I think. I am a little panicked. Are men allowed to do the handshake with women or is it like the Jewish injunction, *bli yadayim*? No hands? No touch?

I guess they're here to keep an eye on their investment. When all the formalities are done, they gather in two rows to one side like a choir, each to an appointed place. Men at the back, looking long-suffering; the women boldly in front.

Can I now call 'action'? What the hell is that in isiZulu?

'Are we ready to go?' I whisper to Moe.

'Let me ask Khumalo.' He turns to talk to the Half-Nelson.

Khumalo turns to Our Lady of the Cones.

They converse in isiZulu and then he turns to tell us. 'She says they would first like to pray.'

It unravels like a dream rolling away to its own purpose that begins as a movie crew that morphs into a prayer meeting. In isiZulu, *nogal*. Moments before, I am about to begin to cue an actor to walk across camera in a furtive manner. It is supposed to be the easiest cue, and one to ease us all into working together for the first time.

The oldest of the three men steps forward, drops his head and folds one hand over the other. His voice is a surprising deep, warm baritone. He says a few words that I imagine go something like, 'Lord, bless us in our enterprise. Make this *Timer Joe* the most blessed of all time.' And then they are all singing like it is Sunday by the water; it is a 'Down by the Riverside' in a language I don't speak. I'm down for an African church choir any day, but not this one.

When they are done, Moe tells me, 'We're good to go, but don't say anything in English. We have to do this all in isiZulu.'

'What? Why?'

'We don't want to lose the subsidy. Maybe there's an informer here.'

Now it's a James Bond movie. This is all a bad dream.

Do I really need *tsorres* in my life? My career as a political cartoonist is in full bloom. Drawing cartoons is, after all, what I have always wanted to do. What am I doing here?

But there is the *dybbuk* that has been dormant in me since childhood. It is the Walter Mitty who has always wanted to be in the movies.

And this is his time.

Right here is where I should start making notes for that memoir.

CHAPTER 3

Fade into Memoir

Fade. In the editing of a film, the term 'fade' is used to describe a transition to and from a blank image.

Interior: daylight. Wide shot. A small kitchen of a lower-income Jewish family, circa 1945, Johannesburg. There are four people in the room. The mother fusses in the background with kitchen tasks while the men sit at the table. A young boy, lost in reverie, rests his head in one hand while he holds a yellow pencil in the other and draws. An older boy sits with a screwdriver, fixing a numbering machine. The father reads a newspaper. All are absorbed in their tasks, lost in their own daydreams.

A thought bubble, as in a comic, appears above the head of the older brother and becomes an animated object. It begins as a numbering machine whose parts disassemble, become a more complex machine, and then reassemble to the relatively simple numbering machine again.

The artist reaches for a dark-blue coloured pencil from a box of Eagle pencil crayons. The father sits opposite reading *Der Forverts* (The Forward), a weekly Yiddish American newspaper.

We zoom in on the younger boy's drawing, which is a violent fantasy of a semi-naked boy fighting a giant spider that threatens to engulf him. It is this dark, menacing creature that he colours in vigorously in an attempt to obliterate it. The drawing becomes an animated sequence in the untutored hand of the boy. There are flashes of cuts from *The Thief of Bagdad*. The boy's drawing shows promise.

Cut to the father and his fantasy. A great newspaper print machine rolls out the day's headline: S. FEDLER APPOINTED EDITOR OF *DER FORVERTS*, and features a photo of the father/editor. A copy boy picks up the paper from the pile and runs past an army of reporters hammering away at their Remington typewriters, to the editor's office. On the smoked-glass window of the door, it reads 'S. FEDLER – EDITOR'. The boy knocks and enters. The editor sits at a desk the size of a snooker table as he is handed the paper. The scene is governed by the roar of a printing press, which fades back to the kitchen to become the voice of the mother who feeds a steady stream of grumbles about her husband's lack of concern for his sons' futures.

Mom: Are you listening to one word?
Dad: Every single one.
Mom: Tell me one thing I said.
Dad: Tell me one thing I said.
Mom: I asked you should talk to the boy.
Dad: Okay! Okay! I'll talk. (Looks at the artist.) You will be a dentist. (He goes back to his reading.)
Fade out.

CHAPTER 4

Fail Safe
(1964)

Released the same year as Dr Strangelove. *Both deal with the breakdown of the fail-safe system created by America and Russia to prevent a full-on nuclear war.* Dr Strangelove *treated it as a black comedy. Its competitor failed for being serious.*

There is always an argument at our table. There is one for every season. We should have a Festival of the Arguments. I have learnt we are a stiff-necked people, whatever that means. Maybe arguing strains the neck? We even have a few angry words for God Almighty. Dad often engages Him even in the middle of soup.

'Why did You curse me with such a stubborn son? Why can he never open a book? He has no ambition.'

He addresses my big brother and the Almighty in the same breath. Sometimes the argument is about me and what I will become and do. 'Become' and 'do' are one and the same thing. Dad's ambition for me is that I be a dentist. What I want to do is draw. I am only the baby, the *mushinikel*, a mistake, born eleven years after my sister and six years after my brother, and am not as yet allowed an opinion. I don't know what I am talking about because, I am constantly reminded, I have no experience. I haven't had time to have much history. At six, almost seven years, I am hazy about my first three or four; so, in all, I have maybe three years to draw on. There can be no argument about what I will be. That one is settled.

But tonight is all about Motty and his lack of ambition. I know that Mot wants to do something with electrics and radio. Isn't wanting to do something ambitious? There is no ducking Dad's lectures on life. He has a master's degree from The University of Life. He's been a puppet, a pauper; never a pirate, a poet, a pawn, or quite a king. Becoming his own boss is a royal enough achievement. In his time, he sells vegetables and is apprenticed to a tailor. After the Revolution, he is forced to dig roads and clean public toilets. He doesn't want us to enrol at his institution of real learning.

He looks up at the ceiling as if there is an overhead teleprompt when he recalls it all, where every step along the byways is recorded in vivid detail for retelling. It's like the Passover story that has to be repeatedly retold so that it is not only imprinted in memory but is like an internal GPS that guides us down the right paths. Oh, he understands that youth is driven by dreams; but soon, just after bar mitzvah, a boy must think responsibly and turn to serious thought about what to do with a life. A life is not to be frittered away. I don't remember when the word crept into his vocabulary, but there comes a time when we hear no end of it. Time wasted messing with radios is frittering. At the top of the fritter list are radio and motor mechanic, and choosing a career that earns no respect, like tailoring, selling vegetables, digging roads and cleaning toilets. Our lives have to be better than his.

'Do you think you can just fritter with radios? Fritter! Fritter! Sometimes read a book. Don't waste time. Time is not for fritter.'

But Mr Reese, the headmaster of John Ware Primary School, has summoned Mom and Dad, and tells them they had better make other plans for Motty as he is unlikely to get to matric. This is like a knife to Dad's heart. Dad can only think in terms of university diplomas and degrees. That is what our ambitions should be. He wants us to be respectable, and the road to respect is through book learning. That is in Dad's book. Mr Reese has recommended that Mot attend trade school, but Dad still wants to rescue some respectability out of that. Mot must go to Commercial High, which really is a trade school thinly disguised as providing a real education. At Commercial High, you get taught bookkeeping, shorthand and typing. It's a respectable institution of learning to which to send a daughter in the hope that there she will learn a shortcut method to finding a husband. Daughters are for marriage and sons are for careers. The best careers are university careers. Trades are for peasants and for poor boys without opportunity, such as Dad is himself.

Dad's English has its own convolutions.

'If only I had the opportunity, what I couldn't have been – anything!' Dad wants us to have a less tortuous learning curve. One must be ambitious for the right things. It is okay to be a poet like Mom, something to do at a kitchen table after the day's work is done. What money is there in radios?

Why doesn't Dad see Mot for what he is? He's a genius with machines. It is plain to see, even for me. Is that so bad?

It is Dad's song of regret. He sings it often like an aria from a tragic opera. He wrings his hands. He paces up and down the kitchen floor as if he were in a courtroom appealing to a judge.

'He is going to have to go into the printing. What is left for him? What he could have been. No ambition. Imagine, in our house, we couldn't afford a book. A book? It was like a treasure, like in the film about the island. Better than gold – a book. Look! A bookcase full of books. One he never picks up.' It is an accusation against which there is no defence, especially after Mr Reese has passed sentence.

'Oy! If my father was here, he would cry. You don't understand the meaning of opportunity. Where's your ambition?'

Mot takes the barrage, mumbling something incoherent every now and then, but is wise enough to dodge an argument and let the storm rage itself out. Besides, he can't wait to get to the radio he is busy building.

'What am I going to do with him? He is going to have to go into the printing. What else is there for him?'

He reaches to the heavens. It is no good appealing to any earthly power.

'Ambition!' he cries out like Kane's 'Rosebud'. A lament.

Mrs Melamed arrives at the front door, worried that something terrible must have happened having heard the *gevalt* and the *tumul* from her own kitchen across the wall. I go to let her in.

'Someone died?' she asks, almost eager.

'Dad's seen Mot's report from school.'

She pauses at the threshold, considers it for a moment, and without a word, turns and retreats.

CHAPTER 5

The Paper
(1994)

An average comedy drama about the inner workings of a newspaper.

'What does he do with all the paper I bring?'

It is my turn at disappointing Dad.

'And what he draws? Cowboys with guns. Naked boys fighting spiders. What for subjects are these? Why never something with a Jewish theme? Always he draws Hitler. Such nice drawings from the Bible he could make. Moses, a burning bush. Moses in bulrushes? No! Cowboys! Killing! It's because of his big brother – a bad influence.'

Great, it has switched back to Mot. But it switches right back.

'Like a sheep, he follows. Reading comics and always talking bioscope. He is already at school. Time to read a book. When I was his age, enough books my father couldn't borrow for me.' Dad sighs at the end of this marathon *kvetch*.

How long before we have to hear it all again? Not long, I guess.

Mot and I are bound to disappoint him. He eventually gives up hope of Mot becoming a scholar but tries constantly to rouse in us a desire for study. He has high hopes for me. I am earmarked for a university degree. I am to fulfil his dream of having a son, a graduate. What more is there for a family to strive for? I will be called doctor but will never be called out at night. Such is the perk of being a dentist. He has the whole thing mapped out.

I only hear Dad's lament as an underscore to the roar of the world. At six, I live in the shadow of my brother's failure. Mot starts at Commercial High when I begin Grade 1. It is doubtful that Mot will get past Form 3. It is bitter times for Dad.

On Friday night, he tries to teach us to read Yiddish in the hopes of something we are unable to fathom. If school cannot educate his sons, he will teach them. It is exquisite torture for Mot, and I am scared he will grind his teeth to dust as he strains to read out loud. I am better at it, but my participation is more informal. The whole exercise is an attempt to kick-start Mot's ambition for classical education.

Dad will ultimately concede defeat.

It's a pity he will have to go through it all again with me.

CHAPTER 6

Stagecoach
(1939)

A classic Western that made a star of John Wayne.

We stand – from my left to right: Hennie, the Half-Nelson, Mogul Moe and me – facing the cast. The praying is done. The committee of investors stands politely to one side. Time to get real.

'So how do we do this?'

Moe steps back like a referee before a match to bring the Half-Nelson to face-off with me.

'You tell him. He tells them. He speaks Zulu,' is our introduction. 'And English,' he adds as an afterthought.

The Half-Nelson's right shoots out and we are into another round of the handshake.

'Howzit? Pleased to meet you.' I get in first as he pumps away like Muhammad Ali.

'Khumalo,' he jabs.

I come back with my own name and an appeal to the referee. 'Is he going to be with us for the whole shoot?'

Khumalo gets back in the ring to answer. 'The what? No shooting. Nobody with guns here. All good people. No *tsotsis*.'

With a sweep of his hand, he indicates the cast.

'All my guys.'

'So, who are you – their agent?'

Moe stands, listening to the exchange, and likes what he hears as he chews and muses. Agent. He likes the titles idea. Agent. Producer. Director. They give status to the enterprise.

'Ja, and dialogue coach,' he adds.

I guess titles look good when you are out to impress the subsidy committee.

'Have you read the script?' I ask the Half-Nelson.

Moe tilts the mirrored Ray-Bans to the tip of his nose and zaps me a dumb-question look. Is he about to confer another title?

Moe likes things short and simple. He likes titles but not extra costs. I am just getting to know him. All he ever wants for *Timer Joe 3* is a simple outline – two, three typed pages at most.

'Write a script,' is his instruction. He means, 'Write me an outline.'

The word 'write' in my book means pages. Lots. You have to put in a ton of words to pan out the few nuggets, if you're lucky. It's the old 'How do I get to Carnegie Hall?' principle. 'Practice, man, practice.'

My late mate Sam Dembo, a copywriter with whom I work in a couple of ad agencies and who dreamt of being a pulp-fiction novelist, talked me into buying a typewriter and got me started. The lesson is 'take yourself seriously and write'. So here I am, trying to get to Carnegie Hall.

Moe wants a Blake Edwards-type comedy, something *Pink Panther*ish. What he means is he wants something slapstick. He wants the kind of comedy Al Debbo makes for Afrikaans audiences around the 1950s. He doesn't know to actually say, 'Blake Edwards.' He doesn't know a director from a dentist.

I take to calling him the Man; sometimes, My Man; at other times, as the Irish do, Himself. Also, Mohandas, Manischewitz, after the kosher Passover wine and, finally, Munchkin.

What makes Moe run is business. His soul is that of an old-style Hollywood huckster – a wannabe Zanuck, a Goldwyn or a Warner, a hustler whose attitude is: 'Time is money. Just shoot it. Who has time to read a *megillah*?' Three pages are already too much. This tome just slows things down.

All my nights at the ten-year-old Olympia typewriter, agonising over typing and dialogue, of what A says to B, all my delicate humorous touches over which I slave, are a total waste. The hell with language. Let the camera roll.

But I am the director and don't begin to know how to roll.

I check out my dialogue coach for the first time, realise that the Half-Nelson is my passport to KwaZulu-Natal. It is with him I need to connect. Right now, I need a friend. I reach for his hand and another shake.

'Howzit, Coach!'

He loves the recognition and forever he is Coach. Are we now brothers? I hope we don't turn out to be Jacob and Esau, or worse, Cain and Abel.

'Would you like to read the script?' I offer my inheritance. Incomprehension jigsaws his brow.

'The what?' He looks the thing over, looks at the title page and begins to read.

'Scene 1, Take 1: Day. The city. Pavement. A man dressed in overalls walks down a busy pavement moving from right to left looking furtive.'

I know it off by heart. An impulse has me reach for my pen and grab back the script. I scratch out the word 'furtive.'

The director in me springs to life. I have a word.

'Tell that guy to walk like a *tsotsi*.'

CHAPTER 7

My Brilliant Career
(1979)

Great Australian movie starring Judy Davis.

My earliest lesson in life is, 'My life is not my own.' As far as I can ascertain, it is my parents who will determine everything for me.

It is only Mom who assesses whether I am well or not. She does this with just a glance or touch of the back of her hand to my cheek or brow. I may protest all I wish, and even, were it possible for me, supply a report from a doctor, and one from the second opinion, which concur in the declaration that I am in the very best of all possible health: '*Uf alle Yiddishe kinder gesogt.*' It should be said of all Jewish children, she would dismiss all opinions. Mothers know best.

How I feel is her business.

The business of my career is Dad's. What a son's career should be is a decision only a father can make. My cousin Sike gets to choose to be an architect all on his own. I want to be like Sike.

My big brother Mot knows exactly what I do and do not know and fills my head with all kinds of invented nonsense that I believe. I am his Chicken Little from the kids' story of my first lessons in reading.

Dad sends Mot for lessons in 'culture' and plies him with books. They pile up and are never opened, and so Mot will be a printer.

Rae, our older sister, is also under instruction, mainly from Mom, to find a husband before she turns twenty-one and lands up on the shelf, as she is constantly reminded. It is Rae who mostly tells me what I can and cannot do.

Mot takes me to the pantry and points to the top shelf. 'That's where she's going to be put if she doesn't quickly find a husband.' I check the pantry to see which shelf she will have to occupy and wonder how long she will have to stay there. She will never fit. It sounds like a rubbish story Mot would make up to tell me. He catches me out all the time.

Mot and I sit at the table, pursuing our passions. He has a cigar box, some batteries, a soldering iron and wire, and is making a radio. Mot can get hold of anything. How he has been able to find a cigar box, no one will ever know. Who in the whole of Mayfair can afford to smoke cigars? I sit across from him, drawing comics, using his Eagle pencil crayons, for which he has no real use. There is just one rule. I mustn't touch his tools he keeps in a metal box under his bed. How he acquires the box is another mystery. Mot loves a mechanical or electrical puzzle. A cigar-box radio is going to be something special. Mot can fix any electrical appliance. Even now, I have trouble with a simple light switch. But Mot is going to become a printer and work in Dad's factory, like our big sister Rae. Making radios will have to be his hobby. I want to work for Walt Disney, but Dad says I will be a dentist. I think I will also end up at the factory.

Why can't we follow our natural talents? Why does everyone seem to work so hard to bury them? Why did God make Mot a master of machines and make me draw all the time? Dad keeps telling me that I will keep drawing as a hobby. I think that, should God and Dad ever get together on the matter, there could be an argument. Dad is not afraid to argue, even with the Almighty.

God would say, 'Let the *boykie* go. Let him be a radio mechanic. Let the little one draw pictures. Why else did I make them?'

Dad would answer, 'He never reads a book. He is going into the printing. And he's a bad influence on his brother.'

Mom says Dad has a hard head. I want to be like Dad. I love Mot but he is soft. Even at my age, I know it's better to be strong-willed.

When I can get away, I run across the road to my friend Raymond Kudsee's house.

Raymond is like Dad.

A history of comedy
Part 1

CHAPTER 8

Abbott and Costello

A comedy duo famous for their 'Meet' films.
Abbott and Costello Meet the Killer, Meet Frankenstein,
Meet The Invisible Man, Meet The Mummy,
Meet Dr Jekyll and Mr Hyde.

'Abbott is the fat one,' I argue. 'I want to be Abbott.'

'No, he's not! I'm the funny one! What do you know? You're only seven and I'm nearly nine. My cousin is a comedian and he is going to be making films just like Abbott and Costello. I'm two years older than you, so I'm right.' Such is the logic of children. 'Have you got a cousin who's a comedian? No, you haven't. I know what's really funny! So, I'm Abbott.'

Raymond always prevails. He is my best friend and the law in Dodge City, but I believe I'm funnier. What neither of us knows is that we have our Abbotts and Costellos mixed up. In reality, I have the part I want, like the role as director I am now losing.

Raymond and I are crouched in the zinc tub that Lizzie, our domestic worker, uses to do the washing in our backyard at No. 21, Eleventh Avenue, Mayfair. Raymond lives across the road at No. 16. When we play Abbott and Costello, it is always at my house because that is where the zinc tub is.

For some reason, Abbott and Costello are always in a boat, or pirate ship, at sea. We play Abbott and Costello when we return from seeing our weekly Wednesday movie at the Mayfair. Sometimes we play Roy Rogers and the bad guys. I am always bad. But I get to ride a broom and wave a finger like a gun, making loud spitting noises that are supposed to be gunfire.

Mom allows me to go with this seven-year-old because he's 'a nice, polite, responsible, young man and not *a ghooligan, a vilde chaya*, a wild animal' like some of my associates.

I am out on parole here, having earlier in the year left kindergarten to go on an unscheduled walking tour of the mine dumps with two other boys. Our leader that day is Bokkie Baron, who is a year older than me. I do as I am told, and we go walking. When the police find us in the late afternoon, I think I am being arrested. I am a known felon with a record.

I'd never mention Abbott and Costello to Bokkie Baron. They would make no impression on him whatsoever.

CHAPTER 9

Room Service
(1938)

*Not the greatest, but how bad can a
Marx Brothers romp be?*

The Kudsees have a great covered porch at the back of the house that is their and my favourite room. It has a proper ping-pong table and soft comfortable armchairs. It is a room dedicated to recreation. It is a playroom. Maybe it is something only Lebanese families have, but then the Kudsees' is the only Lebanese home I know. I will bet there is not a Jewish home in Mayfair that has such a room.

In the homes I know, families are lucky to have a dining room. In most homes, rooms double up. The dining and living room are generally one, or the kitchen is often the dining room as well, and three brothers can share a bedroom designed for one and a half children. I even know of kids who have to share a bed. The lounge, if there is one, is strictly for visitors, and the furniture, which is covered in sheets, is never to be disturbed. If you are lucky, the single toilet is inside. The Kudsees' ping-pong table is as large as some kitchens I have seen. The Kudsees are definitely ahead of their time. Their world fascinates me. Nowhere in all the Jewish homes has anyone made alterations to their home. My *shtetl*-bred grasp of meaning tells me that alterations are something that only tailors and seamstresses, like Mom, do. Are alterations to homes another exclusive province of Lebanese people?

The Kudsees have built a guest room in their backyard where Mrs Kudsee's nephew, Al Debbo, comes to stay when he is in town. He travels around as an entertainer. He is known as the county's best Afrikaans stand-up comedian. Why is he not known as a Lebanese one? When I grow up to be a cartoonist, will I also be known as being Afrikaans? My parents will never stand for that. I am to be Jewish from start to finish, and that is that. The Kudsees are devout Catholics, and their faith, like a chapel, echoes all over their home. I am scared of the crucifixes but Jesus in the pictures always seems happy to see me.

There is, however, a dark cloud that hovers over the Kudsee home. It is the ghost of the oldest of the three brothers, Claude.

'He died of fits in the night,' my big brother tells me and then slams me with this incontrovertible truth. 'You were just a *pikkie*.'

Fits in the Night sounds like the title of a Hardy Boys book. Mot's friend Julian has lent him *While the Clock Ticked*. Fits in the Night would fit right in, but Mot will never read the Hardy Boys even when he gets a few of their books for his *bar mitzvah*. Mot says he saw the ambulance arrive 'in the dead of night' to take the body away. But Mot makes up a lot of stuff. It is hard to know what to believe. Claude died about the time I was born and the only reference I have is my brother. Claude's picture hangs next to one of Jesus, and I am never sure of how Claude is looking down on me. His bedroom door is forever closed, keeping his ghost locked away.

CHAPTER 10

Enter Scowling

*Enter Laughing (1967) is a semi-autobiographical play
made into film about Carl Reiner's entry into
show business. Reiner is most famous for his
association with Mel Brooks.*

Does Raymond Kudsee's cousin Al Debbo actually exist? I begin to have serious doubts. It seems he only arrives late one night from Bloemfontein. He sleeps all day and goes off to work at night. When he is staying over, Raymond and I don't play in his backyard.

'Don't make a noise. Al is sleeping. My mom tells me he only came home at three this morning.'

I look out the window of the Kudsees' playroom towards the face-brick room at the edge of the property. A curtain is permanently drawn across the window. I don't dare to ever peek in there even when I know that Raymond's cousin is away. All I know about the cousin is that he is a lot older, more of an uncle than a cousin, and he is the man who has everyone in Africa laughing. Why have I never seen him? What other secrets are the Kudsees hiding? Did someone else die there, like Raymond's older brother who died of fits one night, and whose bedroom is forever closed like a tomb? And if I am so close to Raymond, might I not also contract the fits in the night that killed Claude, like the infantile paralysis did in the scary time when we were never allowed outside our homes and had to beware an evil eye and wear garlic lockets our mothers had made for us to ward off the curse of disease? And strange that the Kudsees, being Lebanese, used the same garlic remedy, plus the crucifix Raymond is made to wear ever after. Secretly, I wish I had a crucifix in case of an emergency.

And suddenly, one Sunday afternoon when Raymond and I are laughing and playing ping-pong while Desmond, Raymond's older brother, watches, the back door swings open. The cobwebs of mystery are swept away. He stands at the door like a gunfighter entering a saloon.

Raymond has shown me photos of his cousin making pop-eyes and wearing a stupid hat. He looks like he could belong with the Three Stooges, Moe, Larry and Curly. Al Debbo is scowling. Has the sound of the ball plock-plocking across the table disturbed his bearish slumber? He doesn't look funny at all. No one bothers to introduce us. I am seven years old and not yet eligible for that formality.

He walks in to stand at the net, his arms crossed, to watch like an umpire. He takes over calling out the score. He throws me off my game, if I have the cheek to call my efforts that. I am still learning to serve and mostly miss. But Raymond is not critical of my skill. He revels in being my mentor in everything.

Al mutters at every mistake I make.

'How long you going to be?' he asks, with naked impatience.

We are playing ping-pong. When he gets to play, he wants a game of table tennis; and when I am grudgingly allowed a turn to play him, it is 'get it over as quickly as possible' and 'pulverise the *pikkie*'. He slams every shot across the net like a cannonball, rarely hitting the table. It's like playing against King Kong.

It is twenty-one love and no laughs at all.

CHAPTER 11

'When You Wish Upon a Star'

Song from Pinocchio *(1940),*
Walt Disney's second animated feature.

I go to *cheder* every day to learn about the Almighty. We live next to the *shul* and can never get away from there. The *shul* is like the post office where you learn everyone's business. Many boys are giving up the opportunity of a university education to go fight for Israel. Even girls are going, to become farmers wielding guns. If this is what *Hashem* wants, why did He make me want to go to Hollywood? Mom doesn't want any of her children going to fight for Israel. Hitler has already taken her family. It's enough. We must fight for Israel from here, but we must have no fighting in this family.

I don't spend much time musing about the future Dad has planned for me. He's as vague about dentistry as I am passionate about movies. But he insists that dentistry is a career that will provide a guaranteed income and will make me happy. Art is a respectable hobby for a doctor, but artists cannot be respectable. They get consumption and die young, as they do in the opera *La Boheme*. But Dad has the same aversion everyone has to dentists. He staggers home one day with a towel over his mouth, having had most of his teeth pulled. He spends the next day at home vomiting. Is that what he wants me to do with my life?

Not only do I want to be an artist, I want to be cartoonist. What do they die of? Just listen to the word. Cartoon. How can you take such a word seriously? It rhymes with baboon and balloon. It's a nonsense best forgotten. That it is not a career for a Jewish boy. It does not even warrant mentioning since it is taken for granted that any true son of Israel would, from the cradle, know better than to pursue such an absurd notion. His core good sense will navigate him towards a more profitable and socially acceptable choice. When I am older, Dad is certain, good sense will make me want to be a dentist.

This grand fantasy falls apart one Saturday afternoon.

Mom stands behind me as we check my image in the tall mirror of her wardrobe. She reaches over my shoulders and straightens my tie. She smiles then takes a comb to my hair to straighten my parting. She stands back to survey her handiwork, resting her hands on my shoulders and smiles.

'My big man.'

It is a big moment. I am all of five and am going on a date with Mom and Dad to the movies in town. Just me and them.

This afternoon is to be the ruination of me and the beginning of a great love affair. I am already in love with Walt Disney. I have no idea that Walt Disney might be a person. I am in love with Walt Disney as my big brother Mot is in love with Meccano. For all I know, Meccano might, too, be someone. Walt Disney is a universe in which I am to become a frequent flyer. I already possess a colouring book full of Disney characters, like Clarabelle Cow, Goofy and Pluto, in which I refuse any contamination by any crayon. That would be a sacrilege, which is a concept I have already grasped. We are going to town in the car to see the new Disney film called *Pinocchio*. Mot has better things to do, like dream of making radios.

All the way home after the show in the car, Mom and Dad rave 'such a vonderful film'. I am too overwhelmed to speak. It has been too big an experience to absorb. I sit between them as we drive home in the Hudson as they chat enthusiastically.

'Walt Disney? A genius!' says Dad. I have rarely seen them so animated.

I never hear Dad ever praise Friedman, the dentist. The truth is they are as excited by the film as I am. These are my true parents, without masks, in a naked moment of disclosure. I sit in silence. Ever aware of my moods and health, Mom checks my forehead with the back of her hand, for it is rare for me to be quiet.

'I think the boy has a fever. Maybe it was a mistake. He's too young to spend a whole afternoon by the bioscope. Too much excitement. He needs maybe an enema.'

I don't remember what follows and whether Mom subjects me to her universal panacea for all ills, from cut fingers to sniffles, or whether I have to wear a garlic locket to ward off any pestilence. Whatever penalty follows cannot diminish the grandeur of what I have seen this afternoon. My parents have no inkling of the tectonic shift that has occurred in my burgeoning world. Nor, indeed, do I. But a compass has been set inside me that is unwavering in its course. It spoils all hopes of me ever being called doctor. Career? Schmareer! I will be a cartoonist.

That magical afternoon never dims. For me, *Pinocchio* is simply the best animated film ever made. It is produced in 1940, the year I am born, with no computer-generated help. Everything is drawn by hand. Even after an extended lifetime as a cartoonist, I still wonder at the artistry that is *Pinocchio*. Its background paintings alone should grace a great gallery.

My parents use me as front for their own enthusiasm for Disney. Cartoons are locked into our collective DNA. They are thrilled by them. Yet, they take me to the summit of Mount Parnassus to gambol with the muses and expect me to come down and want to pull teeth. Dentistry would be the Monstro that would swallow my hopes. Whatever are they thinking?

By taking me to see *Pinocchio*, my parents have murdered the dentist. This is the day he dies and is buried forever. Over the years, long after Mom is gone, Dad will make futile attempts to resurrect him. But when he begins to tell me about the magical world of dentistry, I watch to see if his nose will grow longer.

It is inevitable that cartoons become my life partner. That marriage is made in heaven. But it is the mistress, movies, that fills my fantasies.

CHAPTER 12

From Russia with Love
(1963)

*The second and the best of the James Bond movies.
Stars Sean Connery, the definitive 007.*

Mom and Dad are talking Russian again. They have finally caught on to the fact that I understand Yiddish perfectly and am learning all little bits of gossip of so-and-so who has a *shiksa* girlfriend, the time Mrs X walked in on her husband in bed with Mrs Y in Mrs X's own bed – would you believe? – and how Mrs X tossed out Mrs Y along with the sheets that Mrs Y then had to launder. A *shande*! A *gevalt*! A scandal, a disgrace to the entire neighbourhood. And caught in flagrante delicto Mr X had declared unashamedly, almost proud, 'I come when I want. And also go.' I listen to these disclosures wide-eyed until Mom twigs that I am eavesdropping and following every word. I am no longer just an object, like the sugar bowl on the table. I've been caught in the spotlight, like Mr X, and am immediately excluded. They instantly switch to Russian.

Mom has discovered my secret pleasure of trying to decode adult talk. I have yet to understand the mechanics of sex and marriage, to assimilate all this secret knowledge. Now it is all in Russian – the language of secrets. It is impenetrable, except that like all spoken words, it cannot help but reveal its content – there is the unspoken part of language, given away by the glance, the shift of an eye, the hushed tone. This is the last time they will converse freely in front of me. But I listen attentively to the shift into the stiffer gear of the steppes, and my ears, like antennae, decipher names that come without disguise. I am left to imagine what it is about Mrs T or Mr and Mrs R that demands the hushed tones, and who might have to launder sheets.

My big brother and his mates too have their secret codes. It is a while before I learn the meaning of who is bent, who's a puss, and whose son has to sit in *cheder*. 'Gone to *cheder*' is argot, slang for 'put in prison'. That too takes a while for me to decode. Language unfolds slowly as my comprehension creeps forward. Like what is a 'puss' and how does one 'fray'? I know that to call someone a puss is the deepest insult. A cunt is worse. But what is a puss and what is a cunt? Only years later, do I decipher that some of the words – like *poes* and *vry* – come from Afrikaans.

I listen even more intently to the Russian and begin to decipher content. I miss most of it but somehow meaning creeps through the barriers. I imagine what might have been said. Mostly, I am off the mark, but I listen attentively and ape foreign sounds. Later in life, engaging people of different cultures, I become a mimic who can speak fluent Russian, isiZulu, German and Italian without a trace of the language.

Now, on the set of *Timer Joe*, I feel I am back at the kitchen table, trying to decode a foreign tongue. I get a lot of it. I realise very early on that in the eyes and ears of the cast, I am a figure of some ridicule whom they discuss quite openly within earshot. I detect that they are discussing, 'What is this *umlungu* doing, trying to direct us?' I feel at the outset that my leg is being pulled.

Though we struggle to maintain it, the 'Only speak isiZulu' clause quickly falls apart. It is obvious from the very outset that the instructions I pass on through Coach are perfectly understood by the players. 'Stand here' and 'move there' are followed long before the tortuous translation is passed on. They stand. They move. In perfect English. Nevertheless, we adhere to the rule. And over the three weeks that we spend together, I become aware of the conversations surrounding me. The cast assumes a vaguely mocking attitude towards me, especially when I display my anxiety, and there is a lot to be anxious about.

A clan gathers to a tight circle that this outsider cannot penetrate. They form a laager. Mom and Dad do it in Russian; Mot and his mates do it with unfamiliar phrases I cannot fathom. Here now, there is another language to penetrate. Here is spoken the argot and slang of the township. The cast is bonded in a common cause, and I am not a part of it.

I imagine fantastic conversations. They belong in a musical comedy movie.

CHAPTER 13

The Talk of the Town
(1942)

*An American comedy/drama film directed by
George Stevens, starring Cary Grant, Jean Arthur and
Ronald Colman.*

Timer Joe Shoot. Scene 1, Day 3. And action!
Coach calls out names from a clipboard. He and the cast speak only isiZulu. He addresses me in English. The subtitles are all in Yiddish.
    Coach (*reads from a page on a clipboard*): Dube?
    Dube: Present!
    Coach Khumalo works through a list. All but one answer.
    Coach: Tshabalala?
    He calls the name a number of times until someone else responds.
    SE (Someone Else): He's not here.
    Coach: Where is he?
    SE: Jail.
    Coach: What's he done now? Planted a bomb?
    SE: No. Sleeping at his girlfriend.
    Coach: Sleeping at his girlfriend? Illegally?
    SE: What else?
    Coach (*mulls it over*): Will he be here Monday?
    SE: Maybe yes. Maybe no.
    Coach: Okay then – Tshabalala?
    SE: Present!
    Coach (*hands Dov the list*): All here.
    I check it and point out the shortfall. I also notice that the same 'someone else' answers twice.
    Dov: How come he answered twice?
    Coach: No, only once. And once he was just answering for his brother.
    Dov: Where's his brother?
    Coach: Coming.

Dov: When?

Coach: Just of just now.

Dov: What does that mean?

Coach (*checks his Rolex*): Hmm . . . Maybe tomorrow, maybe not.

Moe sits unmoved through this, his chewing gum shuttling from one cheek to another in a futile journey. He finally bumps me reassuringly with his elbow. A couple of words manage to hop off the gum train.

'S'okay!'

'But we're one short?'

Coach flashes his enamels. A diamond sparkles from one tooth.

Very quickly, the set turns into that musical farce of my imagination.

CHAPTER 14

Audition
(1999)

A Japanese horror film.

I come to the audition like I am wearing a pair of Elton John's sparkly specs. I see nothing. Reality has left the building. My expectation is of a hall, nay an auditorium, with hundreds of hopefuls lining up outside, waiting to be discovered, while I sit like a Caesar, passing sentence from a plush front-row seat.

The auditions for *Timer Joe Part 3* are held in a space that has standing room for fewer than ten people. It is the front of Moe's movie-hire shop, too small to even call a lobby. It is a space divided by a counter. The twenty or so applicants spill out onto the pavement. It is like a school assembly. All that these people have had to do is show up, mumble 'Present!', get ticked off on the list and depart. In little or no time, it is over. They are officially featured actors. The preceding scene comes later.

We are not introduced as yet. For now he remains the Half-Nelson, who stands facing us across the counter as he and Moe consult a list. He, it appears, is the Man, who takes his instruction from Moe and Hennie. Moe's interest in the proceedings is just in the body count and the wages he'll have to hand out. He is too busy moguling to care. He has the subsidy; he is clearly in the black. Already in profit. He is out to shoot this thing as quickly and as cheaply as possible. Khumalo, the Half-Nelson, seems to be in charge. Whatever authority he lacks in his command of English, Khumalo is obviously the boss in isiZulu, I will learn later.

In principle, an audition is a simple process. Hopefuls come along, strut their stuff before a panel, the panel makes choices. An actor can be chosen for a variety of reasons. It is not always talent that dictates the pick. Sometimes it is just looking right for a part that secures it.

This is not the group's first such audition. Mine is the only unfamiliar face. I suspect that they were all here for *TJ* 1 and 2. I look at the checklist I have ready for this. Like it or not, I have my players. I get to make one suggestion. Furtive Frank, who is to open the movie, is my choice. He stands out in the crowd – okay, the few – by looking furtive. Would that I had watched Frank strut his stuff before singling him out so impulsively. Would that I had watched him take just a few steps. Of all the lousy picks, he is unforgettable.

In minutes, the whole audition thing is over, and we stand in the empty shop.

I feel like I am being played in a Jamie Uys, or Leon Schuster's shucks setup, or some practical joke my brother Mot would dream up. At any moment, I expect someone to rip off a disguise and shout, 'Smile! You're on *Candid Camera*!'

Already, I have a sense of what is to come. A vague idea tickles. The movie I should be making is the making of this movie. This is the stuff that comedy is made of.

CHAPTER 15

A Chorus Line

(1985)

A musical turned movie directed by Sir Richard Attenborough, brother of the now more famous David.

The time: 1983.

The place: the front lobby space of Megacity Films and Flame Productions at the eastern end of Jeppe Street, Johannesburg City, just before Doornfontein. The room is divided by a counter. It is a shop that hires out 16-mm movies and projectors. On the wall behind the counter are three movie posters. Two of them advertise the first and second *Timer Joe* movies. The other is a tattered poster of *The King and I*. Beyond that is a minute office space. Behind the counter stand the producer, the director, and cinematographer – just dim figures for now.

The lobby space is packed like a subway train at peak hour. It is standing-room only. A spotlight falls on Furtive Frank, at the centre of the crush. Music is continuous under the vocal.

The music is from *A Chorus Line*: 'I Hope I Get It.'

Director Dov (*spoken in rhythm*):

Step, kick, kick, leap, kick, touch. Again!

Step, kick, kick, leap, kick, touch. Again!

Turn, turn, out, in, jump, step.

Step, kick, kick, leap, kick, touch.

No one is able to move for lack of space. Furtive Frank stands dead still, responding to none of the commands. He has no room to move whatsoever. The music fades to silence.

Dov: Okay, can I see you walk?

A black man in a suit and tie, like a character out of *Guys and Dolls*, leans over the counter. It is Coach Khumalo. He calls out to Furtive Frank without turning to look at him. Their entire conversation is in a language Director Dov does not understand.

Coach: Don't do a thing unless I tell you. Remember, you don't understand English.

Frank (*shrugs, not making sense of it*): Why can't I speak English?

Coach: Because of the subsidy. (*Coach never turns to speak to his back but seems to be talking directly to Moe and Louis. Dov remains a shadowy figure on the sidelines.*)

Frank: Subsi-what? What's that?

Coach: It's a money thing. If they make the film in isiZulu, the government gives them money.

Frank's eyes go wide and he would fall about laughing but for lack of space.

Dov: No, I didn't ask for him to laugh. I want him to walk.

Frank (*unable to stop laughing*): Ha! Ha! The apartheid government gives out money for films in isiZulu? Ha! Ha! Pull the other one.

Coach: It's true. (*He, Moe and Hennie share a wink.*)

Frank: You're telling me PW Botha is paying for this film? (*Another paroxysm of laughter.*)

Dov: Could you please just ask him to walk across the room?

Coach (*to Frank*): He wants you to walk.

Frank (*miffed*): I speak English. (*Looks about him.*) Where am I going to walk?

Coach: Where must he walk?

Dov: Just across the room.

Frank (*thinks it over, shakes his head in silent disagreement*): You might as well ask me to walk across the moon.

Coach: He says he walks better outside.

Dov: That's not necessary. I just want to see a few steps.

Coach: Did you hear what he said?

Frank: Hey, I'm not supposed to understand English.

Coach (*to Dov*): He wants to show you outside.

Cut to exterior (Intercity Films and Aim Productions).

The cast leans up against the window in a row. Moe, Hennie, Coach and Dov stand at one end. Dov holds a clipboard and pen. Frank struts in front of them and bursts into dance with *A Chorus Line* music backing. There is a magical costume change and the cast now wear miners' helmets and overalls. They turn it into a gumboot dance.

Coach (*in isiZulu*):
Again.
Step, kick, kick, leap, kick, touch. Again!
Step, kick, kick, leap, kick, touch. Again!
Step, kick, kick, leap, kick, touch. Again!

Furtive Frank steps forward and does a perfect Michael Jackson moonwalk. Music morphs into 'Billie Jean' in the background. The chorus applauds.

Frank finishes with a flourish. (*Freeze to silence.*)

Dov: Is there any chance I can just see him walk across a room?
Fade to black.

CHAPTER 16

The Wrong Box
(1966)

A novel by Robert Louis Stevenson and Lloyd Osbourne about the last two members of an inheritance, trying to outlive each other by devious means. The comedy stars Peter Sellers, Michael Caine, Dudley Moore and Peter Cook.

I have wished upon a star, and here I am, forty years later, living the dream. I am about to fulfil my second ambition, which is to direct a movie. The dream, however, does not include that it be in a language I do not speak. Maybe up in that celestial adjustment bureau, there's been a mix-up, and what I have been sent in error is the hope of someone from KwaZulu. *Timer Joe Part 3* is quickly running out of my control. Right off, I know that I am wrong for the task.

I have nothing to do with *Joe* 1 and 2, other than to draw the poster for number 2. Up until now, I have been content to be a cartoonist. My reputation as an illustrator is on the rise. I have my choice of drawing commissions from magazines and for newsletters. Major ad agencies keep me busy. I produce three different comic strips. I design logos and mascots, and I am constantly drawing for *The Star*. Business could not be better.

A word of advice, which is the only preaching I will commit here – always *think* outside of the box but be careful when you *step* out of it. It ain't all clover. There is a lot of dog shit everywhere. This is my second venture into the movie business. The first is easy. I write and sell the script QED. No headaches to follow.

Right now, I am standing at the bottom end of Bree Street, a little like the great Joel Mervis would begin another brilliant instalment of his *The Passing Show* in the *Sunday Times*, of which he was the editor, with his classic opener: 'I was sitting drinking slivovitz with Ossil Broz waiting for a war to break out.'

I am standing with Moe Mankowitz, waiting for a film to get started. My show is passing before me. It feels like a war.

My war is with a language I don't know. *Timer Joe 3* is Word War II.

CHAPTER 17

Haak Timer Joe

That first movie script that I write and sell is called *Haak Vrystaat*, which a fan will immediately recognise is about rugby. My thin appreciation of the game, as a true white South African boy, is less than passable. For this reason, the phrase *Haak Vrystaat* is one I simply don't get.

In spite of being six foot one and weighing ninety kilograms at school, I am a bitter disappointment to my rugby masters. After one scrum, I scram. Very early, I determine that this is a game for watching rather than playing, unless one has a death wish. So it is somewhat surprising that I should entertain a scenario about the game, a comedy about a botched plan to kidnap a key Springbok player before a big game in order to win a big bet. I got the motive from real life: the shooting of a horse, Sea Cottage, in 1967, just weeks before the Durban July. He was the favourite to win that year.

I write in English, which is the only language in which I have any competence. *Haak Vrystaat* is a title chosen by its producers and investors who decide that the movie should be in Afrikaans. I want it to feature young actors. It stars has-beens. It is supposed to be a shoo-in hit. It is a miserable flop.

Even now that I understand it, *Haak Vrystaat* is foreign to me. It comes from the depth of the rugby-soaked Afrikaans soul and means, 'hook the ball, grab, brace, catch, clasp, clench, get it at any fucken cost to life and limb'. It means total commitment. Therein lies an intractable problem with language. Translation always falls short of true meaning. *Haak Vrystaat* is a war cry in victory or defeat. By comparison, the Maori haka plays like a fake call to arms, a piece of performance art. It feels staged, whereas the anguished cry of *Haak Vrystaat*, from the belly of a Free State supporter belching beer, brandy and boerewors, is the cry of a bleeding brave heart. It is more authentic, though in general, the All Blacks play better rugby, which makes *Haak Vrystaat* so much more poignant. Translation doesn't grab, catch, clasp and emerge from the scrimmage with true meaning.

That is the precise problem with *Timer Joe*. I don't understand my own movie title. This is the third movie in what is now known as a franchise. The two previous ones were obviously profitable. I doubt my posters in any way contributed to their success. But it is through that avenue that I have come to both write and direct this one. I am told that *Timer Joe* means a cool, older, well-dressed township dude who is sussed. He's a 'township type', information that is supposed to enlighten me, but in fact alienates me further. A *Timer Joe* is not someone within the circle of my experience. I am back in *Haak Vrystaat* territory – an outsider. There is a whole vocabulary buried in the hinterland of white understanding, an entire culture, denied to me. *Timer Joe*, though it is an English of a kind, isn't. It means many shades of cool and more, and I am not ever going to get the full spectrum of that. I am certain that it is a compound idea created outside the Johannesburg circles I move in. TJ is the old number plate of a Joburg vehicle. T stands for Transvaal. *Timer Joe* is a kind of paste-up moniker, street talk in the townships, I am led to believe.

What I learn is that there is a chasm between writing and realisation. One's first intention rarely makes it across that ever-widening gap. In the beginning is the word, but it soon grows into the Tower of Babel.

Right now, here in Jeppe Street in 1983, the title of my movie is of no concern. All I need is to know what is isiZulu for 'furtive', and for it to have all the nuance of *'haak'*, so that the cast can follow my direction.

Moe has done this all before. Maybe he knows the language.

'Do you speak Zulu?' I ask hopefully.

His gum makes a slow journey to his other cheek as he considers this dumb question.

'Do I look as if I speak Zulu?'

CHAPTER 18

Don't Bother to Knock
(1952)

Noirish. Marylin Monroe is impressive as a neurotic babysitter.
Richard Widmark plays a pilot staying in a next-door
hotel room whose concern is for the child's safety.
Anne Bancroft (Mrs Mel Brooks) makes her film debut.

He tilts his Ray-Bans and gives me what will in 2001 come to be known as a Derek Zoolander pout. Every move or utterance that he makes follows a camera direction in his head. He faces me, favouring his right profile.

He would like for there to be batwing doors so he can swagger in like John Wayne or Clint Eastwood. My door is always wide open as my angled drawing board faces the entrance. It has been open for fifteen years, since May of 1968. Mostly, I am absorbed in my drawing, my head down, my view cut off. Anyone can, as some snatch-and-grab artist once did, step in unobserved and swipe, in that instance, a broken pencil sharpener. I remain blind to the crime for two days after. The creak of hinges and springs, and the *wap-wap* of batwing doors as they swing open and shut, if I had them, would alert me to a visitor, welcome or otherwise. But even that could escape my notice. Chasing deadlines is focused work.

A deliberate cough has me raise my head.

He lounges in the doorway. Lounging in a doorway is the next best thing to pushing past batwings. Lounging too is an art. Marlon Brando and James Dean were masters of the lounge. Dean made the most of it. His version was to hide his face behind an upturned collar as he sank his head deep into his shoulders in a rebellious show of nothing in particular. Brando did it in a vest. No hider, he. Stanley Kowalski's lounge was a tiger about to spring.

This stranger goes for the Dean option, his expression a collage of everything from *Shane* to *Streetcar*. He pushes his leaning shoulder to the jamb, hands deep in his skin-tight, designer-washed Levi's, and straightens up to saunter over to the edge of my drawing table. He wears cowboy boots. Thus far, he remains the Man with No Name.

A deep impulse has me greet him thus: 'Howdy, stranger?'

He leans over to look down on me and goes for a hoarse whisper.

'Hi, I'm Moe. I'm in movies.'

Who would have guessed?

CHAPTER 19

Writers

My fondest memory is of Mom and Dad at the dining-room table, writing. Dad writes letters to his father every week. They are epic. The envelopes he sends them in can barely close. Writing has to be performed at the dining-room and not the kitchen table. Writing demands respect. But this memory is of them in tandem, working on the two books of Mom's poems that Dad edits and finally prints.

Dad respects writers above all beings. He has some dubious Yiddish 'pen pals', essayists and poets who bum off him shamelessly. He loves to feel the names of great authors like some exquisite confection in his mouth.

'Ah! Dostoyevsky – a dark chocolate marinated in cherry vodka, something Lindt might make?' 'Hmm, Chekov! Gogol! Tastes of coffee, no?'

Mom's reading is limited by her education, but her passion equals Dad's. Her history is of dire poverty and slave labour. She tries to keep up with his greater word count but is an equal match as a comic. It is she who has the reputation of being the witty one. In Mayfair, both are regarded as intellectuals. Yiddish is their all. Mom is an aspiring poet.

When we move to Greenside and her heart fails in 1949, though everyone pretends she will rise from it and live a long life, the writing is clearly on the wall. She will die in four years. She is fifty-five at the end.

The four years leading to that drives the writing together at the dining-room table into high gear. Dad has promised that when the printing business is established one day, he will publish a book of her poems. Their twenty-fifth wedding anniversary is to be in 1951 and that deadline looms large. Every evening and on Sundays, Mom and her editor are at the table with the manuscripts stacked high.

I like to think these are the best days of their romance.

My second daughter, Joanne, picks up the writing gene, though she never gets to meet Mom. Jo is only born in 1967 and Mom dies in 1953. Jo becomes a writer's writer. She writes like I draw.

I believe that it is written that someday I too must follow the scribbled path. We are what we learn. I get commissions to write because unconsciously I present myself as a wordsmith. Writing captions, speech balloons and comic strips is not a bad apprenticeship.

I get the offer to write *Haak Vrystaat* under that guise.

I rescue the Olympia typewriter that Sam Dembo talks me into buying from a dusty closet to finally take this writing seriously.

I place it on the dining-room table and begin.

CHAPTER 20

Play It Again, Sam

A misquote from Casablanca. *The phrase is 'Play it, Sam. Play "As Time Goes By",' spoken by Ingrid Bergman.*

'How ya doin', Dave?'

Thus, Sam Dembo greets me every morning when he arrives in his battered Valiant to give me a lift to work.

'Not so great today,' I want to reply. 'That bomb at Park Station has rattled me. I know that guy Harris's face. I used to see him come to Chesa, the coffee shop in Rand Central in Jeppe Street just off Eloff. He could have planted the bomb right where I sit.'

But I say nothing. I want to have happier thoughts this early spring day of 1964. Everything beckons. I am just twenty-four, two years married, and yet to become a father or to make my mark.

Sam drives from Sydenham and picks me up on the corner of Fortesque Road and Page Street in Yeoville, which is the address of Finchley Cross Court where I have lived since 1962, when I became a husband. Sam is a copywriter and I am a visualiser at Forsyth Marketing, an agency in Loveday Street in the heart of the city.

Sam's wife, Rae, sits in the front passenger seat; I am in the back. Rae is a secretary or bookkeeper to some company. Rae does little talking. She doesn't get much chance but, like Jack Spratt's wife, she is a perfect complement to her husband.

Sam has a lot to tell. Every morning, he has something brand new. It is always about reading and writing – his twin passions. Around lunchtime, he will switch to talk about food with an equal passion. 'Whatcha wanna eat today, Dave? Boy, what I could do right now to a pastrami on rye. Don't even ask!'

Sam's enthusiasm is a roller coaster. If pastrami is his call, we will be having pastrami for lunch. But words are Sam's real staff of life. Every word he utters is to do with writing. He sounds American because he is testing dialogue for yet another pulp novel. He has enough rejection slips to paper a wall.

Writing is always his first thought. He insists on calling me Dave while everyone knows me as Dov.

'Dov' doesn't sit right amongst the dramatis personae of Sam's fictional world. A shamus with the moniker Dov Spade just doesn't cut it. Dave, I am.

Sam's career as a copywriter is about to end any moment, when one of his many manuscripts is accepted by some great publishing house and becomes a runaway best-seller, and his name an instant literary legend. That outcome is in no doubt – in Sam's mind, that is.

Sam's rightful place is alongside Dashiell Hammett, Raymond Chandler and Eric Ambler. A crown awaits him, and every day he is ready for his coronation, which makes Sam a totally upbeat kind of guy. We share and pursue similar dreams. I hope to make it big as a cartoonist. I am presently called a visualiser, that which in this new age is called an art director. You had to earn your stripes to make it as art director then. This job is just a step towards my greater dreams. Unlike my buddy, though, I am plagued by doubts that tend to bring me down a notch or two. Often, a black dog nips at my heels. But every morning, Sam raises my spirit with his infectious enthusiasm.

Sam has one book published. It does not set the world on fire, nor does its failure dent his ambition. Nothing will bring him down. When he drives up to the kerb in the morning, he is bubbling over with inspiration for his latest potboiler.

It's a murder mystery, or a high-adventure drama, inspired by what he is currently reading. Correction – has read. Once Sam starts to read a book, he finishes it. His eyes bounce around like pinballs. Superman could not read that fast. Sam claims to read some three to five novels every night and so the story changeovers are really rapid. He totally inhabits his fictional worlds, assuming the characters of his various personae. His first draft is already written in his head and these drive-in talks are just previews.

Whatever he reads, he remembers – verbatim. He repeats dialogue and hopes to come across like a New York cab driver or, even better, as Philip Marlowe. I quite expect one morning that he will arrive wearing a fedora, a Borsalino, or a New York Yankees baseball cap.

It is also my ambition to end up working in New York, amongst my real peers. All the great cartoonists of the world work out of New York, London or Paris. Dreamland is a funny place to occupy constantly, but it is Sam's permanent residence. I wonder who he might be this morning. Whoever he is – secret agent, assassin or private eye; Sam Spade, Simon Templar or James Bond – he wants to share his love of life. Even the news vendor from whom he buys the paper every day gets a slice of joie de vivre. 'Hey! What's new, pussy cat?' The vendor breaks out in a wide gap-toothed smile. Once he has the paper, Sam seems even happier. He would be happy reading a telephone directory. He would savour the names he found there and create characters of them all, given enough time.

The secret of Sam's happiness is simple. In his mind, he is a triumph. It is reality that needs to catch up. He has that puppy-dog quality of a true optimist. If Sam had a tail, it would never stop wagging.

As I slide into the back seat, I slip into a conversation that began in Sydenham this morning or late last night, interrupted only by the four-word greeting. Sam never loses the thread of a monologue. Driving with him is like my family tells me of my own driving – harrowing.

Sam does not appear to know which side of the road to be on. He veers from side to side, rather like his writing does.

Rae remains amazingly calm. Magically, we never have an accident. Bumping into a kerb, the occasional scrape, doesn't count.

'Hey, Dave, wha'chu reading right now?'

I am ashamed to answer that I am only a third of the way through the novel – on the prescribed list he has supplied me – that I started two weeks ago. So far, thanks to Sam, I have discovered Eric Ambler, Gavin Lyall, John D MacDonald, Ross Macdonald, Delano Ames – all great writers of pulp fiction.

Just say *The Mask of Dimitrios* and *The Flight of the Phoenix*, and Sam is in raptures. He salivates as when he is eating.

'Hey, Dave, how's the writing?'

We have stopped at some store one lunchtime to buy a ribbon for the typewriter he has at home. I admit to him that I have been swept up in his passion and have been romancing the Word a little.

'Dave, you must take yourself seriously.'

We leave the store, Sam with his ribbon and me with a brand-new, portable Olympia. I am going to be in big shit when I get home.

'When I make it, I am off to Hollywood,' he declares with unwavering faith. 'The minute I get that letter from the publisher, I'm outta here, Dave! Yesireebob! Holy Wood! That's where the action is! California, here I come! And I'll be writing for the movies.' He attempts a soft-shoe shuffle, a ridding of the restrictive, copy-writing coil. Dancing is not his thing. Sam has the flattest feet.

When he talks about where the action is, I'm not sure that it is the movies that he is talking about. Knowing Sam, he wants to stalk the seedy side of LA, picking up the ghost of the trail left by his undisputed hero, Raymond Chandler. There, we may yet see him in the fedora, wearing a Bogey trench coat, slow stepping the sidewalk (no soft-shoe shuffle here), a cigarette dangling precariously from his lip, his expression a mask of world-weariness.

Cancel that last bit. Sam could never do world-weary. He would be grinning from ear to ear. I will never tell him this, but he would never come up with a character better than himself.

He drops dead at thirty-seven, playing with his dog in his garden in Sydenham, Johannesburg, one Sunday afternoon. He never gets to write another thing.

Tomorrow is Day 2 of my movie shoot. I have some rewriting to do.

Tonight, I have to play Sam.

CHAPTER 21

You Can't Call Me Al

*'You Can Call Me Al' was the lead single from
Paul Simon's seventh studio album,* Graceland *(1986).
Its lyrics were partially inspired by Simon's trip to South Africa
and it was recorded at what was once the Royal Cinerama –
then, a sound studio – in Louis Botha Avenue, Johannesburg.
I begged an invitation from director Koos Hattingh, with whom I had
worked on the Zibi commercial, but it was strictly no visitors.*

Mayfair lies buried in the past. Al Debbo no longer lives with his aunt but in his own home in Honeydew somewhere near, or on, the Crocodile Ramble. It is a mission to find his smallholding. He stands at the gate, waiting for me with anything but welcome written on his face.

'You're early.' The greeting sours in his mouth.

'I didn't want to get lost.' My explanation sounds lame, so I add, 'Listen, if it's not convenient, I'll just take a drive around.'

That sounds even more lame. I've barely stepped onto his property but have already outstayed my welcome. I saw no sign on the gate that read 'Beware of the Comedian'. He frowns as he considers this option.

After an uncomfortable forever, he says, 'I still have to set up.'

I am all of twenty minutes early. Maybe he should have set up before I came? Why is he so resentful of my presence?

'You'd better come in.'

If there were subtitles that spelled out what was really being said, these would read *'Voetsek!'*

My visit to Al Debbo is at the behest of the Sullivans, a father-and-son team of film producers who want me, the writer, to look at what their chosen director has made of my material, of a film to be called *Haak Vrystaat*.

I am here to see some of what has been shot. The Sullivans have paid me R3 500 upfront for my script. Since the deal was concluded, I have had nothing to do with the further development of the project. It comes as a double surprise to hear that Al Debbo is the movie's star and director. Neither of these surprises pleases me much.

'I've had to rewrite most of it,' Mr Debbo says accusingly. It's like being told at school that your essay's no good.

He talks as he sets up a reel on an editing machine. 'I hear you got paid upfront.'

Since he already knows, what's the point of denying it? I nod. Again, I feel this need to somehow apologise.

I tell him how I grew up loving *'Hasie, hoekom is jou stert so kort?'*, the song that made him a legend on radio. The sucking up leaves him unmoved. My overtures just make things worse. It is hard to recognise him right now as a comedy icon. His bitterness rises like a toilet that won't flush and threatens to spill over.

I know that he doesn't have my name right.

Al Debbo has never heard of me at all. He is not a reader of *The Star*. His paper is *Die Vaderland*. He knows none of my aliases. Whatever name he chooses to know me by now is brand new.

I scramble for some common, safe ground. I'm here on movie business. Let's go for broke.

'I loved *Kom Saam Vanaand*,' I lie, mentioning the groundbreaking comedy in which he starred with Frederik Burgers. It was a hit, and the whole country fell in love with Al Debbo. In Bloemfontein, his hometown, Al and his pal, Fred, are still national heroes.

Citing his past glory just underlines his current failure and illuminates my newfound success. I have stepped right on the landmine of his resentment. To have to meet and have to show a reel of his film to a nobody-writer, whose money is safe in the bank and who awaits his approval, is too much.

'I made that bastard rich,' he spits out.

'Who?' I ask in all innocence.

'John *blerrie* Schlesinger. We got nothing. *Niks*.'

Made John Schlesinger rich? That's rich.

'He took everything. I made them millions,' he spews out.

Killarney Film Studios has been going since 1913, when Isidore Schlesinger, an immigrant, brought his New York City sass to Joburg and became a genuine movie mogul.

He becomes a king of real estate and insurance. He also likes the movie business and finds partners to form African Film Productions in 1913. Three years later, he builds Killarney Film Studios. The studio becomes famous for its African Mirror newsreels. He then buys Africa's Amalgamated Theatres, then Empire Theatres Company; forms the African Theatres and Films Trusts; and thus gains the monopoly over the importation and distribution of films throughout the country. And Daddy Big Bucks leaves it all to his boy, John.

Made him millions? Schlesinger? They owned Zebedelia? He made his millions in oranges? Movies were just a hobby.

Looking around me, I see that Al Debbo has made no big killing. It is a long way from 1949, when the movie was made, to 1976, where he and I are now. His audience is forever contained in the laager of boer humour. Even in the platteland, tastes change over twenty-seven years, years that have not been that kind, financially, for our Al. There is no Schlesinger for backup like in the golden days of *Kom Saam Vanaand*.

I tell him, Mr Debbo, that he and I once played ping-pong in his aunt's house in Mayfair, when I was seven and he was twenty-three, but, as an apartheid apparatchik once says, 'it's like duck's water off his back'. I was his first cousin Raymond's best friend? None of our memories conjoin to any intimacy.

Not that I saw Al Debbo that often in the Kudsee home. He was always on the road like an old-time travelling salesman, peddling his worn *schtick*, leftovers from vaudeville and burlesque, stuff now relegated to circus clowns. But still, it would be nice to be remembered.

With this rugby movie, he is going to resurrect himself. *Haak Vrystaat* is going to be his new *Kom Saam Vanaand*, another seminal event in Afrikaans film history.

It would be nice to have a thank-you.

Al longs to be up there with Jamie Uys and Leon Schuster. Just one more hit. Perhaps he already has a sense that this movie is tired and that he is not going to be getting any cheques from the producers. He needs a better story.

'Did you really get paid upfront?' he asks as he looks over what reel to show me.

'I did.'
'How did you manage that?'
'I had a good lawyer,' I tell him.

CHAPTER 22

Pitch Perfect
(2012)

About an all-women a capella *group in a college.*

In early 1975, Chris Rowley, a movie maker, comes to my studio to commission some artwork. He makes feature movies and not only commercials. He has just finished shooting a major production in Lourenço Marques (which has now been called Maputo for more than four decades). This impresses me and I start jabbering on about my own this-and-that ideas for movies. I pick one whose opening scene I have choreographed in my head.

'I've got his idea for a comedy,' I tell him wistfully. 'It's about rugby.'

I have him at 'rugby'.

'Tell me about it,' he says, crossing his legs to show off his hand-tooled cowboy boots, as he eases back in the chair to listen attentively to my idea.

Twenty minutes later, he says, 'If you write down that first scene, I have an investor for you.'

Haak Vrystaat is born.

CHAPTER 23

I Never Sang for My Father
(1970)

A widowed college professor tries to break from his domineering, ageing father and plans to leave. Based on a play. Stars Gene Hackman as the son and Melvyn Douglas, a leading man of yesteryear, who once played opposite Greta Garbo. Greatly depressing.

'What for a nonsense is this? You are now making a film?'

I am thirty-six years old. Dad talks to me like I'm six.

I have been in business on my own since 1968, established for eight years as both a political and commercial cartoonist. Dad retires in 1974. He wants to leave a printing legacy behind and, for his last major personal project, produces a collection of my cartoons. Evelyn Haddon, the giant company, donates the paper. Dad has been their constant customer for over forty years. The book is two hundred and fifty pages, which is a substantial-sized for a book of cartoons. I decide to call it *My Son the Cartoonist*, which is an apt title since Dad drives the project. He's a slave driver when he has to get something done. It is a beautiful book but for the really mediocre cover that I design. It really is one of my worst pieces.

Dad, like Frank Sinatra, cannot remain retired. Not working is not an option. The book behind him, he embarks on writing his autobiography. He writes it in English, and he commandeers my sister Rae and me to help edit it. Even that is not busy enough for him. He goes to the factory every day though he no longer works at the stone producing settings. Instead, he sits in the office and checks the administration of the business, the task delegated to my sister and her husband. His presence is disruptive. No matter our age, we all remain his children, and Father always knows best.

My having an office, a place of business, is a godsend for Rae and Boomie. Now that I too am finally a responsible member of the family, it is time to assume some duties, like having the old man breathing down my neck at every turn. Mid-morning, Boomie drives him from Central Road, Fordsburg, to the corner of Harrison and Commissioner streets, and deposits my father at Victory House. For the rest of the morning, he is mine. Unbidden, he takes over my administration and, of course, now I am constantly monitored in my business decisions. I am, after all, still the *mushinikel*, the baby, never mind that I am now myself a father.

Dad gets to share the golden years of my career, my 'bohemian days', where my studio is a great gathering place. He is there when I first share the space with John Meyer before he goes off to conquer the world and paint portraits of Madiba and the Queen of England.

If it were the Queen of England herself visiting the studio, it would not impede Dad in trafficking my world and seeking her accord.

'How do you do, Mrs Majesty? Do you know what for a nonsense he is doing now? Films. Bioscopes. This now he wants to do for a living. Go speak to children. Do they listen? Never!'

His concern is that I am going to jeopardise the business of which he now approves. It is his duty to see I do not stray.

It is eight years since I have left my last job in advertising and have been working on my own.

Clients, in various shades, come and go. I am open to anything and everything that will bring in a buck. I already have two children, and a third is planned. Kids are entirely Dorrine's idea. I love 'em but have never longed to be a parent as much as I want a meaningful career.

I am a dependable, diligent husband and father and my ambition is tempered by my duty to my family. But I am forever dreaming big. Some giant opportunity is going to come along and shoot me straight into the stratosphere of success.

My practical friends, John Meyer and Romain Orlin, recognise that I am not the stuff that true success is made of. True success is financial.

'You have too much self-gratification from whatever you do. You're just not hungry,' says Romain, always on point.

John puts it differently. 'As long as people are paying ten cents to see your cartoons in *The Star*, they are never going to pay real money for your work.'

They both have it right. Every cartoon I draw for *The Star* is like a major commission. John watches while I work and shakes his head. 'You put in too much work. Put in as much as they pay you.'

I cannot make this kind of calculation. It is what it is. Self-gratification takes all.

The problem in my perception is always skewed by what I want the thing to be, rather than by what it is. And now I am left with just my father to try to steer me right.

'What for a nonsense is this making films?' he presses me.

'I'm not making a film. I'm writing one,' I have to tell him repeatedly.

This encounter with the movie industry does, however, present a minor fork in the road, and the Walter Mitty-me is pulled to follow it.

Sheer luck has brought me an office in Victory House. My landlord is Cecil Amoils, one of my dad's oldest customers. The bright dream of becoming another Charles Schulz, Al Capp or Walt Kelly dims in the deadlines of every day. Bringing home an income at the end of every month is what drives me. Also, Dorrine and I have a special-needs child. Carolyn, our first daughter, is born with a hearing impairment. My focus is on making money.

Against all my expectations, things look up.

I don't ask my family to print me any stationery, half-expecting to have to go back and find a job. I have no confidence in Dov Fedler, businessman. But – it would appear – I am a business.

I have no idea how to write out an invoice or a cheque. My ignorance is astonishing. Even though I am using my neighbour's phone, which is an enormous inconvenience for both of us, work keeps coming in. It takes me a year to learn that I need not have to run to Aubrey Kushner, the photographer – who lets me this space in the first place for fifty rand a month – to use his phone. I am his sub-tenant. Cecil Amoils is the overall landlord. At any time, I am free to apply for a phone of my own. Also, I learn that I can become independent, have an office and become a fully fledged tenant of Cecil's. Some self-imposed stupidity tells me that, within a given physical space, only one telephone line is allowed.

Live and learn. I've been living. Learning? Not so much.

'What do you want on your letterhead?' asks Dad. The family business letterheads read: S. FEDLER PRINTERS & STATIONERS (PTY) LTD.

I struggle to answer.

'So, *nu*, what are you going to call yourself?'

This is a seminal moment. Whatever it is I want to be, the moment has arrived. There is no going back to being a madman. There will be no more invoices written out in an invoice book bought from the CNA.

So far, I have two steady customers, as Dad refers to them, *The Star* and Group Editors. Things are going good. This was never the career he wanted for me. It would be nice if I could be called doctor, but every other day, to see the name Fedler in the newspaper is maybe better. Maybe after all I am making something of myself. This film nonsense will make of me a nothing – a *laydik-gayer* and a nightclub-johnny.

I leave my last job before I get fired. It is inevitable when a new boss is appointed over me. My alternative is to murder him. I choose the cowardly option and thus am here in Victory House.

I resign at the time that I commission Aubrey Kushner, a photographer, for an advertising shoot. It is to be my last job in an advertising agency. We need to take shots of someone in a canoe negotiating a stretch of rapids. The product is Sparletta.

I confide in my photographer that I am looking for a studio. Everything moves rapidly on the banks of the Vaal, where I strike a deal and secure an address.

I cross over into the world of freelance. And very shortly, there is a steady flow of work. A lot starts to come in from the advertising agencies. *The Star* and Group Editors are my bedrock. Pretty soon, the whole industry knows about me. All sorts of ad people now seek my counsel. I am the pioneer of freelance. An old colleague wants to know, 'Should I, shouldn't I?' He too finds space in Victory House. Another soon follows, and another after that.

'Way to go!' I tell 'em all.

Victory House becomes a veritable Tin Pan Alley, but for the music. It is a hive of graphic excellence. It doesn't matter to whom the credit is due, but here, I am, at last, a 'Pty', or whatever.

'So, *nu*, what do you want on the letterhead?'

I tell Dad.

'Is that Pty Limited?'

'I don't know, Dad.'

'You're going into business. You should know.'

'I'll learn.'

I am trying to worm my way out of a *huck*. A *huck* is a lecture by a father to a son on things a son should know. There is no escaping a *huck*.

'A letterhead is not a place to learn.'

But I have this revelation of what I am.

Calling myself DOV FEDLER – CARTOONIST on a letterhead is a thrilling day. It is what I have wanted all my life.

Dad makes a note of precisely what to instruct Mot to set for my printing, which he carefully folds and puts in his wallet. That done, it's back to the real business of this day.

'So, what for a nonsense is this making a film?'

CHAPTER 24

The Midwich Cuckoos

Village of the Damned (1960) is an English horror science-fiction film. It is adapted from the novel The Midwich Cuckoos *by John Wyndham. Women of the village of Midwich give birth to an alien race of blonde Aryan-looking children. The children's glowing stares create havoc.*

'I know Al Debbo,' I boast to the kid standing behind me in the queue outside the Rex bioscope one Wednesday afternoon, waiting to get a ticket to go see a film starring my old friend Raymond's cousin. None of my usual buddies are with me to today to see *Kom Saam Vanaand*. There are a lot of short-cropped blonde heads and bare feet about. It is easy to pick up, from the exciting conversations all around, that these kids are mostly Afrikaans. This blue-eyed kid is one of them. I desperately want to be part of the crowd. I need the cushion of friends at a movie so that when I shout at the screen, they join in.

'He's Lebanese, you know?' I throw over my shoulder as a lure.

'*Wie?* Who?' Great. I've broken the ice. He's talking.

'Al Debbo. He's Lebanese. I know him from Mayfair.'

His brow clouds over as he turns his back on me to talk to the kid behind him. I shrug, turn to face front, reconciled that, today, I am indeed alone. There isn't a Greenside Primary uniform to be seen anywhere. I am left pondering my own thoughts. If I didn't know Al Debbo, would I bother to come today? To see a film all in Afrikaans? Being such a bioscope addict, I would. A flick is a flick is a flick.

I know all about the making of this film. It is a great moment in the history of Afrikaans films. It is a first – a musical comedy. Can I really claim to know its star because he once played a game of ping-pong with me? I am nonetheless excited at the prospect of seeing someone I actually know up on the big screen. I imagine my excitement if it was Bud Abbott or Lou Costello with whom I had once played ping-pong. Wouldn't that be exciting?

'Hey you?' I turn to the voice. Confronting me is a large Aryan lad. His eyes are a pitiless blue and his hair so fair as to be almost white. Even his eyebrows and lashes are white. The hands at his side are clenched in loose fists. I know instantly that I'm in some trouble. Behind him is a phalanx of Midwich cuckoos, all blond and bent on destruction.

'Hey, *Jood, ek praat met jou.*'

This can only go badly.

'You talking to me?'

My version in no way compares to Robert De Niro's. Mine is the sound of a chicken on the run.

'Did you call Al Debbo Portuguese?'

'No, I didn't.'

'So, what you call him?'

'Lebanese.'

'Leba-wat?'

'Nese. Leba-nese.' I need to clear up the misunderstanding, not realising that I am digging a grave.

His hand shoots out and pushes my shoulder, making me stumble out of the queue. I quickly straighten up, but the line quickly closes like attracting magnets. The law of the line is: step out and lose your place. No one is going to play fair and let me step back in, especially blond-with-blue eyes behind me who has summoned this axis of evil. I have always heard of pogroms. Am I about to fall victim to one now?

My aggressor advances on me further, pushing me again until I stand in a ring of his aides.

'*Bliksem hom, Willem.*'

The arm keeps shooting out. The hand is now a fist and it punches my shoulder. I am being goaded.

'Who the hell you calling names?'

'I didn't call him anything. I just said he's Lebanese.'

He now has me by the shirt and pulls me close. We are head to head.

'Listen, *Jood*. Say that again and I take out your lights.'

He doesn't wait for my reply. His head-butt has me flying and I land flat on my back. The world spins, and, though I have never had one before, I know instantly that I have a broken nose.

At supper, I sit with Dad, Rae and Mot at the table. Thankfully, Mom isn't here. She's been in hospital for two months since she had a heart attack. I haven't been taken to see a doctor but have been to the pharmacy with Mot, where a plaster was put on my nose and I was given two aspirin.

Since Mom is in hospital, Rae takes charge. Dad mostly just sits silent, almost as if he is not there. Rae just has to give me a blast. She is still looking for a husband and is practising for when she gets married and has to deal with children.

'How many times do you have to be told not to fight?'

'I wasn't fighting.'

'And why must you always tell lies? So, what were you doing?'

My voice takes on a defensive whine. 'I was standing in the queue at the bioscope, and this boy comes and starts an argument.'

'What did you say?'

'I said, Al Debbo is Lebanese.'

'You must have said something else.'

Rae stands, arms locked, legs akimbo. Is she going to head-butt me as well?

'What is Mom going to say when she sees you with a plaster on your nose? She can't take any more shocks. What are we going to tell her?'

'We can tell her I got hit by a cricket ball.'

Mot laughs into his soup. 'Ja, she's really going to fall for that. Even Mom knows he can't play cricket.'

I want to head-butt him for that. Rae won't believe anything I say.

What hurts most is that I never get to see *Kom Saam Vanaand*.

CHAPTER 25

The Winners
(1973)

South African movie. Released overseas as My Way *long before Frank Sinatra had his.*

'You'll never believe it. I've sold a movie.' I have had to rush next door to my good friend Cliff Webb to share the good news. 'They're coming over to discuss a contract.'

Cliff looks up from the logo he is designing, unmoved.

Webb/White has designed the graphics for the hit movie, *The Winners*. They have major clients like Nedbank, Barlows and AECI. Cliff, a laconic Englishman, is wise in the ways of business.

'When are they coming and who are they?' he says, crossing his arms like a magistrate.

'They. Them. I don't know who the hell they are, but they want to buy my script.'

Cliff has grown to know my erratic ways of conducting business and hears my dad berating my inefficient practices, like not sending out invoices and statements, when he comes to use the photostat machine that we bought together, but which I barely use. Dad never pauses in his lectures when Webb walks in. Webb, as Dad calls him, is like family.

Dad is absent for this moment and so Cliff is my counsel. He prints out a name on a piece of paper.

'We got burnt on *The Winners*. We lost money. Be careful, the film business is full of sharks. You phone this number immediately and you do nothing until then.'

Deflated at Cliff's lack of enthusiasm, I go back to my office carrying the slip of paper. I read his perfect calligraphy and make the call.

CHAPTER 26

'Good Old Reliable Nathan'

Song from Guys and Dolls *(1955), a musical that stars Marlon Brando, with Frank Sinatra playing Nathan Detroit.*

'Could I please speak to Mr Wunsch?'

I go through directly, no assistant or PA to screen his calls. I imagine a sordid space, a desk and filing cabinet, something out of a cheap private-eye movie.

Could he possibly see me urgently because . . .?

Tomorrow morning.

This guy must be small potatoes and hungry for customers.

* * *

The law firm Edward Nathan & Friedland is like a small airport located in Innes Chambers, which is directly over the road from the Supreme Court. Maybe this Wunsch is someone after all? It is busy, busy, busy, a rush of coming and going of lawyers in suits and robes, clutching portfolios and stacks of documents. I have to wait my turn at reception to be directed to Mr Wunsch's office. I can't afford this place.

Sheepishly, I knock on the door and am bid to enter. He is on the phone finishing a call as he beckons me to a plush leather chair.

I pick up that I am dealing with a very senior partner of the firm ENF, which is not a firm to mess with.

'Look, Mr Wunsch, I think I've made a terrible mistake. I can't afford you,' I blurt out, anticipating what this short interview is going to cost.

'Sit down,' he commands. 'Call me Basil. What's your story?'

I sit like a hoop-jumping dog and tell Basil all.

'This is how it works,' he says, having listened. 'You get paid R3 500. You do not negotiate. You do not deviate. You have them sign on the bottom line, or you walk out.'

I get the thou-shalt-nots.

'Come back Thursday. I will have the contract ready for you.'

All of my doctors will attest to my being the best possible patient. One naturally respects a doctor's opinion. That is the way I've been brought up. Respect and doctor. The words are virtually interchangeable. Every Jewish mother wants her daughter to marry a doctor. I wonder, had my mother lived, how she would feel having her son marry one?

My respect for doctors is threefold. Dorrine's father was a doctor, and my eldest daughter has followed in their footsteps. In my household, doctors are revered. A doctor's opinion is like a rabbi's. It is law. So whatever my doctors prescribe is law.

I follow their counsel to the letter. There is no negotiating with an expert. I apply this rule to any expert whose advice I seek. One goes to a specialist for a definitive opinion in the first place. Basil Wunsch is a contract specialist.

I listen as if I am Moses on Sinai. The contract may as well be carved in stone.

CHAPTER 27

The Producers
(1968/2005)

Originally just a madcap comedy about a crooked producer and his accountant accomplice. First with Zero Mostell and Gene Wilder, and then as a musical with Nathan Lane and Matthew Broderick.

Chris Rowley collects the proposed contract. He flips through it like he too is a specialist.

'Upfront?' he says finally, a little amazed. 'I don't know if they will go for that. Let me take it to them.'

I feel a need to apologise and explain my position. It would not make sense to him if I did. These are The Five Pages of Basil.

My bill from Basil Wunsch is all of R350. It is nothing if I'm going to be paid ten times that.

Dad tells me, '*Dos is aroys-geworfene gelt.*' It's money thrown away – money wasted. He and John Meyer are always in agreement.

The first time Dad walks into the studio and meets John, he wanders over uninvited to look over his shoulder and watch him work.

'Good,' he says finally.

'John, good? What does he know from drawing?' I tease.

'Maybe he doesn't know. But good he is.'

The joke is back to haunt me now. John is long gone on his way to success, and here I am messing with movies.

'Why are you always messing with nonsense? Always with you is bioscopes. Life is not all bioscopes. Look at John Meyer. John is a businessman. Already, a big success. What is a bioscope? What *meshugoyim* will pay you so much money?'

What madmen indeed?

Chris Rowley and the Sullivans come to call at Victory House. My office in no way resembles the suites at Innes Chambers. Mess is my order. It doesn't exactly inspire business confidence. Dad nags me about that too.

The Sullivans come in wielding a copy of the document Basil Wunsch gave me for R350 of my hard-earned money. Treat it with respect. What are they doing tossing it onto my desk like it was trash?

'Are you serious about this?' Sullivan Senior picks the document up from the desk and tosses it down again. I get the sense that the only thing keeping him from slamming his fist down is that the desk belongs to me. 'This is outrageous. No one gets this kind of a deal.'

I want to explain my doctor/expert/respect thing. Now is not a good time. There is a lot of spluttering and anger, and they leave. *'Aroysgeworfene gelt'* indeed. Maybe I won't mention it to Dad and just cut my losses. What I fail to notice is that the Sullivans remember to take their copy of my outrageous terms.

Chris Rowley calls the next day. The Sullivans want me to meet with their lawyer soon.

Sure. Where?

The address is in a block in Eloff Street. Eloff Street is the oldest prestigious address in the city. It has my unconditional respect even before I walk in the door. This suite is super-plush.

I'm offered a range of any beverage of my choice. I go for water. The lawyer sinks back into his leather chair and gives me the steepled hands so that I get a close look at his all-gold cufflinks.

There is no reaching in the drawer for the document. It sits there as a centrepiece, as if placed by an interior decorator to draw attention to the proceedings at hand. I sit across this tennis court desk to one side, the Sullivans to the other. I get the feeling this guy has made it big in divorce.

'This contract is ridiculous,' he says. He begins a slow rhythmic swivelling from left to right. This is going to be like Wimbledon. 'Nobody gets this kind of a deal.'

Maybe now would be a time for the respect speech.

Now begins a series of alternative deals. A little upfront. A little behind. A little after. In between. It is a crossfire of cannonballs. I return every serve. Ours is a long tennis match. Back and forth, back and forth.

I keep returning with, 'Look, this is the only contract that I will sign.'

Sullivan Senior finally explodes under the pressure. 'Then the hell with you!' he says, banging a fist on the court. If he had a racquet, he would throw it.

I pick up my *'Aroys-geworfene gelt'*, thus ruining the careful desk arrangement, and walk to the door.

Someone calls, 'Hang on a sec.'

The proceedings at the *seder* table on *pesach* begin with the holding aloft of a piece of *matzo* as a token of what the order of business is about. We recite, 'This is the bread of our affliction.' It is about remembering being delivered from bondage.

I turn in the doorway, holding my paper tablet aloft. Right now, I could be Charlton Heston.

'Guys, this is the contract. There is no other.'

I leave Eloff Street R3 500 richer.

In my fractured mind, I am already driving down Sunset Boulevard to lay my hand and footprints at Grauman's Chinese Theatre. If only Sam Dembo could see me now, having hacked away at the trusty old Olympia. Holy Wood! Here I come. Maybe I'll get a real Remington and even smoke a pipe like Raymond Chandler. I can hear Sam say, 'Here's lookin' at you kid.'

That *Haak Vrystaat* is an abject failure is no fault of mine. Other than writing and selling the script, I have nothing further to do with the project. Having written it, I am elbowed out. No big deal. It's the easiest money I have ever made.

CHAPTER 28

There's No Business Like Moe Business

There's No Business Like Show Business (1954).
Star cast, but only Ethel Merman is ever remembered
for her grating rendition of the title song.

The contract for *Timer Joe 3* is vastly different. When Moe Mankowitz lounges into my office unannounced, we slip into an easy relationship. He loves talking about his achievements and I am a willing audience. Like Chris Rowley, he has come to commission me for some artwork. He knows what he wants – a Mort Drucker-like drawing, like a *Mad* magazine cover in colour, of the principals. These are to be serious billboard posters. I am impressed at his ambition.

'I make films for black audiences. Black people like the same movies we do, but they like them with black people. Last year, we made *Timer Joe 1* and it was a smash. This time, we're going all out. I want great posters. We're going to advertise all over the townships.'

The posters read in English, 'They're back again, funnier than ever!' So I assume that the dialogue follows that route.

Timer Joe 2 is released and is another smash hit. A very buoyant Moe soon pays a visit. This time, it's *Timer Joe 3* he has come to discuss. What that might be, he is not sure, but the posters are a must. 'Triple the fun. The greatest comedy team are back yet again in *Timer Joe 3*.'

'What's it about?' I ask.

A comedy, he assures me. Yes, but what about a story? Surely he has that in mind? By now, we are talking a lot about film, and my own enthusiasm fills the spaces with many cross-references, which are the great comedies and directors. I quote from Billy Wilder movies. Frank Capra, Chaplin, Buster Keaton, the Marx Brothers. Moe recognises only a few, like Chaplin and the Marx trio. Moe thinks he is dealing with a movie maven.

'Would you like to write *Timer Joe 3*?'

Dreams do come true. Would I ever? Time to get the Olympia out of the cupboard again.

I type very slowly and inaccurately, but soon I present him with an outline. He reads it very quickly and asks, 'Would you like to direct it?'

The Walter Mitty within me *kvells*.

Soon I'll have to play Billy Wilder, Frank Capra and Charles Chaplin. But right now, it is Sam Dembo.

CHAPTER 29

Walk on the Wild Side
(1962)

Stars Jane Fonda and Laurence Harvey. It follows the lives of women in a New Orleans bordello.

The writing is done; the directing begins. The cast is assembled, and the camera is ready to roll. 'It's showtime!'

I tell Coach to tell the actor to walk across the screen from left to right. Somewhere in my lexicon of filmmaking, I have picked up that some great director – John Ford, or whoever – always places his heroes to the left of the screen and the baddies to the right. My guy walks from left to right to indicate that he is bent on no good. The *boffs* are going to love me.

The *tsotsi* was the shiftiest guy in the room at the audition, which is why I chose him. I have the role marked as Furtive Frank.

At that very moment, a delivery truck to the left chooses to deposit its load at the building next door, thus denying any access to that side.

Out comes my pen.

Enter Furtive Frank right.

Coach tells Frank to switch sides and Hennie has to move the camera. We have not begun to shoot and are already deep in compromise country. But the shot should still be a walk in the park.

'Action! And roll camera!'

Frank's walk not only stops Hennie, but some curious passers-by as well. There is no need to yell 'Cut!' Hennie does that unbidden.

'Are you making a zombie movie?' a curious spectator asks the boom operator. The mike man shrugs. He doesn't speak English.

What the hell is Frank doing? Is that gait a result of poor translation?

'What did you tell him?' I ask Coach.

'What you told me. I told him to walk like a *tsotsi*.'

'Do *tsotsis* really walk like that?'

'Not where I come from,' says Coach.

CHAPTER 30

The Wages of Fear
(1953)

A harrowing French adventure, starring Yves Montand, about a group of desperate men transporting nitroglycerin to snuff out an oil fire.

Off camera, Furtive Frank is everything I want. He breathes the part. He slinks, sidles, displays the entire repertoire of the sly, the shiftless, the stealthy. Call 'action' and he becomes everything I don't want – a live version of Edvard Munch's *The Scream*.

Frank suffers from stage fright. He is terrified of the camera, which is not an advantage for someone who aspires to a movie career. There are technical names for the condition: scopophobia, scoptophobia, or ophthalmophobia. It's an anxiety disorder characterised by a morbid fear of being seen or stared at by others.

Scopophobia can be a pathological fear of drawing attention to oneself. Turn on a camera and Frank walks as if concrete has just set in his joints. His arms swing out of rhythm. His natural gait is gone. He swings left foot forward together with left arm, and then comes the right side, as if in opposition. Each step is a peculiar, deliberate staccato. Fear grips Frank's very eyeballs. He is only able to stare straight ahead. His face looks anaesthetised, like it has been overdosed on novocaine. As a Boris-Karloff-in-Frankenstein impersonator, he does a fine job.

I too am gripped by the spectre of something uncomfortable. While everyone on set is merely trying to contain their giggles, I'm having an attack of atychiphobia – fear of failing. Moe, who has been standing on the far side of the vague ring around the action, comes walking across to confer with us. He must be pissed at this first demonstration of my skills as a director.

'That was great,' he beams.

'That was terrible,' I murmur.

'But this is really funny. I want to go with it,' he burbles, just in case I don't exactly understand whose movie this is going to be. When this project is through and hopefully, successful, I know The Munchkin is going to claim to be the sole genius behind it all. Now he wants the director's role as well. Suddenly, everything is his idea. He has paid for it, so I guess it is.

If I broach the idea that what we have filmed is inappropriate, wrong, bad for the scene, there will be no appealing to some sense of good taste. The movie *dybbuk* that possesses Moe is Ed Wood, reckoned to be the worst movie director ever, on the planet.

I watch Coach walk over to have a word with Frank while Moe continues to worm in my ear. I have to listen to the full Mankowitz/Munchkin Philosophy of Comedy and The Art of Profit Maintenance.

Hennie moves the camera with no intention of consulting the director. No one pays attention to what I want.

An ancient resentment rears its whiny head.

'You think you're so *blerrie* funny?' I scream in frustration at big brother Mot. He is teasing me again because he is bored. His idea of amusement is making me lose my temper. I am an easy mark. It just takes some poking me in the ribs at dinner as I try to get a forkful of peas in my mouth. They spill just as the fork is about to reach my mouth. I am proud to be able to eat peas off a fork, which shows I'm not a baby. Of course, I lose it and I jump out of my chair, trying to punch Mot who easily holds me at arm's length, laughing.

'Leave me alone!' I punch fresh air as he cups one hand over my head and holds me at bay.

'Leave your little brother alone,' Mom orders.

I hate that – the 'little' part. That is exactly what he wants. Now that he has shown exactly what kind of a baby I am, he is beaming. I swear one day to be avenged, but we grow up.

Moe Mankowitz's smug look on the issue of Frank's walk is like a poke in the ribs and my peas are all over the place. Moe is delighted with himself. His tone becomes imperious as he proclaims.

'That's what comedy is about.'

CHAPTER 31

The Comedians
(1967)

A political drama starring Richard Burton and Elizabeth Taylor based on Graham Greene's novel.

Raymond and I think we are comedians. Even though we are but two, we play *The Three Stooges* and then switch to Laurel and Hardy. We read a lot of comics and do a lot of drawing. It is something other Jewish boys seem to shy away from, like eating *treif*, non-kosher food. The smells of Mrs Kudsee's *treif* dishes make me salivate, but I dare not eat any of it. There appears to be no restriction on what Raymond is allowed to eat. He happily feasts on anything my mom offers without fear of divine retribution. He has the best of both worlds. Life is not fair.

When we sit down to supper, there are things that have arisen in my argument about Abbott and Costello that need resolution. I have a query for Dad. I want to understand the word 'abbot'. I know that it has something to do with the church. I must ask. Mom won't know. Her English is not that great. It is useless asking Mot because he'll just make up some shit and have me believing it. I won't ask my big sister Rae because she will turn this into an interrogation. 'Why are you asking about the church?' She will turn to Mom for support.

Rae is like my other mother. When Mom had a breakdown when I was two, it was Rae and a neighbour, Mrs Steinberg, who took care of me. Rae likes being in charge. Rae tells me she used to put ribbons in my hair. Thank God, I don't remember that, though I do remember Mom's breakdown. Rae is someone with whom I can never argue.

'You see what he's asking? About the church! You see with who he is mixing? I bet he is eating *treif*!'

If we go down that road, they will all be making me confess about the one time I think I really did eat *treif*.

When Raymond and I are with the Khouri boys and I am trying to worm into their group, I am compelled to eat a lemon. It takes years before I trust that lemons are indeed kosher, even though at home we drink a lot of lemon tea. The boys could really force something truly non-kosher on me, like a piece of sausage, but they understand that kosher just really means meat and know perfectly well that all fruit is allowed. It is exactly the kind of diabolical off-the-cuff joke my big brother Mot will conjure in an instant, like his telling me after I have eaten a mealie and drunk water that a mealie field is going to grow in my gut. Then I feel like Jack who has swallowed the beanstalk. I am worried for days, long after Mot has forgotten it and come up with some new bullshit to stir my wild thoughts.

The tease begins with the boys grilling me on why I won't eat in Raymond's house. I lie. I say that I will. So it turns into a dare. 'Oh yeah? Show us!' We are in their backyard, which is back to back with the Kudsees' house in Twelfth Avenue, and we happen to be squatting in a circle close to a lemon tree in fruit. One of the boys gets up, plucks a lemon and hands it to me.

'Show us!'

If I don't, Raymond might stop being my friend. I eat the lemon, keep my friend, and wonder if it will be God or Jesus who will come to get me. But I fail as a Lebanese boy by crying in our bathroom when I get home. No one must know. If I tell the story to Mom, the word could leak to one of Mom's great friends, Mrs Seftel, who lives in Twelfth Avenue and who knows Mrs Khouri well.

Knowing Mrs Seftel, she could get angry on Mom's behalf, as she had done with Mrs Sachs, another neighbour in Twelfth Avenue, who had accused Harry, Mrs Seftel's genius son – the meekest, shyest boy in Mayfair – of defacing her front wall and then forced him to wash off the graffiti with a bucket of water, Vim and a scrubbing brush. Mrs Seftel might very well cross the road to Mrs Khouri's house and confront her as she had confronted Mrs Sachs. 'Tell your boys they make the Fedler boy eat *treif* and I will come and *bris* them all. And remember – you leave my Harold alone!'

Even the Lebanese know that a *bris* is a circumcision. Mrs Seftel probably means 'castrate', but her English is a lot like Mom's.

Mrs Khouri, who is also no linguist, is bound to get the message and the true content of the threat. It is more than possible that Mrs Seftel, driven that far, could, like on the previous occasion, shove Mrs Khouri back into her own house and bang the door shut. That would not be a good idea. The Khouris are cousins of the Azrams who live up College Street. The name Azram is feared beyond the borders of Mayfair. Even if they weren't cousins of the Khouris, such an act would be a call to arms. There is about to be war in Palestine. We don't want one here in Mayfair.

* * *

I wait until Rae leaves the table to ask. 'Dad, what is an abbot?'

Dad sucks on a Domino sugar cube, pondering the question, and sips from his glass of Russian tea with the slice of lemon. I know all my dad's moves. The sucking on the cube and the sipping are a prelude to a lecture. He is going to turn this into something long, complicated and cultural.

'First, there is good, and then there is bad.' The lesson begins. I have no idea of where this is going but I know it has something to do with church.

Is Dad about to say something bad about Jesus? That is not like him.

'In life is important to know good from bad. Very easy in life to do bad. Lazy is bad. Swearing is bad. Stealing is bad.'

Oy! This is going to take forever. Dad really knows how to stretch a point.

'I get it already. Please get on with it,' I want to call out. Of course, I sit silent, feigning attentiveness.

'Eating too much is bad,' Dad continues, reaching for more examples. Thank God, he finally runs out. 'Ve must try to become wise. Visdom is good. Visdom you get from reading books. Never reading a book is bad,' he says pointedly, looking at my brother.

Mot just rolls his eyes.

'In life, we have to cultivate.' He pauses. Dad loves important words like 'cultivate'.

He repeats it. 'Yes, ve must cultivate.'

He pauses, savouring the word one last time.
'Ve must cultivate good 'abits.'
I leave the table none the wiser.

CHAPTER 32

The Longest Day
(1962)

*An epic about D-Day, the day the Allies invaded Europe.
Starring everyone who was anyone at the time.*

None of my peers are compelled, beyond *bar mitzvah*, to attend *cheder*, Hebrew school. It is a moment of great release for a thirteen-year-old. His bondage is over, and he is free to pursue the fleshpots of assimilation. I get another four years of detention. Dad rules that I study Hebrew until the end of matric. It's an extra subject. More work, no play. I sit alone with a teacher who hammers me with further lessons of Torah.

There are no *Goldilocks, Hansel and Gretel,* or heaven forbid, *Three Pigs* stories to fill my childhood or adolescence. From the beginning, it is 'In the beginning'.

Even at the outset, it is all grim fairy tales – so much *Sturm und Drang*. Banished from Eden. The entire world drowned. And this is the Good Book? Much of what is in the great book strikes me as being clearly impossible. Noah and his Ark trouble me. When the ark came to rest on Mount Ararat, which we know is somewhere near Turkey, how did the kangaroos get to Australia? One giant leap for kang-kind? There is a period of my life when I become wholly religious, when I believe it all, but the inconsistencies finally make me somewhat sceptical. Nevertheless, Torah echoes through my life. Even now, why do I feel compelled to write 'the Ark' in capitals?

The Five Books are easier read as allegory. They are lessons of life that are meant to guide one to be a good citizen, and, yes, to be an artist. Creation is all about the Creator – the Artist. Genesis is a great handbook. In the beginning, He creates heaven and earth. And the earth is without 'form and void'. In the original Hebrew, 'without form' and 'void' is 'tohu va-vohu'. The sound of it tells it. *Tohu va-vohu*. Translation fails. The translators would have done better to use a phrase like 'mish-mash' to give one a real sense of it. Recent translations use the word 'confused'. Always remember, we are talking about the Almighty – the Perfect One. Lest we forget, this is the Bible – respect, folks. Let's keep the language up there. We can't have, 'And the earth was a mish-mash.' Who would dare to suggest He was confused? Bring back the Inquisition!

'Without form and void' is grander. But in my book, it is mish-mash.

Creation begins with raw material, sometimes a bad mix of colour, a poor choice of brush or pen, an uncooperative piece of paper. If it is modelling and sculpture, the raw clay is too grainy, too soft. As Stephen Sondheim, that great composer and brilliant lyricist, points out, 'Art isn't easy.' Things need correction and editing. Such is the hard graft of the act. It doesn't all come out with twittering birds and cherubs mixing the palette, grinding the pigment.

It takes the Almighty six days to complete His work. And get this. On the seventh day, He has to rest from all the work that He has done. Rest? Remember who we are talking about here. The One who is on call 24/7, 365, to infinity, needs six days in which to finish His work, and is in need of rest. There is no quick *zap*! Hello, folks. Welcome, universe.

Heaven is okay, but it is the earth that has problems from the outset. There is darkness on the face of the deep. Why the problems?

The Omniscient, the Omnipotent, begins with *tohu va-vohu*? Impossible. Not if you think allegory.

* * *

I arrive on set as a god with my great plan. There is to be no messing about. There are to be no hiccups. It's to be plain sailing. No mish-mash, no Tower of Babel where no one speaks the same language. Mine is to be the perfect epic.

My first day has barely begun and right off I am in deep shit. Frank's expression of terror and his Frankenstein-monster walk are his best furtive effort. As long as we don't allow him to walk in future scenes and shoot in extreme close up, we're okay. So we cut any scene that reads, 'Enter Frank.' There will be no entering. I make frantic corrections to my notes and instead of writing 'Frank' I scribble 'Frankenstein' as some kind of reminder. It makes me think of Mot.

I am desperate to steer things right, but it is coming out *tohu va-vohu*.

CHAPTER 33

Abbott and Costello Meet Daisy de Melker

One day, I am going to murder Mot. Only he knows my secret fears. Like an idiot, I have told him of my fear of Daisy de Melker, Thuys and his gang, and Frankenstein. He tries to tell me that the monster's name is not Frankenstein, but I know it is. I am barely seven and he tries to fill my head with all kinds of shit.

I know the story of Daisy de Melker. She poisoned several husbands and her sons and was hanged. Mom and Dad talk about her sometimes so I know it's a true story.

Mot has seen the film *Frankenstein*, which you have to be twelve to be allowed to go in to. Only Mot could get a ticket at the age of ten. He says it's the scariest film he has ever seen. When he's bored at home and wants to get me going, he tells me about it. He shows me how the monster walks: he holds his arms wide, his fingers curled, and advances stiff-legged, with a madman's grin, his eyes fixed on mine. Bastard! He knows I'm getting scared. I shout as loud as I can, 'Shurrup! Shurrup!'

Mom comes running from the kitchen.

'From where you learn to swear?'

It's me she's cross with. It's not fair.

'He made me do it!'

Mot shrugs like he doesn't know what I am talking about.

Mom knows better. 'Leave your little brother alone.'

'I did nothing,' he says, all innocent.

'Maybe nothing, just don't do it again.'

But today, I want to follow wherever Mot leads because his best friend Julian Wesek is busy, so he lets me drag alongside him. Mot doesn't like to do anything alone. We are going to Mr Fine's hardware store on Central Avenue to look at tools. Mot looks at tools like I look at comics on display at Feldhun's café. Mr Feldhun lets me look but checks my hands first to see if they are dirty.

'Did you vash?' he always asks as I step inside his shop.

I learn a long time ago to come to Feldhun with hands scrubbed red.

'Good!' he nods, granting my pass.

'It's good to cultivate good 'abits.' I think Feldhun has been talking to Dad.

I'm okay on my own. Just give me some comics, pencil and paper, and the world can pass me by.

As we are cutting round the back in Eighth Avenue, and we come to the Levers' house on the corner of Bird, Mot says, 'You know Daisy de Melker lived in that house?'

I want to turn around and run as fast as I can back home.

'Ja, she poisoned everybody in there. Even visitors. If she offered you tea, you better not drink it. Otherwise, tickets.'

Icicles of terror sprout on my scalp. Mom and Mrs Lever are friends, and I have had lots of tea there. Oh shit!

'You were crackers if you ate her biscuits.' Mot laughs at his own joke.

I don't think it's funny. I'm going to die. I just know it. I love Mrs Lever's biscuits. How long does it take for poison to work? Mrs Lever doesn't intend to poison anyone, but that stuff must still be in the air all over the house. I know about ghosts and haunted houses. There is the haunted house on the corner of Ninth and Dolphin Street, across the road from the swimming bath. All the boys say there was once a murder inside that house, which is why it is covered in creepers and vines. You don't go in there because murder, like poison, hangs in the air. Bamboo grows there but no one will go near it to steal any in kite season. Not even Motty. When I go with him to swim, as we walk past on the far side of the road, he never fails to say longingly, 'Lekker bamboo, man.'

Now there are two houses in Mayfair that I have to avoid. Today is the very last time I will ever walk to the corner of Bird and Eighth Avenue. Next time, I am going right up Church to Central Avenue where there are lots of people. I'm not going where there are ghosts, haunted houses and murderers.

Mot never misses a moment of my fear. It's all in my eyes. The Daisy de Melker story becomes another one for his arsenal of tortures for me. Now, when he really wants me out of his hair, all he has to do is strike his Frankenstein pose and walk stiff-legged towards me. It is the time in my life that everyone calls me Davey. He advances on me with his arms wide, wearing that killer's grin as he sings through gritted teeth like a ventriloquist, 'Davey, Davey, give me your answer do. I'm half crazy. I'm going to poison you.'

I shut my eyes tight like clothes pegs and hold my ears as I scream and swear, like trying to ward off a spook, but a *klap* to the ear quickly opens them and shuts me up. This time, Mom doesn't stop to ask questions, and Mot gets one too. Good job.

When Mot tells me long after this that *Abbott and Costello Meet Frankenstein* is coming, I don't believe him. This time, I'm not falling for his *kak* stories. He knows how much I love their films. He knows I won't hear anything bad about my idols. For sure, it's rubbish.

I'll never step into the Levers' house ever again, but nothing is ever going to stop me from seeing my heroes. But when I find out that it is all true, and that Abbott and Costello do indeed meet Frankenstein, I'm not sure I want to play in the zinc tub any more.

CHAPTER 34

Heist
(2001)

A film by David Mamet about robbery. It twists and turns in plot as much as dialogue, like only Mamet can do it. Gene Hackman and Danny DeVito make it crackle and pop as they relish their roles.

Day 1 seems to stretch out to infinity. The heist has yet to be filmed. There are three scenes that make up the robbery. Beginning at the getaway car across the road, it progresses into the building. There is a security guard who is also an accomplice. That requires a number of setups. Lastly, we arrive at the workshop. Again, we set up the scenes that make up the actual robbery and have to go back and out to the street for the getaway. The boss of the gang, whom I have named Getaway Gus, waits to drive off in my Datsun. We plan to shoot Gus at the steering wheel last.

It is the guns that have everyone nervous. It is just make-believe, but the robbery setup at the diamond-cutting factory is somewhat tense. There is a sense of reality about it all. No one is comfortable, though two of the weapons are completely fake. It is the presence of the one real gun that has everyone on edge. That one is wielded by Furtive Frank. It isn't loaded, and it's been checked repeatedly for a forgotten bullet that may have slipped into the chamber, but we've all witnessed the man walk and it seems likely he is bound to do something surprising with it. In his hands, the bloody thing is still likely to go off. A gun is a gun is a gun.

The weapon belongs to Hennie, who knows his way around cameras and guns. We need not worry. But we do. The other two guns are plastic replicas, an automatic and a snub-nosed cap gun which are mine. I keep those at my studio as reference for the comic strip *Jet Jungle* that I draw. Men with guns are always jumping off my pages.

The location is a cubic zirconium workshop owned by Benny Gavin, father of Louis, a close friend of mine. This is our diamond factory. We have only two hours, which Benny has generously allowed us, so we are dead serious and focused. At the entrance to the building, we confer with the cast. Coach passes my instruction on to the three robbers. As he explains, I hand over the fake weapons to the actors. Hennie only hands over the real one to Frank once we're inside. A better idea, as it turns out.

Our activity in front of the workshop attracts a small crowd of curious onlookers. A neighbouring shop owner – who steps onto the pavement to investigate and sees no camera, only the passing of weapons by a large Caucasian man to two black men – is alarmed and runs back inside his shop.

We start our shoot in the lobby where a security guard frisks the robbers as they enter. It is the security guard who passes a gun, the real one, to Frank. A single-scene shot generally needs three different cameras' points of view, from an overview, to middle, to close-up. On a big movie, there might be three cameras, even more. We have just the one. The tedious part of filmmaking is the length of time setups take between shots. Lights have to be moved. The boom mike has to be placed elsewhere. Something needs pasting down, propping up. The tasks mount. It is a while before we get to Benny's workshop, which mainly consists of two long tables facing each other, on which are numerous polishing machines manned by an operator. There is a problem. Benny has given his staff time off. We have twenty stations and no extras. There is a frantic request to other offices in the building to loan us staff as extras. We manage to find five in all. They sit behind the machines, which are turned off. My script reads, 'Hive of activity'. Five very confused office workers stare at these intimidating machines, trying to look busy. They manage to look plain scared. It looks like an epidemic of scopophobia, scoptophobia and ophthalmophobia is breaking out all over. Thank heaven they don't have to walk. The clock ticks.

Our three robbers, supposedly workers, come in to work, sit down and, on cue, pull their guns. We move the camera three times for each shot.

The 'workers' at the benches are bewildered by each camera shift. We do a panning shot across the benches as they sit like children with puzzle pieces that don't fit anywhere. We have the first three run behind the camera to sit at station 6 to 9. There is no whine or grind of machines to be heard. It looks like Benny employs a lot of twins. But it makes it to the final cut as, I will learn, does everything that is shot for *Timer Joe 3*. Good, bad, ugly gets spliced into the final product. The cutting floor remains pristine.

We cue Frank, who does fine work as he springs to his feet, brings out Gat 1, and waves it about. We all flinch in expectation of some mishap. Hennie keeps it rolling.

A voice from the door calls out, 'Put your hands in the air and put down your weapons.'

A cop wearing a Kevlar vest fills the doorway, his wide-legged stance exactly mirroring that of our robbers. No one is more bewildered than I am. The cast don't know what's coming next. Is this what has been scripted? If the movie is in isiZulu, how come this new guy is speaking in English?

Frank looks to me for direction. How is this scene supposed to play out? Oh fuck! Frank points the weapon at the cop, thinking that this is something that he is expected to do. The cop, who is going for this Mexican standoff shit, holds his ground and barks out an order.

'Drop your weapons – now!' Good acting, thinks Frank, checking out the cop.

I duck as I run between them. 'Drop the gun!' I scream at Frank, who needs no help from Coach to understand my frantic instruction. Thankfully, he lays the weapon on the floor.

There follows a Kafkaesque ballet of having us all stand facing the wall as we are frisked and questioned. Coach comes into his own here. There are four cops in all, all armed for an invasion. The leader listens with a lot of sceptical nods and grunts, his disappointment growing as the situation is clarified.

Pity. It would have been a good day to shoot someone.

I see everything I have made, and behold, it is crap.

And this is just the first day.

CHAPTER 35

The Brothers Scaramouche

The Brothers Karamazov is a classic Russian novel by Dostoyevsky, filmed in 1958, starring Yul Brynner and William Shatner, later Captain Kirk of Star Trek. *Scaramouche is a lesser French classic by Rafael Sabatini, filmed in 1952, starring Stewart Granger and Mel Ferrer. The best duels ever on film.*

There is always a movie that comes along to stir my blood and compel me to emulate it, which results in some truly wild activities. Nineteen fifty-two is a year that has me create some bizarre practices into which I lure new friends, who display poor judgement in following my lead. Here, if I want to play both Abbott and Costello, concurrently, my new friends wouldn't know the difference. There is no one to share my passions like Raymond once did. This is the year I introduce my followers to both jousting and swordplay, inspired by two big MGM films, *Ivanhoe* and *Scaramouche*, released in the same year. I simply have to somehow engage in these sports. The more dangerous of the two proves to be the jousting.

Since we do not live in a rural community and have no horses, only bicycles, I adapt the idea. I find two long poles, and we use dustbin lids for shields. It is a lot to carry and ride a bike at the same time. I referee the first contest. Two innocents come at each other full tilt across the playing fields of Greenside Primary one afternoon. These are the days before tall gates and locks deny us free entry to use it as our after-school playground. If any of our teachers should happen to work late and witness this insane contest, no doubt we would all face the headmaster, Mr Nesbitt, the next morning to be censured. And having investigated the case further, he might conclude that I, being the architect of this suicidal pastime, should be sent to a reformatory and there, placed in solitary confinement for being – that worst of offenders – a bad influence. That Cyril Strul is not impaled but merely flung back some feet off his bike and suffers no mortal wound is more than lucky. The game dies instead after that first charge.

Swordplay is sexier. It is all fancy moves with rapiers and lots of vocal interjection, like 'En garde!', 'Have at you, varlet!', 'Touché.' If we knew any Shakespeare, we might add, 'A hit, a hit, a palpable hit!' or other gibberish utterances. Duelling requires acting and jumping up and fighting from rough-hewn benches and stools designed for kids at which to enjoy their break sandwiches. We would, if it were possible, swing from chandeliers like Gene Kelly does as D'Artagnan in the earlier 1948 version of *The Three Musketeers*, where, like his singing in the rain, swordplay becomes dance.

Unlike lances, rapiers require some invention. Sticks will not do. There are four basic parts to the weapon. There is, of course, the blade, the length that forms the sword; the guard, the metal piece that keeps an opponent's sword from sliding down over the hilt and cutting your hand; then the hilt, the handle of the sword, usually made from leather, wire or wood; and lastly the pommel, the end of the sword that the hilt is on. The rapier fills me with a wild lust. I long to wield one. Toy manufacturers even that far back shy away from producing such a lethal weapon because – like every mother's other nightmare, the pellet gun – it could cause the loss of an eye. I need a pair of duelling foils. I just have to find a way to make them. Clearly, they cannot be made of metal. No mortal wounds must result. They will have to be springy so that they swish through the air. There is a large palm tree in our garden. As luck has it, it has been recently trimmed, and the cut fronds lie in our back garden. I have a Eureka moment; I know exactly how to make them. This is the day I become a prop maker.

I grab the topmost leaves on one side of the stem and tear down. I do the same with the other side and test the spring. It is perfect. But I need to saw away the thicker, bottom part to get the right length. For that, I need to use one of Mot's saws, which he would never allow. But that's okay, he's at work at the factory. I know I will get punched, but reality has no place in this venture. I'll suffer the consequences of that breach later.

I swish my find through the air. It would make a great cane for cuts too. Mot will no doubt find an opportunity for using it to whack me.

My head buzzes with ideas as I go. For the guard, I find a large Nescafé coffee lid amongst the junk that is in the coal bin in the yard. I need thick wire. It is a scavenger hunt. What fun. Mot collects all kinds of bits and pieces of trashed mechanical and electrical parts: rolls of all kinds of wire, six-inch nails, nuts and bolts, ball bearings, old spark plugs and more. It is a treasure box. I rummage through it all to find everything I need. I take two of the large nails to make crosspieces. But the points need to be filed down, so it's back to the toolbox.

The tin lid needs to be hammered out into a cup shape, so yet again it is back to the box, which Mot keeps tidily packed under his bed, to retrieve his ball-peen hammer. He has a tool for everything and I have learnt to use most of them. We share the room and I know all his hiding places. When he finds out I've used them, he's going to kill me. He is so unbelievably neat. I don't have to search. I know exactly where he keeps the hammer. What the hell is a ball peen?

CHAPTER 36

The Swordsman
(1947)

*A Romeo and Juliet story in eighteenth-century Scotland.
Features Larry Parks, best known for starring in* The Jolson Story *(1946).
His career died in the McCarthy witch-hunt.*

'Don't spend all your money on tools,' Dad tells his printer's apprentice every Friday when he pays him his wages.

'I won't,' Mot lies.

Mom is also on his back about him spending all his hard-earned cash. Every Friday afternoon, Mot sneaks into the house hiding something under his leather lumber jacket. He gets into big shit for buying the garment. A *shande*, a disgrace.

'What respectable Jewish boy from a respected Jewish home wears a leather lumber jacket? Only wild *chataisim* and *skotsim* wear leather jackets. Only peasants and lowlife gangsters dress like that.' There is a lot of, 'You're not going out looking like that,' and 'Aw, Ma, all the appies wear them. It's like a uniform.'

'And what respectable girl is going to go out with a boy that wears such a uniform?'

'Ma, I'm not going out with any girls.'

'That's right. Are you listening to yourself? Of course not. What respectable Jewish girl is going to go out with you in such a jacket? In a jacket like that, all he will bring home is *shiksas*,' she says in an aside to Dad, in search of his support on the matter as he sits quietly reading the newspaper.

'Maybe he needs a jacket?' Dad shrugs.

'Needs a jacket? This you call a jacket. The next thing is he's coming home with a motorbike.'

'Not with what I pay him,' Dad says without glancing up or intending any humour. There is a moment of silence, and suddenly, it is all laughter.

Mot's jacket is safe. The jacket turns out to be good for hiding stuff when Mot comes home after his spree every week. Mom hears him from the kitchen and calls out as he runs for the bedroom.

'What did you buy today?'

'Nothing, Ma,' he answers in a whisper, which gives him away. He's a lousy liar, just like me. I wish that, one day, I could have a black leather lumber jacket but know I never will. I'll have to become a printer's apprentice to have one of those and that is never going to happen.

'Don't blab on me,' Mot pleads as he hides his latest whatsit under the bed. Heaven knows why he does that. Mom and Dad would never rummage in his toolbox and wouldn't know which tool was bought this week or last. This hiding stuff is just temporary. He'll move it later in the dark when everyone has gone to sleep.

I'm going to get off easy.

'I used your saw today,' I tell him.

'Did you bugger it up?'

He goes up like a flare and as quickly douses it. Now is no time to bawl out a kid brother.

'You little shit. I bet you made it blunt.'

He's too busy hiding his new gadget to give his anger his full attention. I'm safe for now. Now is not a time to get angry. Right now, he needs me as an ally.

'I also used your ball-peen hammer.'

Later in the week, or the next, the punch will come, and I will cry to Mom that he hit me for nothing. That will get him into shit with Dad. But not much.

'He started it,' Mot defends himself. 'Why do you always take his side?'

'Because you're older. You should know better. Don't fight with your baby brother. You got nothing better to do. Go, improve yourself. Go read a book.'

Nothing makes Mot grit his teeth like being told to read a book. Why can't the old man, for once, say, 'Motty, the car won't start, go look at the engine. Maybe you can fix?' He'd be there in a minute even if it was after midnight, and at five past twelve the car would be fixed.

Mot glares at me. I grin back. But for the next week, I am waiting for that punch out of nowhere.

Later, in the dark, he uses a special torch to check out the tools that I have violated, looking for telltale scratches. Of course, there are. 'What the hell were you making?'

Proudly, I go to the back of our wardrobe and I take out the Scaramouche swords. His anger dissipates in a moment as he examines my work by torchlight.

'They look like shit,' is his final judgement. My heart lifts. I know what that means. Tonight is *Shabbos* but at sunset tomorrow, he'll be helping me fix them. This brotherhood thing is complicated.

I cannot wait for Sunday afternoon to run over to my new friend, Solly Nissenbaum, who lives a few houses away. With me I have two foils, modified by my brother, that have copper wire and different-coloured flex wound tight like an armature making the hilts. He has rounded the points and caps of the nails on the grinder he has bolted to his workbench in the garage. He is saving for an electric one, but I'd better keep my trap shut. He ball-peens the second cup as if it were clay fashioned on a wheel. It is beautiful. They are ready for combat.

If Solly's mother is at home and sees me coming through the gate carrying these weapons, she'll chase me away as if I were a stray dog. She knows what happened to Cyril Strul. But if she is out, I will be Stewart Granger, and Solly will just have to make do with Mel Ferrer.

'En garde!'

CHAPTER 37

With a Song in My Heart
(1952)

A biopic starring Susan Hayward and telling the true story of Jane Froman, a singer and entertainer who is involved in a plane crash that leaves her partially crippled. She makes a comeback entertaining troops in World War II but has serious romantic complications.

The most profound words I know are the ones pasted to the posters outside a cinema that read: NOW SHOWING. I study the posters like a rabbi reading the Talmud. My sages are Burt Lancaster and Gregory Peck. My new circle of friends wouldn't know Jonah from a whale. All they know is Donald Bradman, Dennis Compton and Stanley Matthews. Everything is soccer and cricket. One day, they will make fine examples of South African citizens. Rugby is a distant state we will only encounter in high school. We don't even talk of girls yet.

These new buddies only argue over who gets to play Roy Rogers. I let that one slide, knowing that next week I will be *The Crimson Pirate* and, the week after that, *Captain Horatio Hornblower*. Let them have Roy Rogers. I am conducting auditions, assigning roles, building props. But Abbott and Costello get cut.

I should be in the movies.

Even now, I want to see every movie ever released. Back in 1948, I am mostly first in the queue to see anything that is showing at the Rex bioscope in Greenway Road.

The scariest person for me in Greenside is Taki, the owner of the café next door to the Rex. There is always a gang of boys hanging out, waiting impatiently for a turn at Minstrel Man, the one pinball machine Taki keeps at the far end of the narrow space. The boys try to cheat the machine by making fake sixpences out of washers. When Taki catches one, it is scary. He gives him a solid *klap* across the ear.

'Mi kleveis ta glyka mou, ee tha kopso ta podthia sou!' His gestures translate easily. 'Don't steal my sweets or I will cut off your legs.'

'I will make you *kleftika*! Wap! Wap!'

'If you ever step inside my shop I will make you into a kebab!'

The next day, the boy is back, with a real sixpence. An honest sixpence buys all of Taki's forgiveness. The boy will never, ever come in again with a filed-down washer.

It is Saturday afternoon and I stand devastated under the porte-cochère of the Rex bioscope, tears streaming freely down my chubby cheeks. My nine pence, six for a ticket and a tickey for a roll of Maynard's Wine Gums, had fallen out of a hole in the pocket of my short pants as I ran all the way to be first in the queue at the cashier's window. It is a special day: Walt Disney's *Song of the South* is showing. I have been trying to draw Br'er Rabbit for weeks, knowing that it is coming to Greenside. The film is a mix of animation and live action. There's been nothing like it before.

I ran all the way to the Rex. My shirt is soaked with sweat but that's just fine because I am first. I tremble waiting for the box office to open. Today, I will occupy the centre seat of the front row.

Instead of which, an hour later, I am left alone outside while everyone is inside, waiting for the lights to go down for the big picture. I loiter outside, hoping, by some chance, to somehow see what is going on inside. The sound of excited voices trickles out to tease me. The laughter seems to cheer my loss as I stand transfixed in stunned shock. This is how I am to feel four years from now, when I am thirteen and Mom dies. I am rooted like a rock on the beach as the waves break over it. At interval, the kids flood out to rush to the café next door to clamour for Wilson's toffees, penny bubble gum, peppermints, liquorice, Lifesavers and Maynard's Wine Gums. They then rush back past me like the tide returning. I sob uncontrollably as the usher at the door watches me with a smirk.

His name is Jannie. He wears a maroon uniform with brass buttons, his arms crossed with one hand showing all the torn tickets, watching me like a hawk. Jannie, who is about seventeen, knows me. He could let me sneak past, but he won't. He's enjoying watching me blub. He has seen this baby-*kak* film three times already. His job is boring. He'd probably rather be somewhere else, watching a game of rugby or playing pinball next door at Taki's. I bet Jannie has washers in his pockets. But watching this fat *Jood* kid is a good-enough spectator sport for this afternoon. There are other ballsy kids who manage somehow to sneak in, past Jannie. I don't know how they preserve their anonymity. I would never make it. I am the biggest and loudest kid in my group, and he knows me and calls me *Jood*. I stare into the lobby. I don't want him to see me cry because that will just confirm his belief that all *Jode* are just big sissies. I can't drown in tears. Not here. But I am going to miss Bre'r Rabbit and all his friends. My heart is broken like it was the day we leave Mayfair.

'Hey boy, why you cry?'

Taki leans in the door of the café, one leg crossed over the other, lighting a smoke as he watches me. Business is suddenly quiet with all the kids inside the bioscope. Taki is better looking than the actor Ricardo Montalbán. I already know so many film stars' names. I am afraid to look Taki in the eye.

'Hey, boy, you, wha's your name? Come here.'

Reluctantly, I walk to him, trying to contain my tears, expecting him to *klap* me for blubbing. He looks down on me, one step up, like a god from Mount Olympus. I am nine but look twelve.

'Wha's your name?'

'Fedler.'

I spit out my surname, like an alias that he won't be able to track if he ever needs to. But then why would he? I would never think of filing down a washer to try to cheat Taki. He studies me for what seems like forever.

'No more crying. You too big. What happen?'

My sob story gushes forth like a confession. He crosses his arms as he listens. For sure, one is going to swoop down and *klap* me. I pull out both my pockets like a suspect being searched for a contraband coin and show him the hole as evidence.

He looks me over again and flicks his cigarette to the gutter, like something that Humphrey Bogart would do.

'Come!' he commands as he walks into the shop.

For sure, he's going to *donner* me. I follow like James Cagney in a film going to the electric chair.

Taki steps behind the counter.

Oh shit, what's he bringing out – a baseball bat?

He punches the till and reaches behind him, and the next moment, I have a sixpence and a roll of wine gums in my hand.

'Run!' he barks.

I fly with a song in my heart.

CHAPTER 38

A Getaway Car Named Desire

A Streetcar Named Desire (1951). A Tennessee Williams play-turned-film, set in New Orleans. Shot Marlon Brando to super stardom. Vivien Leigh, famous for playing Scarlett O'Hara in Gone with the Wind, *is equally memorable as Blanche DuBois.*

It should be easy enough to film Getaway Gus as part of the heist scenario. All he has to do is sit in the car, drum his fingers on the wheel and watch the entrance to the building. Again, it should just take a few minutes. My mistake in my instruction to Coach is to ask Gus to look anxious. He simply can't. I need some villainy, something threatening in his expression. Take 1 doesn't do it. I ask Coach to be diplomatic and ask if Gus could possibly stop smiling in the scene. 'Anxious', like 'furtive', becomes another casualty of translation. Coach cues Gus. Take 2.

Gus listens carefully. Their conversation is an extended one, where Gus makes many gestures regarding the interior of the car.

'What's the problem?' I ask, anxious to move on. It is barely noon and it has been the longest day.

'He wants to buy your car,' says Coach.

'I like this car. You must sell me this car.'

If only my actors could deliver their lines so convincingly. Not today, please. All we need is a cutaway shot, just a close-up of hands then a cut to Gus, his eyes moving. It's something that Alfred Hitchcock does so well, showing that the character is, well, anxious. Gus likes this drumming thing. Sitting at the wheel, somehow he believes that already this car is his. Possession is, after all, nine-tenths of the law. He beams and gets into a groove, his head and shoulders move in counterpoint to each other, dancing while sitting down.

But I insist on a moment of him looking serious. I have one of my greatest moments of genius as the camera starts to roll. I whisper to Coach, 'Tell him that I will never sell him my car.'

We get the shot. First take.

Dear God, let me call it a day.

CHAPTER 39

Tales of Hoffmann and Horror

The Tales of Hoffman (1951) is a film for lovers of ballet, partially directed by Michael Powell who also collaborated on the direction of The Thief of Bagdad.

Mom's biggest fear is that I will run off and disgrace the family. There is the time I stray from kindergarten across the mine dumps and the police find us kindergarten delinquents. It is an affair to remember. Never to be forgotten. Who at five knows that you don't do stuff like that? Why else have we learnt to walk?

It's my passions that worry Mom. She doesn't want me to waste my life with comics, movies and the piano. I've been getting lessons and I show some promise on the instrument. These are wastelands, inhabited only by the fallen, the lazy, the *no-goodnik*, the nightclub-johnny and the *laydik-gayer*.

Laydik has no sexual connotation. *Laydik* means 'empty' and *gayer* means 'goer'. Someone who goes around with his hands in his pockets, doing nothing. No good can come from any of these areas. Artists starve, do drugs and (God forbid) die of consumption.

Comics ruin young minds. They stop them from reading a good book. The music can only lead to one thing: nightclubs. With nightclubs come *shiksas* and drunkenness. These are three separate things but, like *laydik-gayer*, it is a compound idea.

Shiksas are non-Jewish girls. As for the bioscopes, they are filled with nightclub-johnnies, *laydik-gayers* and nightclub pianists with their *shiksa* girlfriends. There will be no hope for me unless I strictly follow the precepts of my parents. Like all parents, ours lie to us a little in an effort to lead us up the right path. The Right Path is one of Dad's major sermons.

'Be careful,' he warns, 'is always someone wants to lead you up from the straight and narrow garden path.'

It surprises me when Dad, though he mangles it somewhat, comes up with such a quintessential *goyish* reference. I doubt that he ever had a garden when he was growing up, but he quickly loses my interest when he reverts to the Jewish route.

'There is a right path and a wrong. Important to know right from wrong.' This is Jewish Talmudic juggling, the playing of opposites against each other. Right from Wrong. Good versus Evil. Success and Failure. War and Peace.

It's a seesaw. Once it gets going, it is forever. It is a never-ending daisy chain of opposites.

But he will suddenly surprise me with a song, 'De Prince of Vales is going to jails, parley-voo', or even 'I've come a million miles for vun of your smiles'. He slips easily into 'California, here I come.' I look over the table to Mom who has a broad secret smile dancing on her lips. This is a 'tell'.

The 'tell' is a story once told. It is a confession that begins as a sermon but drifts happily into reminiscence. The lesson tonight is about Saving and Waste. It comes long after Mom has died.

Dorrine and I are treating Dad to a movie. For some reason, my stepmother, Fanya, is not with us tonight. We take him to see Stanley Kubrick's *2001* and the Royal Cinerama in Louis Botha Avenue. To watch that particular movie at the scale at which it was intended is extraordinary. Reg Park, who was once Mr Universe and was Arnold Schwarzenegger's idol, just happens to sit behind us. It is impossible to miss his bulk even under dimmed light. He too is built in Cinerama.

At the end, Dad smacks his lips. 'What a vonderful film.'

Driving home, he asks how much we paid for the tickets. We tell him.

'So much?' We can almost hear him mulling this over in the back seat.

'Let me pay for my ticket,' he says, having added it all up.

'Not a chance. It's our treat.'

The wheels of cogitation turn over in the back. Dad knows to the penny what I earn. He likes to check over my invoices and statements. Can I afford such an extravagance? He considers his verdict.

'Thank you very much.' There follows another pause. 'You know what? Worth every penny.'

The confession unfolds. 'Oy!' he begins. This is going to be a story of tough times. 'We had it so hard. You can't imagine. A tickey for tram fare, I never had. I walked every day, miles. The Depression? Don't even talk. Every penny we had to save for something for the table. Never any *mazel*. No luck. Like poor *schwartzes*. That was us. Nothing was easy. Mommy kept the books. Always red, never black.'

I know him so well. Something new is coming.

'But once, it came in our horse. We got paid. We saw a little profit. We could pay off our debts and be free. But there was a show in town. *Swan Lake*. A once-in-a-lifetime opportunity. Not to be missed.'

'Not to be missed' is like a rabbinical injunction, like there is no freedom of choice in the matter. I have heard that one before. He uses it in 1954, the year we are mourning Mom, when Maurice Schwartz, the Jewish Laurence Olivier, comes to play Shylock in a Yiddish version of *Merchant of Venice* at His Majesty's Theatre. Mot and I, being official mourners, are disallowed any entertainment by custom, but Dad is bound by no such restraint.

Here is an issue in conflict of the Straight and Narrow that our parents have averred is the correct way. 'Be like Javert, follow the path of the righteous and have our reward.' But *Swan Lake* versus Responsibility? It was never going to be any kind of contest. And now Maurice Schwartz, *Merchant of Venice*? And in Yiddish *nogal*? Who could miss? Once in a lifetime...

Dad is torn with guilt that he should even want to go. It should be all sackcloth and ashes. How can any idea of entertainment be entertained? What a shallow piece of work is man.

But if it were Mom here now, we'd be going through the same thing. Like Dad, she too would be in tears about this once-in-a-lifetime opportunity, never to be missed, and going along to see Maurice Schwartz, the Yiddish Laurence Olivier is, well... a Godsend! God forgive us for thinking that a show could override the observance of a mourning.

But culture is not entertainment.

Culture is what feeds the soul. The whole of the Torah is nothing but culture. If not for culture, there is no Torah. And vice versa.

Which is Right? And what is Wrong? Mot and I have no desire to go watch the Jewish Laurence Olivier.

With great magnanimity, we grant Dad permission to go in the name of culture. Like the time they didn't pay their debts and went to see *Swan Lake*. But now I want to know about the time they went to see Al Jolson, the Russian-born Jew who performed in blackface in *The Jazz Singer*, and what it cost. I like it better when Dad talks of Jolson and not of Hoffmann.

CHAPTER 40

The Best Years of Our Lives
(1946)

Academy Award-winning film about US ex-servicemen returning home.

The whisper 'not to be missed' is in our home once more. It comes round like a festival. I know that, come *Shabbos*, Mom and Dad will be taking us to town to a matinée. We drive there because, well, one should avoid handling money on the Sabbath.

The seats are booked in advance, so that more or less puts a *hechsher* on the enterprise – a sort of kosher stamp of approval. There is always this concern to somehow observe the day of rest but with sliding rules – like it being okay to go see a really good movie, something that is cultural and will improve our minds. Tickets on a tram involve a financial transaction, so the tram is out, and it's nice to drive to town in the Hudson.

We dress up as if we are going to *shul* on *yom tov* in our best clothes. We wear ties, and brush and comb our hair as we stand in front of the mirror.

Mot tries to crowd me out. 'Stop bloody copying me,' he says, giving me the elbow. My big brother teaches me everything I know.

Mot makes a mix of Brylcreem and Vitalis with which we paste our hair to our scalps. Brylcreem is a cream and Vitalis is a clear eau de cologne. Men of the world who smoke Max are divided between the cream and the cologne. My brother has engineered the perfect combination of hair grooming to straddle both. My head feels as if it is coated in wax. This is how you look smart, dressed for an occasion.

I copy Mot as we put on our ties. He has taught me to tie a Windsor knot. It is an exciting event. The 'fillum' we go to see is an important, cultural one. Our family would not violate the *Shabbos* to go see Johnny Weissmuller, the Deutsche who plays Tarzan, or Roy Rogers, the cowboy, the *shaigets*, who is nothing but a peasant. No, the rules of the holy day can shift up a seat to accommodate something that improves the mind.

Today we are to see *The Best Years of Our Lives* at the Metro in Bree Street, one of the best bioscopes in town. Its credentials are impeccable. It could almost carry a Beth Din stamp. This is the fillum 'not to be missed' that everyone is recommending. There are other families with the *Shabbos* sliding-rule policy whom we are bound to meet at the Metro.

Rae is too grown-up to come with us. She's a teenager, busy with her friends, and doesn't want to spend an afternoon with baby brothers. So it is just Mom, Dad, Mot and me who go.

I am a bit apprehensive because my friends tell me, 'There's a guy in the fillum with no arms.'

'*Ag, kak, man.* You're just jealous that you aren't going to the Metro. How can you have a guy in a fillum with no arms?'

Mom has filled her bag with sweets. Maybe Dad will buy some Black Magic chocolates.

The Metro is a grand place. The Colosseum in Commissioner is more exciting. There, the ceiling looks like the sky with twinkling lights, and Charles Manning comes out from under the floor to conduct a whole orchestra as part of the supporting programme. Sometimes the supporting programme is the thing we enjoy most. But the Metro is also great. It shows *Tom and Jerry* cartoons and *Pete Smith Specialties*, which are hilarious.

It turns out, though, that *The Best Years of Our Lives* is just the worst, and anything but funny.

And there he is, the man with no arms. I squirm in my seat every time he appears on screen. I will only appreciate later that the story is about three war veterans who come home and have difficulty adjusting to their previous lives.

Harold Russell, the man with no arms, is an actual veteran and casualty of the war, and wins an Academy Award for his performance. He haunts me still, like Dad's glass eye in the glass at night.

Films that are supposed to improve the mind are usually about bad stuff. Driving to town, I ponder my previous two encounters with Culture and Mind Improvement. They were more like going to the dentist. Maybe I'm not going to enjoy this outing, my past experience nags.

Maybe what my friends told me is true after all. I'll just have to wait and see.

We have violated the *Shabbos* before to first see *The Red Shoes* and then to see *The Tales of Hoffmann*, neither of which remind me of the best years of our lives. Both are ballet movies and forever ruin any chance of me ever enjoying the ballet.

In *The Red Shoes*, the ballerina, Moira Shearer, puts on these red ballet slippers that won't let her stop dancing. It's a horror story equal to *The Pit and the Pendulum*, the classic comic I read where the victim gets sealed into this grave from which there is no escape.

In *The Tales of Hoffmann*, this guy Hoffmann first falls in love with a mechanical doll who breaks his heart, and then he's in love with this other woman and she breaks his heart. There is a scene where there is this duel with rapiers on a gondola and Hoffmann kills the guy who is in love with his girlfriend. He looks into a mirror, he can't see his own face, and the girl runs away with a dwarf. His heart is broken again. It's a fucken nightmare.

For me, *The Tales of Hoffmann* is a film to be missed. No one talks. Maybe if they did they could all get on better. All they do the whole time is dance.

Hoffmann is not a happy guy at the end. He doesn't get any of the three girls. He's such a loser. I'm sure Hoffman must be Jewish because Jewish stuff is always sad. Nobody gets anything in the end.

We go to the Bijou bioscope in Jeppe Street to see a film in Yiddish, *A Brivele der Mamen*. A Letter to Mother. Not only is the mother broken-hearted at the end, but so is the whole tearful cinema. I hate these movies that are improving my mind. They are all telling me that life is *kak*. The heroes are always doomed from the start.

It doesn't matter what happens to Roy Rogers in a movie. He is always going to win. Roy Rogers gets everything, even the girl.

Driving home after *The Best Years*, Mom says, 'What's wrong with Dovid? From him not a peep all afternoon.'

'He peeped at interval, Ma,' says Mot, deliberately misunderstanding Mom's mangled English. 'And he nearly *poeped* himself in the movie,' he adds, giving me another *eina* elbow punch on the arm in the back seat where no one can see.

'Maybe you should have *poeped* first, Shitpants?' he whispers.

He knows exactly what is going on with me. Bastard! He knows I'm shit-scared right now of losing my arms. Oh, he is going to have such fun with that. Punching me on the arm is just to get my boiler heated.

There are two messages in that. Watch your arms and watch out for the next elbow. Later, he'll have me explode and cry, then he'll be bored. The next hours are going to be hell. The whole way home, Mot keeps noodging me and sneaking elbow punches.

I grit my teeth, but eventually I lose it. I attack him with a flurry of ineffectual blows that he dismisses with laughter. That makes me madder. He is having such a good time.

'What are you doing in the back? Stop fighting,' says Dad. 'We take you to something special and you fight. Did you learn nothing? Fighting makes war. What comes from fighting? You can lose your arms, even your hands,' he adds as an afterthought.

How can you lose your arms without losing your hands?

CHAPTER 41

A Farewell to Arms
(1932)

This classic film, based on the famous Ernest Hemingway novel, won many awards. It starred Helen Hayes, Gary Cooper and Adolphe Menjou.

Saturday-night suppers are simple – scrambled eggs, jam, rye bread, cheese, sardines and tea. I'm not really hungry because I can't stop thinking about the guy with no arms. Just as I can never forget that sad sack Hoffmann and the girl in *The Red Shoes* after that afternoon nightmare.

The surprise is that, this time, it isn't Mot who starts it all up again. It's Dad.

'That boy in the film. He really was in the war. He lost his hands fighting the Nazis. Now he makes a film. Okay. But what is he going to do to make a living now? From what kind of job can he find? Believe you me, too many films with a boy without arms, they aren't making, not even one.' He pauses and looks to us for affirmation. 'Absolutely nothing,' he concludes.

He's happy now that he has resolved that. If this is what culture and improving the mind lead to, I don't want any of it.

Dad finds some solace in putting an extra sugar cube on his saucer to suck with his Russian tea. He stirs and sucks as he ponders further. 'Imagine if Bill Mallett came back to me after the war without hands to pick up his job. Without hands. What could he do?'

Bill Mallett has been Dad's number-one machine minder in the printing factory since it started during the Depression.

'Even a machine minder needs hands. The machine does the work and a minder has to watch. Still you need a pair hands. To switch on, off. To minding is also necessary, hands.'

Mom, who is at the stove making the scrambled eggs, sees a joke.

'If a man can pick up a job without hands, you have to hand it to him.'

Dad and Mot chuckle. I get the joke but can't find it funny. Hopefully, that will be the end of it.

We eat quietly and then Mot starts up again. 'You know how they made those things?'

'Made vot?' asks Dad, still as deep in the injustices of the world as Mot is deep in the mechanics of everything.

'Those claws.'

Damn him. He knows exactly which word to choose to freak me out.

'Do you know how they work?' Mot says, grinning wide. He sees no horror in the prosthetics but an example of genius engineering. The hairs on my back and neck are standing to attention. I remember every frame of Harold Russell's performance. I don't want to be reminded.

'It works with a spring release. He jiggles the one with the other and that's how he picks things up.'

If Mot tries to build one of those, I'm running away.

He grabs two forks and tries to get Dad to understand how the claw arms work, all the while sneaking smug smiles my way. He can't understand that Dad, a compositor, has no real mechanical skill. Dad can work a Cropper but can't repair a machine.

'There's a lock that opens and closes it.'

Mot has forgotten me for the moment and caught up with the explanation to Dad. Dad looks bewildered. I'm glad Mot has no friend without arms because for sure he's going to bring out the ball-peen hammer, wire pliers, side-cutter, and maybe use a Nescafé lid to manufacture a pair of Frankenstein fingers.

'You know how the cable works on a brake for a bike?'

Dad shakes his head. He never had the opportunity to ride a bike. Mot gives up. Then he remembers me and innocently does an imitation of Charlie Chaplin's famous fork and knife dance on the table. Dad catches on. He has seen all of Chaplin's movies, and for free.

'From this, you don't make jokes. You know what it is to lose an eye? If they are so clever to make such hands, why can't they make a glass eye that doesn't hurt all the time?'

That's enough culture and mind improvement for one day, thank you.

Rae arrives like the cavalry from being out with friends. The conversation shifts immediately to just her and Mom.

'So where did you go?' Mom is going to be quizzing her for the rest of the evening.

'I was at a social with the Bnei crowd.' Mom ponders this information.

'Did you meet any nice boys?'

'Some,' says Rae.

Mom ponders again. 'Anybody at university? Any doctors?' she asks hopefully.

'I don't know, Mom. This one boy I think is doing accountancy.'

There is a long pause. Mom looks at me and Dad.

'An accountant is good. A dentist is better,' says Dad.

'I don't even know his name. It was just a crowd. He's short anyway.'

There is another pause.

'An accountant will never be short,' Dad says with a half-smile.

Mom never laughs at my sister's prospects, but she smiles at that one.

'Meet any *laydik-gayers*?' I ask. Mom gives me a look. It is time I went to bed.

I am grateful to run from the table.

CHAPTER 42

Zoon at the Top

> Room at the Top *(1959). An ambitious young man from a poor family gets a job in a mill town in Northern England. He woos the daughter of the richest man in town, but he also falls in love with a married woman with whom he has an intense affair. There is more. Stars Laurence Harvey and Simone Signoret.*

On this particular *Shabbos* in 1950, we are unsure whether the film we have booked to see is indeed one not to be missed. Nevertheless, we are going to the Piccadilly Cinema in Yeoville to see a British film called *Cairo Road*. Our move to Greenside took place two years ago, and now that we are living there, our religious restrictions have loosened somewhat. This is the new world. Mayfair was the ghetto. Mom and Dad are not sure whether it is be a cultural event. It could be rubbish. But, being British, how bad can it be?

The reason for going to see the film is a highly personal one. My parents attended the *bar mitzvah* of one of the movie stars. They are not exactly close to his family but know them well. I even remember once driving to their house in Bertrams to fetch or deliver something. It is not that my parents are all that enamoured of this now-glamorous personage, the son of these acquaintances. Dad has had enough trouble with the boy's older brother, and this actor doesn't even go by his given name, which is Larushka Mischa Skikne. One can understand that he now goes by Larry. He is, after all, making films in England. Also, the boy was never much of a Jewish son. What he did is legend. He ran away from home when he was just sixteen or seventeen to join the navy. He was detained in Durban, and his struggling parents had to travel to collect him and bring him home. When they came face to face, the boy said, 'I have never seen these people before in my life.'

'Imagine such a thing a child should say to a mother.' Mom is forever appalled whenever the story pops up. Of course, as always, it becomes an instruction in life.

'You see what becomes of bioscopes? It makes *laydik-gayers*, nightclub-johnnies and rubbish of a good name. From Skikne to Harvey. Look what becomes.'

Her eye falls directly on me for I am the one most likely to stray. What will become of me? Don Fellers? Fellows? Davenport Feathers, perhaps? If I were to do that, it would simply kill my mother. Of that I am reassured. Mom hopes that the threat of her death will be enough of a deterrent.

It is because of Harvey's brother Nahum Skikne, who comes to Dad looking for a job in 1940, that, ten years later, we are at the Piccadilly to see Laurence Harvey in a film. Nahum Skikne, who is not a member of the Master Printer's Association, needs temporary employment as he plans to emigrate to Palestine the following year. A real *chalutz*, a pioneer wanting to build a homeland for our people? How can Dad resist such a request? Dad knows nothing about having to join unions. He employs people as he needs them. Nahum Skikne understands the risk to Dad's business. Dad is still a *griner*, a greenhorn.

Thus, Dad enters into what he describes as the most difficult period of life. Some disgruntled employees report him to the union; a case is brought against him, which almost brings him to ruin. He fights the case with Percy Yutar, who will become infamous for being Madiba's prosecutor in the Rivonia Trials and who acts for the Crown till 1943, when Dad is finally discharged on appeal.

Dad is always forgiving when he proudly tells that Nahum Sneh (Skikne) was to become deputy mayor of Beersheba. Dad feels that he has himself been something of a *chalutz*, a pioneer, and somehow a participant in that achievement. Nahum chooses a Hebrew surname, which means 'burning bush'. Mom and Dad approve.

I wonder at the success of Laurence Harvey. There is a host of better players who never rise so high. He stars opposite Elizabeth Taylor, Frank Sinatra, John Wayne and Paul Newman in major blockbusters. Hollywood likes British voices. Brits bring prestige to the screen. His fame as a performer rockets in the British movie *Room at the Top* in 1959, in which he stars opposite Simone Signoret, considered one of France's greatest actresses and wife of the French singing icon, Yves Montand. She wins an Oscar for her performance. Signoret always speaks of herself as Jewish and fights in all the battles of the Jewish people, from equal rights for Soviet Jews to Israel's right to survive. She is born Henriette Charlotte Simone Kaminker.

'Such a handsome boy,' says Mom after the show, 'but what he only did to his mother is criminal.'

'Worse,' says Mot, 'it was murder to watch.'

CHAPTER 43

Oh Mother, Where Art Thou?

O Brother, Where Art Thou? (2000). *A Coen brothers comedy set in Louisiana during the Great Depression, based on Homer's* The Odyssey.

I imagine sitting in some grand shopping venue with my mother, where there is a tea lounge with a piano player offering tinkling muzak, quiet familiar tunes like 'Somewhere over the Rainbow' or 'When You Wish Upon a Star'.

It is a venue such as the Belfast, John Orr's, Stuttafords, the fashionable shopping stores in central Johannesburg where our mothers go weekly to shop and meet. It is in some metropolis, where all the Jewish mothers of the world meet, daintily drink English tea in China cups with milk and eat fat scones crowned with real cream and genuine strawberry jam, as they confer *durch tsu reiden dem hartz* – to talk through one's heart, take a load off, share their fears and ambitions for their children, catch up on who has been born, who is passing and so forth. But it is the subject of *die kinder* that dominates. Since long before Freud and the couch, Jewish mothers have been lounging in comfortable armchairs, enjoying group therapy, where a consultation is the price of a cup of tea and a scone; and for another week, a mother can acquire the *koach*, the physical and emotional strength, to carry on. What else is one to do? *Oy vey!* They all heave a collective benediction. Such is life. And especially children.

It is quite possible in the real world that Mom has sat in such a tea lounge with Mrs Skikne, swopping tales of *tsorres*. In reality, I would not be included in the conversation, being barely able as yet to walk. But in the fantasy, I am being discussed as if I am a contemporary of 'Larushka, mein zoon', Mrs Skikne's younger son, the one who wants to become an actor.

'*Oy!* I worry about *mein Dovidel*. Always comics, with bioscopes. I don't want he should grow up a *laydik-gayer*, a *no-goodnik* or a nightclub-johnny.'

It remains an eternal mystery how Jewish mothers know from nightclub-johnnies.

Mrs Skikne tsk-tsks in sympathy.

Mrs Livi nods and sighs now that it is her turn to contribute. It is a lot like a game of rummy where you only play your hand to top a story. There is no language difficulty for they all speak Yiddish.

'*Oy*! The trouble I had with my Ivovkele. When we escaped from Mussolini and when we came to Marseilles, what does he want to do? Become a cabaret singer. After all we went through? He also changes his name. For what? He runs to Paris and gets involved with that *schtick* drug addict, Edith Piaf. From this, he expects to make a living?'

Ivo Livi changes his name to Yves Montand, succeeds as both a cabaret singer and movie star, is heralded as the archetypal great French lover, and is considered by many to be the quintessence of worldly Gallic charm. His movie star burns brightest when he plays opposite Marilyn Monroe, with whom he has a brief, and greatly publicised, love affair. Monroe is besotted with Mrs Livi's sexy son, and it is rumoured that Montand makes her pregnant. But by the end of filming on *Let's Make Love*, the affair is over. Ivovkele makes it brutally clear he had no intention whatsoever of leaving his wife Simone Signoret.

Signoret says of the affair, 'If Marilyn is in love with my husband, it proves she has good taste. For I am in love with him too.'

'*Laydik-gayers*,' sighs Mom.

'*No-goodniks*,' adds Mrs Skikne.

'Nightclub-johnnies,' agrees Mrs Livi.

They cluck in unison, regretting the sons they will never have – the doctors.

CHAPTER 44

Whose Movie Is It Anyway?

> *Whose Life Is It Anyway? (1981). First a play. Study of a quadriplegic who requests the hospital authorities to remove his life-support systems so that he may die with dignity. Stars Richard Dreyfuss.*

There is a gap where I find myself alone with Coach for the first time. Hennie is setting the camera on the M1 highway service path for a telephoto shoot of a chase on foot. Moe is at the Braamfontein end, and he and Hennie communicate by a two-way radio, equipment supplied by Hennie. Coach and I stand back watching, not wanting to intrude. The highway streaks over the sprawl of the Park Station stockyard from Braamfontein before it splits into an upper and lower deck, the upper feeding into, and the bottom one feeding out of, the city. We are at the staircase on the top deck, at the city end of the flyover that leads directly down to the western side of the Old Market building. The staircase snakes around a giant supporting pillar down to street level at the southwestern corner of the Market building, which spills directly onto the stockyard. And in days of yore, when this giant depot functioned, it fed the country, and the trains crowded to her like beggars. Now it is somewhat derelict and decayed and has assumed a vague sense of menace. This is Newtown, in need of being called something else. Perfect.

Dad has his first factory at this end of town in the days when he can't afford a tickey for his tram fare home.

Hennie appears to be able to afford anything. He owns a lot of expensive stuff, from lights to cameras, from guns to pickup trucks.

This sequence has Frank with his two pursuers hot on his heels, running the stretch across the bridge, a distance of kilometre or more.

Frank has to run for his life. No stiff-legged zombie steps today, please. This cannot be a Sunday jog. We are asking the actors to belt it across. Hennie is very at home with the radio; listening to him, it is obvious that Moe, at his end, is finding it somewhat confusing. A mogul doesn't know technical stuff. Coach and I stand well back, letting the two sort out their problems. Moe has to wait for Hennie to give the call to cue the runners. It all takes time, time that Coach and I fill in by getting acquainted.

'Have you worked with these guys before?' I ask.

'Hennie, yes. Moe, not so much.' The answer surprises me.

'You did *Timer Joe 1* and *2* with both of them, right?'

'Yebo.'

I remember Moe telling me that he has only made two movies. I am naturally curious that there are more numbers to disclose.

'So you've worked with Hennie before that?'

'Lots.'

'Other movies?'

'Lots. Lots.'

'How many movies?'

He whistles an indeterminate number. 'Eish! I don't remember.'

'What, three, four, more?' This is becoming an interrogation.

He shrugs, unable to provide a figure.

'Ten?' I keep upping the ante.

'More. More.'

'*Twenty?*'

He consults the sky.

'Maybe twenty. Maybe more. Yes.' He returns to earth with an answer.

Twenty films in a year? Forty films in two years? Not possible. This is a very tall story.

'You have worked with Hennie Basson on more than twenty films? So how long have you worked with him?' I begin casually, like Columbo about to trap a guilty party.

'Since last of last year.'

That's two years, tops. 'You have made forty movies in two years?'

'Lots and lots of films.'

Somehow, I believe it to be true.

Hennie signals for silence. He is ready to shoot and cues Moe to start the chase. He makes no effort to consult me at all. He is all about rushing things along. I have these perfect images in mind that I have thought through for so long and so hard that I feel need some discussion. I want my DP and I to see eye to eye. What I am hoping for is some recognition, perhaps, of my efforts.

Though I cannot quote f-stops, apertures and all the minutiae of camerawork, I know precisely what is required. The direction in my script calls for a telephoto because it compresses distance so that further and nearer images appear to be right on top of each other, and Frank's pursuers look as if they are about to bring him down. Do they have him? Don't they? The choice of lens is what is heightening the suspense. Wide angles create other dramatic possibilities. Movie buffs would get me. After all, I have worked with Richard Cutler, Struan Robertson and John Brett Cohen, all recognised masters of photography. Sam Haskins, who is Mr Pentax and is world renowned, greeted at the airports in Japan like a rock star, is a mate I have acquired through collaboration.

But Hennie is not at all interested in anything I have to say. We seem to have entirely different agendas. Richard, John and Sam always take time to consider my opinion. Who the hell does this cameraman think he is? I would dearly love to engage him in a conversation about photography.

CHAPTER 45

Radio Days

(1987)

A middle-aged man looks back on his childhood in Rockaway, New York, in a series of vignettes focused on the golden days of radio. Joe (Woody Allen), who narrates, is portrayed as a teenager in the film by Seth Green.

Our move to Greenside in May of 1948 is a mistake from the first day. It breaks Mom's heart, as the phrase has it, but it takes a year to manifest physiologically. In September of 1949, after Yom Kippur, the Day of Atonement, the day on which the Almighty names names in the Book of Life, He elects to put Mom's on the shortlist in His black book. Maybe not this coming year, maybe not the next, but she has been blacklisted. After the fast of Yom Kippur of the Jewish calendar year 5714, she suffers a massive heart attack and is hospitalised for three months, which renders her a cardiac cripple at fifty-one for her remaining four years.

By the time I am eleven, the idea that Mom is going to die soon is not something I can daydream away. I live in a constant state of terror and I cry quietly in my bed every night. We learn to expect to have to make the midnight call to Dr Josselson, who comes when Mom has yet another attack. Will she go like Claude Kudsee, in the dead of night? How I dread that phrase. But she limps on into another day. We learn to have the kettle boiled to make the tea for after Dr Louis has attended to her, as we sit in the darkest hours of the night and he tries to reassure us that the sun will rise. It is that small act of normalcy, the cup of tea and 'Please, doctor, have a jam biscuit,' that eventually puts a veil over the doomsday thought. This is the way we will live, and I begin to have some hope and return to my childhood and seek out new friends.

When we move to Greenside, Mot's best friend becomes Ivan Cohen. Ivan has two brothers, Max and Tzoddik, one older, one younger. The Cohens, too, are immigrants from Mayfair. Motty and Ivan have their *bar mitzvahs* on the same day at different *shuls*. Theirs is an ancient rivalry. Mot and Ivan share the distinction of not being great scholars, and at sixteen Ivan gets apprenticed to become a motor mechanic working at New Curzon Motors in Kotze Street in Hillbrow. Mot and Ivan share a new ambition, to own a motor car. Ivan aims to own a big garage and franchise Valiants. No one takes him seriously. Even his family. What Jewish father wants his son to be a grease monkey? No doubt, like Dad, Ivan's father, Bennett Cohen, who has a thriving factory called Kaigor making kitchen furniture, has had bigger ambitions for his son. But at least he is pursuing a useful trade. Grease? Schmease! Monkey? Schmonkey! It's not a fritter. It's a living.

Both Dad and Bennett Cohen are wrong.

Ivan is the first to own a car. He arrives at our door one evening, abuzz with pride of ownership. His car is a London taxi, rescued from the scrapheap, abandoned by New Curzon as being unsalvageable. It has no floorboards; Ivan has blown his month's wages, the grand sum of twenty-five pounds, buying it with the dream of restoring it.

Mom, Dad, Mot and I, and even Rae, come out to the driveway on a perfect summer's evening to look at this wonder parked in our driveway. Though as close as brothers, Mot and Ivan share a fierce rivalry. Mot is seething that Ivan has got a car before he has. This intense jealousy is one that persists throughout their lifetime. They are both lifetime friends and lifetime enemies.

Ivan insists on giving us a detailed inspection. A car without a floor is indeed an odd spectacle. The taxi has a sort of makeshift one of planks nailed together. Ivan switches on the engine and the old pensioner trembles, sputters and coughs. We would not be surprised at a big gob of black phlegm spitting from the radiator.

'What do you think?' Ivan glows, his cheeks smudged with grease.

Mom becomes our spokesperson. 'Ivan, this car is going to put you on your feet.'

At last. A parent who acknowledges that ambitions are not just frittering.

'Thank you so much, Mrs Fedler.'

'Yes,' says Mom, the mistress of timing. 'You're going to have to get out and push.'

The taxi survives two weeks.

But Ivan is not one to be put down. He talks and dreams big. Mot surrenders his ambitions to Dad's domination. Ivan's next ambition is to become a photographer. He sets up a darkroom at home and arrives one evening on foot to our dining-room table to declare his new pursuit.

'I'm going to do weddings and *bar mitzvahs*. What do you think, Mrs Fedler?'

Mom was a great friend of Ivan's late mother who died when Ivan and his two brothers were little. Mom's opinion is an echo he needs to hear. Besides, it is an unspoken but open secret that Mom will be meeting Ivan's mom soon enough. Her life is all but over. Her opinion is one to be heard.

'Photographer? That will make something of you, Ivan.'

We all wait for the stomping on his dream. There is none.

Mot goes dark and silent, which is rare. What is he thinking?

Soon after, Mom leaves to join the late Mrs Cohen. Ivan eventually makes a fortune out of radios and kitchen appliances, securing the agency for Kenwood products.

Mot sneaks in one Friday with a bunch of stuff to hide.

'Are you wasting your wages?' Mom calls out from her bed, observing the Friday ritual, as he sneaks down the passage to our bedroom.

'No, Mom,' he lies as he frantically stuffs a cardboard box full of photographic equipment out of sight.

But there is no way he is getting out of the fritter sermon.

CHAPTER 46

Photo Story

Photo Story is a free Microsoft application that allows users to create a visual story (show-and-tell presentation) from their digital photos.

Evening. The film stock is black and white, old, scratched. We follow a boy, Chonny (Dad as a child), dressed in a shabby coat and cap as he walks briskly down the gaslit sidewalk of the main street of a *shtetl*. A similar-looking boy stands on a corner selling newspapers. A banner headline board leans against a streetlamp pole. In Russian, it reads 'War!' There are subtitles.

The vendor Yossel, in the tradition of newspaper vendors everywhere, calls out as people hurry past. 'War with Germany!' A troop of soldiers marches by in the street as Chonny draws level with Yossel.

Chonny: What gives, Yossel?

Yossel: It's war! *Milchoma*!

Chonny: What war?

Yossel: How would I know? I sell the papers. Extra! Extra! Read all about it! How goes it with the photographer?

Chonny: I like it. Better'n sewing buttonholes. For three years, I get paid nothing. I'm an apprentice and they're making me a printer. My boss's son came back with a printing machine from Riga. Now they are making me a printer. How am I going to become a photographer? They never let me in the darkroom.

Yossel: At least you get to work inside.

Chonny: Inside is his daughter, the witch. So ugly she hides in her room. I got to *schlepp* water upstairs for her bath.

Yossel: But you get to print the movie programmes and go see Charlie Chaplin for free. Who has your luck? (He goes back to calling out the headlines.)

Chonny shrugs and continues down the sidewalk, whistling while everything around him suggests panic. People run, carrying parcels, suitcases. Chonny is blissfully unaware of this as he enters the premises with the shingle on the door that reads, 'Stzupak Photography and Printing'. He enters and an unpleasant female voice calls from upstairs.

Ms Stzupak: Chonny, is that you?

Chonny takes off his jacket as he greets yet another boy, Yudel, who is feeding paper into a Cropper print machine that katchoofs loudly.

Yudel: *Dein basherte ruft.* Your beloved calls.

Chonny: Tomorrow, you carry the water. I'll do the printing.

Ms Stzupak (*stridently*): It's late for my bath!

Chonny (*calls*): I'm going to get the water now. (*To Yudel, normal voice*) Where is the bloody bucket?

Yudel: It's in the darkroom.

Chonny: Great. I get to go to the darkroom.

He enters the darkroom through two sets of black curtains that completely block out the light, muttering to himself. The film changes to negative as in a night camera, ultraviolet light, so we can see the action in the dark.

Chonny (*muttering*): Yes, Ms Rochel! No, Ms Rochel. Three bags full, Ms Rochel. Who has my luck? When do I get to the photography? I should have listened to my Zayde and stayed a tailor.

He fumbles in the dark in search of the bucket.

Briefly cut to a sharp hook on the wall that is filmed in positive image, even possibly in colour, a subliminal image, and cut back to ghostly black-and-white negative image as Chonny stoops and his right eye gets punctured.

It is like the Luis Buñuel image in *Un Chien Andalou*, where an eye gets sliced. Chonny cries out in agony, and his cry becomes the whine of a train as in Alfred Hitchcock's *The 39 Steps*.

Cut to Chonny on train. His head is wrapped in a thick, bloodstained bandage covering the eye. His father, a dignified figure with a long beard, holds him close. Through the window, we see a troop train pass close by and slowly in the opposite direction. As the two trains draw level, a soldier, fresh and young in new uniform, sees the injured boy through the window. The boy looks like a victim of war. The soldier stares curiously but Chonny's look is vacant.

Cut to our Greenside kitchen. It is just the three men left in the house, sitting now at the kitchen table, drinking tea. Dad is reading the paper, the headline of which reads, 'WW3?'

Mot: *Jissis*. Can't we get some cake sometime?

Dad: Who will bake? Your mother, *ava sholem*, isn't here any more.

Mot: We could buy a cake at Crystals.

Dad: Buy? Buy? All you know is how to spend your money. To buy cakes is for rich people. Have bread, jam. Sugar is good for you. Don't always look to spend.

Mot: They're my wages. I can spend them how I like.

Dad: I know. I pay them every week. And what do you do? You spend.

Mot: They're my wages.

Dad: Not until you're twenty-one.

Mot: Eighteen. I can vote.

Dad: Eighteen? Twenty-one? What's the difference? *Pisher*! What do you know from vote? When you turn twenty-one, you won't have a penny, big shot, if not for me and your mother, *ava sholem*. We put in a savings account every week. So what new *meshuggas* you brought to the house this week?

'Photography,' I chirp in.

Dad puts down the paper, his interest piqued. He looks thoughtfully at Mot.

'Photography?' The word rolls off his tongue like the mention of a pastrami-on-rye sandwich.

Mot kicks me under the table and whispers, 'Little shit!'

'So, photography? So, *nu*, what did you buy?'

Mot loudly slurps his tea in a vain effort to drown out the interrogation and the fritter sermon that is sure to follow. He manages another kick at the same time. I know it's coming, so I move and he misses.

'Oh, he bought chemicals . . . and photographic paper.' I'm snitching, teasing him, sticking him in the ribs for a change. It's rare to get even with an older brother.

Dad folds the paper and places it on the table. He wants to know about Mot's latest, expensive madness.

'Fritter! Fritter! Fritter!' I say softly, giggling about our own filial code.

'What chemicals you bought?' Dad crosses his arms, ready to hang on every word.

Mot mumbles, 'It's stuff you need for developing.' He hopes this will close it.

Dad squinches his one good eye. 'Who are you telling? You're telling me you need chemicals for developing? What do you do for fixing? You have to dissolve hypo-salt in a glass of water for a fixing bath. So, *chochem*, genius, did you buy trays? One for developing, one for wash, and the one for fixing?'

Mot stops mid-slurp and even I am rendered speechless. It's not that we don't know the story of how Dad lost his eye working for a photographer in the very hour that World War I started, it's that we don't expect Dad to really have any knowledge of photography. Sure, we know he would have loved to be a photographer and that the loss of his eye killed that prospect, but this lively interest is new to us.

Dad stands up. 'Come, show me your studio.'

We head to the bedroom. This feels like it's going to be a search by the secret police. Even I am worried that Dad might, by chance, open our desk and find Mot's meagre stash of titty pictures. Mot has set up a small table in a corner, behind our wardrobe, a place that Dad would never spot on his way to the bathroom. There is no danger of him ever entering our room. Why would he?

Mot has already set up three lights with individual switches, fixed to a board of Masonite mounted with screws to the table – one white, one red and one blue. When you open the packet of photographic paper, you can do it with the red light on as that does not expose it to light. Also, there is a timer, a small clock that you use to time the exposure of the paper over which is laid the negative, all of which gets put into a special press with small clamps.

Dad examines the setup. He takes note of the piece of iron board Mot brought home from the factory, which fits across the small window and completely obliterates any light that may creep in.

'A darkroom it is.' Dad takes note of the three trays on the table and the press. 'You're making contact prints?'

'For starters. I'm looking for an enlarger,' Mot confesses.

'An enlarger would be nice.' Dad nods. He looks under the table and spots the chemicals. 'You must be careful when you look under the table in a darkroom,' he says quietly.

'Why?' Mot asks.

'It can happen, accidents.'

CHAPTER 47

The Last Picture Show
(1971)

Two boys reaching graduation contemplate their futures outside of a dead-end town. Directed by Peter Bogdanovich, The Last Picture Show *belongs in the top ten all-time greatest American movies.*

Desert Legion, starring Alan Ladd, is the feature at the Savoy cinema in town. It is not a memorable movie. The only reason I remember it at all is that it is Monday, the last day of a school holiday, and the last day of my mother's life. She is dead early the next morning, the 29th of September 1953, 114 days before my fourteenth birthday. I sit through the movie with a sense of dread, not daring to look behind me in the gloom for a black-cowled figure lounging in the dark in the back row, his hollow eye sockets fixed on the back of my neck. I just know that something awful is about to befall me. Mom dies the next day at about half past eight in the morning. In those following months, I grow up more than I would have liked. It never occurred to me that my mother actually would, or could, die, even though she'd been so fragile. She was a constant star in my universe – always there.

Dad, Mot and I settle into a whole new array of rigid rituals.

First, there is the rising early in the morning to attend *shul*, where Mot and I have to recite the Kaddish, the prayer in praise of the Almighty on behalf of the dead. I go every morning, deprived of sleep and cold to my core. The prayers seem to go on forever with much repetition, and I find it all unbelievably boring. When the festivals approach, of which there are many, we have to get up really early in order to accommodate longer repetitions. After that, it is home for a hurried breakfast of toast and fish paste and then to school. In the afternoon, I have to attend Hebrew school. After which, it is back to *shul* for the afternoon and evening prayers, which are almost exactly the same as the morning prayers.

Our lives are pretty much dictated by the constant demand to say the

Kaddish. Another thing is that we are not allowed entertainment of any kind. We may turn on the radio to listen to the news and nothing else. We may not attend parties or celebrations of any kind. But the greatest imposition on my life is that I am not allowed to go to the cinema. Not only have I lost my mother but am also being punished most cruelly.

The three Fedler men are pretty much prisoners confined to one another's company. For entertainment, we begin to play chess, which we do badly. I remember Saturday nights confined to the kitchen, waiting my turn at the boring diversion and longing to sit in front of a silver screen.

Yet another change in the order of things is the reading of the newspaper. This is bought religiously every day on Dad and Mot's return home from work. So ritualistic is this practice that they buy *The Star* from a particular corner as they drive past each day. Many paper sellers line the route home, but it is at the edge of Vrededorp, just before the gas works, that the transaction takes place. I travel with them from time to time over the years and am sometimes given the task of paying the seller the tickey he requires as we make the hurried exchange in the flow of traffic. He knows us well enough to pass a greeting of recognition. With the newspaper in hand, Mot, who is driving, asks, 'What's new?'

I have no real memory of reading newspapers before the year of our mourning but now I pick up the habit from both Dad and Mot. When we return from *shul* and have yet another chicken dinner, sometimes provided by my sister Rae who is well off the shelf, married, and living around the block, we adjourn from the kitchen to the dining room where reading the paper is almost equal to writing.

The paper is divvied up. Dad wants to know the political situation in regard to Israel and the rest of the world. That is something like three pages. Mot only wants to read the smalls, wanting to know what is for sale and what is best priced. It can be anything from a washing machine to a set of panel-beating hammers. Every item has his undivided attention. I end up with the middle section of the paper where there's a political cartoon by either JH Jackson, Jock Leyden or Abe Berry. I particularly like Leyden's work.

What really pulls me in, though, is the page that advertises all the cinemas of the city. Centre and large are the major movie theatres, boldly blaring the latest blockbusters. There is the 20th Century, the Colosseum, the Empire, His Majesty's, the Metro, the Bijou and the Savoy. Then follows the suburban bioscopes in a double column at the bottom of the page. I study them all and mourn every movie I am missing.

But I never check what's showing at the Savoy any more.

CHAPTER 48

The Chase

(1966)

Stars Marlon Brando and Robert Redford. Marlon Brando, the sheriff, wades through sin and moral degradation looking to recapture his integrity. Ho and hum.

Coach and I stop talking as Frank and his pursuers get close to where I will yell, 'Cut!' Not that Hennie takes the slightest notice of me. I want a one-on-one discussion with him about how the film is shot, to tell him that I have a long history in photography and film. But it is all in his hands right now.

We are spellbound by Frank's furious pace. He looks like he's going for gold. His pursuers struggle to keep up with him.

'Lekker!' Hennie calls out, holding a thumb in the air to encourage them over the last gruelling stretch to the finish, which is at the staircase where it will all continue down to street level but needs several camera-angle changes. One of these angles is to be a hand-held shot as Hennie runs carefully behind them down the spiral. What it needs is a steady cam, but Hennie hasn't bought one.

We have no skidding or crashing or any of the deafening action that usually accompanies a movie chase. All is played out in virtual silence. On the looped soundtrack, all I want are the sounds of laboured breathing and footfalls. In my naiveté, I imagine we will have foley artists, people who add sound effects to movies, adding these subtle extras. At this stage, I still am under the impression that I will also have something to do with the editing of the movie. I have a lot yet to learn about Messrs Mankowitz and Basson.

We work our way down the staircase in stages, sometimes placing the camera in front of the runners and switching to filming from behind them. We finally get to ground zero. This last shot is wide, well away from the trough of the stairs, showing the highway support pillar behind it on the left and the edge of the Market building on the right. Between that is a gap that leads directly onto the bird's nest of railway that jumbles outside of Park Station, which is at least a kilometre away, at the turn to the right at the shed behind the market side of the Old Market. The edge of the shed makes a natural cutting point, because once the actors have passed that, they are out of camera.

Though this instance is entirely unnecessary, I still call out 'Cut!' Old habits die hard.

This run has been Olympian. Frank redeems himself by setting the pace. The hell with walking. On one of the takes down the staircase, he gives me a sweat-soaked smile. I beam back. Almost before I yell, 'Cut.'

Hennie is loading the equipment into his Kombi, ready to move on to the next location. Only two very sweaty actors return from behind the shed.

'Where is Frank?' we ask. They are like amateurs finishing the Comrades Marathon, too winded to speak. One lies down on the ground like someone being prepared for crucifixion. It takes them some time before they are able to speak.

Coach consults. 'Maybe he needed to make a piss,' is the conclusion.

Curious and concerned, we move like a pack of tracker dogs, searching and sniffing around everywhere. No Frank. We pass the corner of the shed, which gives us a full view of the entire rail network. We limit our search to just around the shed. Still no Frank. He has to be here somewhere. Maybe he's had to take an emergency dump and found a private corner? We start to raise our eyes and look further.

'There!' someone points out.

Five hundred metres or more to the east, where the railway lines converge, we spot the diminishing figure of Frank chugging away like a locomotive, about to disappear into the maw of Park Station.

We watch in awe and amazement.

'Come back!' we eventually call in all the languages we know.

'*Kom terug! Woza! Kommen Sie her!* Come Back! *Bo heina! Kum tsurik!*'

He must hear one of us because he does, eventually, stop running.

It's a pity we don't have all that on film. Tomorrow, we shoot at the Oriental Plaza. Please let this be an easy day.

CHAPTER 49

Gofer Broke

A movie needs a lot of toys. It is not just palm fronds and Nescafé lids. Writing down the story, one mentions things in passing: handcuffs, food on a tray, guns, a security box, rough diamonds, outfits, a ballpoint pen. As a writer, one pays little heed to these details. In the writing, one might not refer to an object at all, but just to its function. For instance, 'He/She writes.' We casually infer things. Write? Ergo, a writing implement and something to write on. But is it perhaps a Koki pen that is implied? Is it chalk?

The writer proceeds with the misplaced belief that someone else will attend to such obvious detail. The required object will just be available without the need to go hunting for it. That is not how it happens on set. There is a lot of desperate, last-minute searching on set.

It begins even as we start to shoot. There is no sign prepared for the International Diamond Co. I have to make a frantic call to my designer friend, Cliff Webb, to help quickly put that together. Someone rushes across town to fetch it. Not to waste time, we find something else to shoot. This sending someone off to fetch or buy something even as we are about to shoot becomes a pattern. Very quickly, I assume the role of prop master, filling sketchbooks and dispatching a runner with drawings of what is required. Carnival Novelty is everything its name implies. Our film requires us to visit the shop regularly. It is able to supply fake cooked chicken, lobster and handcuffs. It is situated in Jeppe Street, across the road from the Johannesburg Post Office, thankfully, just short blocks from where we mostly film.

By the second day, I am wading in mish-mash, up to my ears in *tohu va-vohu* and who knows what. I have much to learn. Having created my world, I expect it to now yield fruit. The Almighty is capable of handling all the ancillary tasks of creation, single-handed. He provides land that grass and trees may grow, water for fish to swim in. He dresses his set long before he lets his actors walk on. He has no need to go in search of fake, uncut diamonds.

Dress? What about wardrobe? How are the robbers dressed? How many are there? Do they wear balaclavas?

It becomes glaringly obvious that there is going to be no rest for me after the sixth day. No one else is doing or finding anything. Hennie provides one real handgun for the robbery. It falls to me to gather everything else. I solve the diamond issue by stopping on the corner of Barry Hertzog Avenue and Troon Road, near where I live, where I collect the remains of a broken windshield from the gutter. It works perfectly as the loot.

As for guns, I go to the Oriental Plaza to find good replicas.

Romain Orlin, another mega-friend who, with his father, owns Kays, supplies our wardrobe. Real Timer Joes shop at Kays – full and Half-Nelsons alike. Romain sees the opportunity to advertise the shop. He asks for no more than a screen credit for Kays. I do better than that. I write in a scene in which Kays features.

We get balaclavas, Nike T-shirts, a Bogey trench coat, a security guard uniform. I can tick Wardrobe off the list.

These acquisitions impress Moe and even Hennie. But they raise all other expectations of me. I become the look-to guy – the grunt, the gofer, the geffer, the guffer, the goofer, the whatever.

But, like Spider-Man, I learn that with great power comes great responsibility.

Palm fronds and Nescafé lids are more fun.

CHAPTER 50

Blade Runner
(1982)

A unique sci-fi film by Ridley Scott. Best of the best.

'Where's the knife?' My anxiety spikes to panic even as I ask Moe, already knowing the answer.

He looks at me blandly. 'What knife?'

Panic mounts to hysteria. What do we do now?

We are shooting the sequence where someone gets stabbed in a busy market. We have no knife. In fact, we need two. One for the stabbing – a hand-wielded-knife-slashing one – and a prop knife, to protrude from the victim's back. This second one should look like the first, but we could somehow fudge that. We need half a knife, one that appears to be buried in the victim's back. As the gofer, I have goffed up. Why did I ever expect someone to keep a check on the props?

'We need a large knife. Didn't you go to a prop shop to get one?' I ask stupidly.

Moe doesn't lose a moment's chewing. Prop shop? As if something like that exists outside of Hollywood. My heart is beating like bongos as the problems and solutions sort each other out in my mind. We are at the Oriental Plaza, where we are shooting the most complicated reel of the movie. This sequence is all about different groups following one another. It begins with the investigative reporter Constance, who follows a trail of suspicious cops while the cops shadow Luki, who has to come to the Oriental Plaza to replace the ghetto blaster that belonged to his boss. It is supposed to have a French farce quality to it. No one really knows who is following whom. It is all about followers – following followers – which results in someone being stabbed from behind a colourful rack of clothes. A hand with a knife flashes from between the hanging fabrics, taking its victim, who falls with the blade lodged firmly between his shoulder blades. The intended victim is Luki, but an error in timing claims an innocent shopper.

It sounds so easy on paper. There are a number of hidden problems with the whole thing.

If we had a prop knife to begin with, the dangers of actually stabbing someone would be eliminated. The stabbing is nothing. It is the aftermath that is the sticky problem. Speaking of sticky stuff, we need blood. Fake blood. Pig's blood. There will be none of that in the Plaza. Whatever it is they use in real movies to fake bleeding is just not available. How is the blade to have any purchase on the body? It is supposedly buried deep in his back. The implied piece inside the victim is the problem. That piece of the knife – wherever the fuck am I going to find a knife? – will have to be sawn off. We have shot up to the point of the stabbing. But now there is another problem. We have shot the entire sequence with the innocent victim wearing a blue shirt. We have to find one to replace that.

'Give me some dough,' I say to Moe, holding out a hand. 'We have things to buy.'

Wielding a handful of cash, I run through a number of shops, unable to find a shirt to match, looking like an escaped convict myself, hurriedly searching for a disguise. In a third outfitting shop I eventually find a white shirt. Which means all the sequences of the victim, now wearing that shirt, have to be shot again.

'What size, sir?' asks the shop assistant

'I dunno, medium, large – whatever you have.'

I grab the shirt, barely waiting for change, and run on. Now I need to find a large knife, a piece of polystyrene, some tomato sauce and a hacksaw. The brother Scaramouche has sprung to life. It is useless turning to the others to assist as I have no time to explain. As they say in the business, we are losing the light and the clock is against us.

I rush out looking for knife, the shirt trailing in one hand. I see an elderly shopkeeper wearing a tupi and loose white dress standing like a sentry in the doorway of a shop. A sign in the window reads 'Daya and Sons'.

'Do you know where I can buy a knife?' I ask, heaving for breath.

Sweat runs from my brow as my dishevelled emotions make a public display. He doesn't answer, but brings a hand from behind his back to point to an identical shopkeeper keeping guard further along the passage.

I run towards this second man, wildly flailing my arms, my shirttails hanging out, the shirt like a banner of someone wielding a flag and running to do battle. The man sees me coming and beats a hasty retreat into the shop. I see a sign that says 'Moosa and Sons'.

When I run in, he has taken refuge behind a counter and looks nervous.

'Do you have a kitchen knife, something large?' I hold a fist to the air, making downward stabbing motions. Too much explaining to do.

'Was the gentleman thinking of something in particular?' he asks, barely masking his alarm.

'Just something long and sharp!' I repeat the stabbing action.

A steady stream of sweat trickles from my scalp in troubled tributaries. I lean forward on the counter, as I struggle to find the breath to speak.

'We stock the very finest in knives, sir. Was the gentleman wanting kitchen or dining? Bone or wooden handle? Most elegant.'

I am irritated and impatient. 'It doesn't matter. Just long. It doesn't need to be fancy or expensive.'

It makes sense. Why take an expensive knife to a killing when a cheap one will do as well?

I pick up the knife and once again, reflexively stab motion down.

'Perfect!' I say, leaving a trail of money in my wake.

In the doorway I stop and turn to ask, 'Where can I find a hacksaw?'

I often think about Daya and Moosa and wonder what went through their minds, witnessing this wild man in search of a knife. Mostly I think about Moosa, who had to deal with this apparition who needed both a long-bladed knife and a hacksaw. What horrors did he imagine this lunatic was planning?

I wonder whether that day I ruined Moosa's afternoon and evening prayers, and possibly the many nights of sleep that followed? I see him scanning the papers, looking for reports of some barbaric horror and finding none. I imagine his conscience and his imagination finding no rest. And I wonder how long it takes him to forgive Daya for pointing me his way.

CHAPTER 51

Paths of Glory
(1957)

*Stanley Kubrick delivers a lesson on how battles should be shot.
It is arguably the best film about World War I. It is inspired by
a real incident, where three innocent men are executed for cowardice
to cover for a French officer who orders a suicidal attack on a German
stronghold. The end execution scene is shattering.*

I fall asleep doing rewrites of the *Timer Joe* scenes we have to shoot tomorrow. I dream of war, of trying to cross no-man's land where there are no trenches or foxholes. There is nowhere to hide. Buried in the mud is a bullet-riddled sign that reads, 'Proceed with Caution. Non-Europeans Only'.

The attack is coming from an elevated position shrouded in darkness from far off as I scramble like a cockroach, desperately seeking safety. I am caught in a bright white light, an easy target. I am covered in makeshift camouflage, clumps of soil and dead brown grass on my back as I scramble frantically, knowing I am in their sights. There is no safety. My observers are like an eagle tracking a mouse. I have no idea of their position. I must make it to my general. I throw caution to the wind and inch forward.

A soldier, a white man, covered from head to toe in what looks like black oil or pitch, like James Dean in *Giant* or Yves Montand in *The Wages of Fear*, walks past me quite matter-of-factly, a man on a Sunday stroll, except he walks stiff-legged, like Frankenstein's monster. He mumbles something incomprehensible. I realise that he is dead. I crawl in his direction, expecting that I too will inevitably become a casualty, cut down in a hail of bullets.

We disappear into an underground bunker, the war room where decisions about forthcoming battles are being made. A bald Peter Sellers wearing horn-rims sits to my left. A second, with a blond wig, sits in a wheelchair to my right. I sit next to Winston Churchill, who is examining a map laid out on the table. The ordeal across the minefield and the acrid smell of his cigar smoke are all too real.

'This does not begin to be funny. This is the beginning of the end of funny,' he pronounces.

And right there, it occurs to me that this is a dream, one I must record. I ask one of the aides to hand me a pen and paper so I can get it all down before it evaporates in the mist of memory. I am handed an old war poster and a house-painting brush thick with black enamel paint, which makes it impossible to write at all.

Churchill moves without fear to the door of the bunker and steps outside into the naked light, smiling smugly, looking younger, and glowing like a just-glazed Toby jug. He tosses the cigar away and, with a self-satisfied smirk, offers me a stick of Wrigley's, which strikes me as odd.

With a war on, he must have got that on the black market.

CHAPTER 52

Lost in Explanation

Lost in Translation (2003). Written and directed by Sofia Coppola, starring Bill Murray and Scarlett Johansson. Filmed in Japan to heighten the breach in communication.

If only I could be bold and tackle this language thing head-on. It's getting in the way of my directing this movie.

But being in charge here is not without a deep, subtexted political agenda. I want to have some authority over how things are proceeding but can I do it without *baasskap* getting in the way, the term used to declare white superiority by the apartheid government? The word literally translates from Afrikaans to English as 'boss-ship', but a more applicable translation is 'domination' or 'white supremacy'.

If only I could confront the issue without fear and guilt. Oh, to be Dad right now.

When he came to this country and found a job at the giant box company, Yserbrand, with little – almost no – English, in less than six months he was made foreman with the authority to issue orders to everyone on the shop floor. He addressed everyone equally. His commands were simple and to the point. His language limited him to a simple do this, do that. No translations were needed. He maintained this cryptic way of giving orders even when his command of the English language improved and he became master of his own shop.

As a child I was never troubled by his apparent rudeness. He never dropped a 'please' or 'thank you' for a task done. When I walked in on him taking a bath, it was, 'Dovidel, wash my back.' A request, not an order – it was his tone that contained the politeness. When I washed his back with a bar of Lifebuoy and a *lappie*, he would sigh and sink lower in the tub and let his fatigue drown in the soapy water. We were both happy.

Boss Solly (as my dad was known by his staff) always spoke with authority and earned everyone's respect. Now, on the set of *Timer Joe 3*,

I too want some R-E-S-P-E-C-T – but without speaking isuZulu, do I deserve any?

To Fedlers, for over thirty years when he was still in charge, my dad brought his Yserbrand persona, his cryptic way of command. A testament to his leadership is the fact that some of his staff have been with him since just after the Depression. There is John, who was the first, who came to him with no skills, a farm labourer who became Dad's right-hand man, learning all about the cutting of paper, parcelling and delivering the print. Jeremiah, George and Samson joined when times were toughest, and under Boss Solly's guidance still have good solid jobs. Everyone, no matter their race, referred to Dad as Boss Solly, and there always seemed to be affection and respect in that title.

As a cartoonist, I am always trying to juggle two balls. On the one hand, I have to be funny; on the other, seriously funny. I confer with editors at *The Star*, who keep me abreast of events. There are cries from all sides to bring down this unjust order called apartheid, to get rid of the 'white man boss'. Now I am caught between the reality of the news and the absurdity that is my movie. I am not a rock and I am in a hard place.

As I instruct Coach what to tell the actors to do, I know that most of it is being lost like bathwater down the drain. The cast say whatever the hell they please, making up their own lines. There is no rehearsal. It's just Instruction. Translation. Action. Sometimes a speech is too long, sometimes too short. It all depends on Coach's commands. It is a game of broken telephone. It's a fucking mess and mirrors the way the country seems to be headed.

Each day when I call Arnie Benjamin, a senior editor at *The Star*, to discuss the cartoon I have to deliver by late tomorrow, and ask him what's going on in the country, what I hear is unintentionally funny, crying out for a cartoon. Like when Carel de Wet, our ambassador to the United Kingdom says, 'There should be more contact between White and Non-White to bring about a greater separation of the races.'

'He actually said that?' I ask in disbelief.

'Verbatim,' answers Arnie.

Other countries are grappling with race issues too – we are not the only one. Our government doubles up on their double standards. Japanese people – a small minority – are granted honorary white status in South

Africa, while the growing Chinese population is denied. But see, we do big business with Japan, little with China. What about the Maoris? Not that South Africa cares a fuck about the politics of New Zealand. This is about how the Maoris who play for the All Blacks are to be classified here. All White? The issue is fraught and *vrot*. Then there is that *'blerrie kleurling'* D'Oliveira who plays cricket for the *blerrie rooineks* in England. 'Can't these people come up with their own sports? Let him play in Hyde Park. We don't want him here. Then all of them are going to want to be allowed in. They will take over our stadiums. *Nooit!*' I can make this funny in a cartoon, but it's not funny.

'How about Botha, Minister of Bantu Administration?' Arnie suggests.

'What's he doing now?' I ask.

'Forcibly resettling the people.'

'That's old news.'

'Wait, let me read to you how he explains it,' Arnie says, reading me this quote: 'The Africans moved to re-settlement areas needed a good deal of persuasion to get them to move – but they are volunteers.'

I listen long and with a heavy heart.

More bombings are reported. Umkhonto gladly claims all responsibility. I can feel it. Everyone can. The time is coming for a proper uprising in the name of justice. How can the ordinary person in South Africa not be angry? I'm angry, and I'm one of the privileged ones.

On set, I wonder about the lives of the actors, where they've come from and how much resentment each one justifiably might have against someone like me, who has it all, simply because Lithuanian Jews have a deficit of melatonin. People can only take so much before something snaps. Isn't that one definition of revolution?

I recall an incident outside Fedlers one Friday morning in the early seventies, back when Dad still held the reins. The factory was a simple one-storey building on Central Road, Fordsburg, with a vast factory floor to the right and a driveway and service alley to the left. George, who always wore a smile and worked at Fedlers with quiet dignity for more than twenty years, had to load a bike to deliver printing before the weekend. As he was about to leave with urgent Friday-afternoon printing deliveries, a car drove up the driveway and blocked the exit.

George politely asked the driver to move his car. The driver ignored

George's request and calmly got out of the car. George pleaded – he was going to be late, it being Friday. The man started towards the Post Office across the road. George followed. 'I'm asking you nice, sir, please, please, move your car.'

The man stopped in the middle of Central Avenue, turned to acknowledge George's presence, and said, '*Voetsek*. Don't you *blerrie* tell me where to park,' and gave George a loud *klap* across his cheek.

A second man, a passenger, emerged on crutches and with his face close in on George, said, 'You deaf? My *boet* told you to *voetsek*.' And with that, he poked George in the chest with a crutch.

At this point John, who had observed all this, ran into the factory and called out, 'Come quick. Big trouble.'

The staff of Fedlers poured out onto the pavement to witness George wielding a crutch as he vented his fury on the man's vehicle that was still parked in the way of his Friday-afternoon deliveries. He smashed every window and headlight, then tackled the bodywork, finally breaking the crutch on the bonnet. Dad, with his one eye, took it all in calmly. He walked up to the two men who were watching in shock as their car was being destroyed, and this short, portly Jew in his seventies who had never been involved in any form of physical contest of which I am aware, delivered a slap (a *frusk*) to each of them.

'Where do you think you are parking? We are trying to run a business here. *Voetsek* from here!' he said, pointing to the wreck. Having said his piece, he turned to everyone and said, 'Back to work.' He led and they followed.

Nothing further was ever heard from the illegal parkers.

Dad earned Mot's everlasting awe and admiration. 'Man, you should have seen the old man. He was fearless. He was prepared to take them both on,' he would often reminisce and laugh. 'Dad thinks he's bloody Johnny Ralph.'

But what of George? This humble, dignified man who had never revealed a temper beneath his veneer, having disposed of the crutch, ran into the factory and picked up a large hammer, intent on returning to the two cowering assailants outside.

'If it hadn't been for Jerry and Samson stopping him, my bet is he would have killed them,' Mot told me.

I often think of this story, and about anger biding its time. When I hear the crew chatter amongst themselves, I'm transported back to when Mom and Dad conversed in Russian. I doubt the actors are talking about the movie, or their performance, or how to be 'furtive'. They must be sharing stories from their daily lives. Discussing what is going on in the country. The injustices that daily weigh them down. The revolution that must surely be coming. The *baasskap* of the white man that must be dismantled.

I am shaken out of this reverie by Coach who asks, 'Boss, what's next?'

A history of comedy
Part 2

CHAPTER 53

Start the Revolution Without Me
(1970)

*A comedy with Donald Sutherland and Gene Wilder,
set during the French Revolution.*

The crowd calls out for more jokes, more laughs. The *chassidim* are clapping, shouting, singing and banging the tables. The *Aiyai aiyaiy aiyaiyais* become a collective chant of 'We want Nat! We want Nat!' It is the night of Purim and the celebration is in full swing. Every year, we attend the great Lubavitch Purim Party, which Jewish law dictates has to be a piss-up. On that day, a Jew is supposed to get so drunk that he cannot tell the difference between Haman, the original Hitler, and Mordecai, the saviour of the people. Check out the Book of Esther.

We all make a lot of effort to provide all sorts of entertainment for the evening. One year we even make a movie called *Kosherjack*, a spoof of the hit TV show *Kojak*, which I write and direct. It stars Cyril Green. Cyril barely needs a script. The doctors and lawyers are recruited to act and read off prompt cards. We shoot it all in one day on Super 8 mm. Ray Perkel, a Lubavitch convert, writes and plays a score. It is a mild hit.

But now the crowd demands some stand-up comedy. They want Nat to entertain them. It has become a tradition of the evening, like reading the *megillah* of Esther on the festival – compulsory. 'We want Nat! We want Nat!' He walks onto the floor. No politician ever had a more enthusiastic reception.

He is not here to deliver something new. His is a comic act that must not in any way be different to last year's. Not a line or a gesture must be added. No one is under the illusion that we are watching another Jackie Mason or Shelley Berman – especially Nat himself, which displays a great depth of character and lack of ego. The fact that his jokes are so corny and familiar is what endears him to one all.

Nat Bregman is a regular at Rabbi Mendel Lipskar's *shiurim* at Chabad House every Thursday night. *Chabad* is an acronym for *Chochma*,

Binah, Da'at – Wisdom, Understanding and Knowledge, the pillars of the movement. We're a mixed bag who attend. The group boasts a few doctors, a number of lawyers, accountants and artists, and what I mistake to be failed comedian. No one has heard anything of Nat since the fifties. I presume he's been scrounging a living working in dingy nightclubs and gin joints, as they are called in the movies. I surmise that Nat is here because he's heard there's a free meal thrown in.

Rabbi Lipskar has become a phenomenon. Fresh out of *yeshiva*, aged twenty-four, he has come to assume leadership of the Lubavitch Foundation in South Africa. Few of us have ever heard of the Lubavitcher Rebbe, and have no idea of his scale of influence across the world. We come not to be sold on joining the organisation but to listen to this this young charismatic emissary. Rabbi Lipskar – Mendel, as we call him – talks Torah in a way we have never heard before. It is cool, like beat poetry and Zen, and exciting. He discusses Philip Roth, Lenny Bruce and Woody Allen intimately and intelligently. His favourite song is 'The Boxer' by Simon and Garfunkel. He doesn't deliver sonorous sermons as from a pulpit, but invites participation. He talks about the portion of the week – the *parsha*. A different chapter of the Five Books is read every week in synagogues.

The mood is laid back, like guys after a game of golf or bowls, and the banter across the table is constant, with many laughs thrown in. Nat, who one would think would dominate this exchange with wisecracks and quips, is strangely silent, hardly contributing to the chatter. There is a meal of roast chicken that Nando's would envy, prepared and served by Zack, Chabad's driver and cook – a Zulu man who wears a *yarmulke*. Our cups run over with Johnnie Walker Black and the conversation runs everywhere. Everyone gets to share and offer an insight into their world. We cool Joburg professionals like this casual, happy-time religion, which brings with it an intellectual core that has us riveted.

We are all much older than this *yeshiva bocher*. We are graduates of the Schools of Life and Hard Knocks, which has campuses in Mayfair, Doornfontein, Berea, Yeoville, Kensington, Bertrams, Bez Valley, Malvern and others, and our Judaism is strictly Friday-night dinners with the family. Over our *l'chaims*, our toasts to life and dinner that come after Mendel's *shi'ur*, we exchange hard-times stories. Nat never contributes. He is forever the quiet one. *Ag* shame, the poor guy must be battling. As we step out of Chabad House, we sober up and pocket our *yarmies*. We don't want to be mistaken for Happy Hebrew Clappers. But Nat Bregman departs silent and sober as a judge, with his head still covered.

It is some months before I learn with some surprise that Nat is, in fact, a lawyer – and by all accounts a successful one. I must shed all previous opinions of him.

As a teenager, I see him on the stage of the 20th Century cinema in a variety show sponsored by Colgate called *Anything Goes*. The show is recorded early on a Sunday evening and entrance is free. I take an early bus from Greenside to the city with Mot and a loose gang of his peers, among whom is Sol Kerzner, to try to get into a live recording. We all but run to queue outside, in the hope of getting in. The show is hosted by Robert Haber, and features Dan Hill and his band, the songstress Artemis (Mrs Dan Hill) and the comedy of Nat Bregman.

We would like to believe we are at Radio City Hall in New York, waiting for Frank Sinatra and the Tommy Dorsey Band, screaming for more, crying with laughter at the comedian. Dan Hill plays a mean clarinet and his beautiful Greek wife can really carry a melody. His real name is Illchillchick, but I guess Hill is cooler – and Artemis Illchillchick would intimidate any MC.

The comedian is adequate. Nat Bregman finds no reason to change his name and is unashamedly Jewish. He loves to play with the immigrant accent like the old vaudevillian comedians, delivering the kind of *schtick* that the two late greats, George Burns and Walter Matthau, give us a taste of in Neil Simon's *The Sunshine Boys*. It is the comedy of minor, on-stage costume changes, of jacket, wig and hat. Speed of delivery is everything; there is lots of face-pulling and exaggerated gestures. It frantically seeks a laugh.

Nat is likeable. Great, he isn't. I would not pay to see him.

Circumstances bring Nat and I together in the late seventies when we are both invited to participate in an evening of Yiddish humour in Pretoria. We decide to drive together and are alone for the first time in his car. Nat wears his *yarmulke* all the time. Our conversation is less than memorable. There are no political exchanges, nothing about our work. I find his conversation reserved. I doubt that he has any a political agenda – just another Jewish boy from one the old neighbourhoods who has found God under a hat.

At the venue, the Pretoria Shul Hall, he is greeted like a rock star. They all want his autograph, to shake his hand. They all remember him for *Anything Goes*. Nat is bewildered and uncomfortable with this wild reception, especially after thirty years. He is uneasy in the spotlight.

Why would he be?

It is somewhere in the early part of the new millennium that I tackle Nelson Mandela's biography *Long Walk to Freedom*. When I come upon the passage dedicated to Natie Bregman, I am at first startled, then riveted. I read it over and over, trying to shape the story in my head.

I put it together in this way: Nat, like all of us, comes from a lower-income Jewish family; he takes sandwiches to work, which his mother lovingly prepares; he can't really afford to eat out. Nothing is too much for Mrs Bregman's son, the lawyer-to-be. Like all Jewish mothers, perhaps, she really wants him to be a doctor – a Jewish mother's first prize. But Nissenke (Natie to his friends) has never been someone for blood and fights. He's a nice, quiet boy, who likes to make jokes. What he really wants to be is a comedian but he would never, God forbid, disgrace his parents with such a low-life career. A hobby? Yes! A career? No! Young Natie Bregman tears the sandwich that his mother has prepared for his lunch today at the legal firm of Witkin, Sidelsky and Eidelman, and hands it to his equally junior colleague, the other articled law clerk Nelson Rolihlahla Mandela.

'Nelson, I am a communist. We share everything.'

In *Long Walk to Freedom*, Madiba's description of the sandwich-tearing is far more formal than described above. It has the ring of an initiation ceremony. It goes like this:

'Nelson, take hold of the other side of the sandwich. Now pull. Now eat!'

Nat, or Natie as he is known to his colleague, then delivers the Sermon on the Sandwich.

'Nelson, what we have just done symbolises the philosophy of the Communist Party: to share everything we have.'

The story is a mind-twister, like something conjured by John le Carré.

In my mental dossier I cannot reconcile all the communist stuff with the *yarmulke* and the comedy. Aren't comedians supposed to be apolitical? Red and funny don't really mix. Okay, Danny Kaye was one to stand up against McCarthy. But he didn't conceal it. At the evening in Pretoria, the fans would be appalled to know that their idol is a red-hot commie colluding, *nogal*, with Mandela.

It's his ability to go on with this annual charade that I don't get. If Nat is ever maybe as drunk as he is supposed to be, and not know the difference between John Balthazar or *Die Groot Krokodil* and Nelson and Oliver, then, okay.

From 1975 or '76 to 1982 and beyond, there is Nat again, doing his Purim *schtick*, mugging it with, 'Vot ve can, we can and vot ve can't, ve can too.' It's a joke the crowd loves about a family canning business.

Where has he been since the fifties?

Surely, he's on the government's death-squad radar? The Civil Cooperation Bureau doesn't miss a trick and is having its busiest time. They're going big-time on taking out the revolution. No *blerrie aluta continua kak. Aluta finita.* 1977? *Totsiens* and good riddance, Steve Biko. 1982? Bye bye, Ruth First. Maybe it is already 1988. Albie Sachs loses an arm and an eye. We'll show these *fokkers* who's the *baas*.

Who the hell is this big mate of the big boss? This *blerrie* Bregman is the *Jood* who started all the trouble. How is he still hiding out here in plain sight?

I read page sixty-nine, over and over again. Sixty-nine is an appropriate number. Hard to know which side is up.

How wrong can one be?

As Mandela ascends to myth and fable, I try to imagine how the praise-singers of the future will tell it. I look towards the histories that will be written, the way the revisionists might record it. Over the centuries, Jesus and Moses have been shaped to suit an Aryan ideology. Jesus gets blonder and more Nordic, while Moses remains more Roman and though in truth he stuttered, he speaks like some great Shakespearian actor. Perhaps the legends will shift to a more African way of telling it all. I wonder how the tale of Nat Bregman will be told.

Few in history achieve the status of Nelson Mandela. His name will stand along with Moses, Jesus and the rest. Like all great historical or religious figures, we want to know every tiny detail of their lives. A Jew, in particular, would like to know the nature of the shared sandwich. Food is always a grand accompaniment to great occasion. Was it, perhaps, a lovely brisket on rye, with mustard and sliced *ugereke* (cucumber)? Probably not. Hard to tear. Brisket you have to tear longways.

Talmudic scholars would, over the centuries, argue over such a detail. What it was is, alas, a footnote lost to history.

In my version, when Nat breaks the sandwich and hands half to Madiba, he intones a *brocha*, a blessing that Jews recite at the beginning of a great occasion.

Baruch ata Adonai, elohaynu melech ha'olam, shehechiyanu, vekiyimanu, vehigiyanu, lazman hazeh.

Blessed are you, Lord our God, King of the universe, who has granted us life, sustained us and enabled us to reach this occasion.

CHAPTER 54

The Conversation
(1974)

Written, produced and directed by Francis Ford Coppola.
It comes in the wake of the Watergate break-in. Gene Hackman is a
very inferior snoop who depends on technology and agonises about his
personal responsibility. He is not a bad man, just doing a dirty job.

'What is "zoom"?' Coach asks. I try to answer as I watch Hennie, who might this moment be zooming, shooting the runners cross the bridge.

Coach has begun to quiz me. He keeps reading my script as if he's swotting for an exam. I constantly have to ask for it to be returned. It is quickly dog-eared. He is the only one on set who understands that the book is everything. His Walter Mitty has been awakened. Like mine, his own *dybbuk* wants to direct movies.

Over the next two weeks, my instructions to the actors get more skewed as he begins to put his own spin on translation. Nothing comes out the way I want it. Coach paces about wearing the gestures of considered thought, elbow resting in one palm while the other hand strokes the pencil line beneath his nose. He clucks approvingly, or not, at the end of each take. He is constantly in my face. In the middle of a setup, he has another question. When I am crouched down between takes scribbling frantic notes, he is looking over my shoulder and mugging me with yet another inquiry.

On Day 3, he walks up to me carrying a copy of *The Star* and holds up the leader page, displaying my cartoon as if it is a piece of vital evidence of some misdemeanour.

'You draw this?'

'Yes.'

He considers my answer and continues the cross-examination.

'You work for the newspaper.'

It's an accusation, not a question.

'Not all the time,' is my truthful return. 'I have other clients.'

He considers this a while. 'So, you write for other people?'
'No, I draw for them.'
'So, you are not a writer.' Another statement.
'Not really.'
'You write all the words,' he asks, pointing at the script.
'Yes.'
'Who draws your pictures?'
'I do.'
'But you wrote this *Timer Joe*?'
'Yes.'
'You wrote the story?'
'Yes.'
He ponders this a long time and comes with the clincher.
'How do you become a writer?'
'You buy a typewriter.' My answer is short and sarcastic. That should shut him up while I concentrate on making my movie.
He paces some more and finally comes back with another question.
'What kind of typewriter?'
'An Olympia,' I reply.
Somewhere, Sam Dembo smiles.

CHAPTER 55

The Color of Money
(1986)

Directed by Martin Scorsese and starring Paul Newman in an Oscar-winning performance revisiting Fast Eddie Foyle, the character he plays in The Hustler, *directed by Robert Rossen in 1961. A wonderful supporting role by Tom Cruise who also deserved an Oscar, but missed out.*

If I want to keep my real job, I have to show my face at *The Star* and confer with Arnie Benjamin. Later today, I have to meet with all the crew at Moe's in Bree Street, from where we have to drive to Beaconsfield Club across town, which is both a tennis and bowling club. The club has allowed us to use their kitchen as the set for the *Timer Joe* kitchen. But when Luki steps out of the kitchen at Beaconsfield Club, we are in fact far away, across town in the set we have built in Craig Wood's photographic studio in the penthouse of Winchester Mansions. We have to shoot that tomorrow. Right now I have a leader-page cartoon to think of.

There is a lot on my mind as I rush into the paper. But then I bump into Barry Ronge, editor of *The Star's* 'Tonight' section, and everything leaves my mind.

Barry's range of knowledge is all-embracing, like a contestant on *Mastermind*. If it is literature, the movies, and arts and entertainment, any trivia one wants to know about, ask Barry. Barry works at speed, never seeming to lag for a moment to reconsider a word or reconstruct a sentence as his fingers flit across his keyboard. He is a Mozart, getting it all down at once. His wide, blue eyes are fixed to his monitor as he tries to keep up with himself. He doesn't have time for long chitchat. A quick Q and A is the best one can get from him.

'Who is Hennie Basson?' I ask. Preambles waste time.

'Probably the busiest filmmaker on the planet,' he answers instantly, not even glancing up as he types.

Later, leading the convoy to Beaconsfield Club, I have an entirely different view of who is who on *Timer Joe 3*.

Dov Fedler is nowhere on the list.

A few days later, I strike it lucky with Barry. He actually has time to talk to me. He has met the day's deadlines and slips into that storytelling mode that I associate with consummate, easy raconteurs like the Afrikaner PG du Plessis or the singular Jan Spies. I am in for a long story. Arnie Benjamin will just have to wait.

The story just scrolls from Barry like a printout.

Over the next year, long after *TJ3* is well behind me, Hennie Basson becomes a pet study of mine. And there is a lot of learning to do.

He not only owns a big stake in *Timer Joe 3*, but without him it wouldn't happen at all. He is the glue that holds this project together. Hennie has *protectzia*, a Russian word adopted by the Jews. *Protectzia* is simply who you know, particularly who you know in high places. Whilst the small and huddled masses feed off crusts, *protectzia* dines finely off the fat of the land.

What a sweet deal. Your friends in the highest places ensure that the subsidies come through and you return the scratching of your back with scratch. The profits are shared. What are friends for? The higher the friends, the greater the favours and flavours. I no longer wonder why my cinematographer thinks it is his movie.

Hennie is the kingpin. *Die Grootbaas* who hides in plain sight.

But to be fair, the man works. Well, at twenty films a year, with the government tossing in a free hundred grand per movie, with two million to pocket before one begins, a little effort would be the proper and decent thing to invest.

But let's watch the costs. Since we work with the dictum that black people like the same films that we do, a fantasy to feed to the wannabe mogul partner, why bother hiring a writer? Take any Hollywood film and just copy it. And why shoot in 35 mm, which is just so bloody expensive. A 16 mm Arriflex is cheaper and easier.

I make a close study of Mr Basson's CV, consulting Barry Ronge whenever I can. But even working in blind ignorance at the outset, it is inevitable that Hennie and I clash.

It is the way he rushes through every scene without even a nod to me that does it. If I were chasing two million rand a year, I would probably also have run over him to the next take. It is Hennie who directs the first two *Timer Joe* movies and should, by rights, direct this third. But Moe's ego has blocked him for now. It is me who is the block and the reason for this passive-aggressive attitude.

The subsidy system is created to produce movies exclusively for African audiences. It is Hennie's baby, one he has fathered with his friends in high places. The *Timer Joe* films are like stepchildren with this new mother, Moe. They do very well, thank you, and grow very nicely, to be seen by over 15 million people. Not many get to see them for free. What is two million times 15? Only 30 million? Times 40 more movies? Is that only R1 200 000 000?

On set, our introduction is brief.

'Hi, this is Hennie. He'll be filming the movie. This is Dov.'

'Hi.'

'*Aangename kennis.*'

'*Is jou naam werklik Dof?*' he asks. He is playing on the Afrikaans word *dof*, which means 'dull'. He is saying, 'Is your name really Stupid?'

In retrospect, considering what I have learnt, I should probably have said, 'Yes.'

Hennie simply lifts storylines from Hollywood. Barry tells me his movies draw throngs in black townships across the country. The anti-apartheid movement dismisses him as a backer of white-minority rule. Hennie makes no apology for stealing intellectual property.

Talk about movie-capture. *Protectzia.*

Clint Eastwood starts making his own movies when he sees how big studios squander millions of dollars. He learns from the Italians that one can make a movie for just a fistful of bucks. You keep the production modest, use unknown actors and, well, if you have been handed R100 000 and the whole thing comes in at, say, half that, you come out with R50 000 to bank. If you're shooting twenty films a year, by my maths that's a cool million.

Hennie starts out owning a construction company. On Saturday nights, he shows Hollywood movies to his two hundred black workers. Good old-fashioned paternalism. How come his workers do not have a home to go to on a Saturday night?

One cannot, however, fault his genius for seeing the opportunity. Who doesn't love a movie?

Hennie gives up his construction company where he employs two hundred black people to go into the movie business, funded by the government. He gives up the big time for a bigger time.

You didn't have to be a rocket scientist to know that movies for black people was the market of the future. Under something called the A-scheme, the government has been subsidising films for white South Africans since the 1950s. There has been nothing available for the greater black audience.

Enter Hennie. Enter Broederbond. Enter Subsidy. Enter Moe. And Moe buys the 'black people enjoy the same movies we do' myth. They just want to see them with their own actors and in their own language.

Hennie is not big on ego. His eye is on the main prize, the money. And on the clock. Let Moe claim the idea. Hennie has nineteen other movies to shoot this year. *'Dit is oestyd.'* This is the harvest season. Make hay while we can. Milk the white government cow and pretend to entertain the restless natives. It is all legitimate.

And why do we need someone who is really *dof* slowing this thing down?

Moe's career begins as a pharmacist, but he sees a bigger profit in hiring out movies and projectors. He and Hennie join forces. They are now into distribution. The whole thing works like a combine harvester. You don't have to go back to the textbooks to study rocket science. You just change gears. You become a Player.

Moe wants to be The Player. He announces himself as a producer of films for black people. Not of the people – for the people. It really is money for jam. Nice work if you can get it – and Moe is getting it, in subsidies. He has three to Hennie's twenty a year.

Who is The Player?

Black actors come in dirt cheap. Even cheaper than dirt. To be a black actor, you don't have to be an actor at all. You just have to be black. Is there a minimum-wage clause for actors in the subsidy bill? You don't go in there for the money. You'll be lucky if you see four hundred rand for a week's work. The subsidy may be 'for' the black people, but the profits are for the white people.

It would be illuminating to know what our lead actor Jabu-Jabu Masondo gets on the deal. He doesn't exactly arrive on set wearing Pierre Cardin and Polo shirts. When we go to Kays, which only stocks top-brand labels, he's like a kid let loose in a toy store. He thinks everything is for free. At the end of the shoot, maybe he gets to keep his red waiter's jacket. As for the rest of the cast, they seem to be hopefuls, looking for casual work, picked up on a corner somewhere. Their only acting skills are pretending they don't understand English.

Hennie is the best actor on set. He underplays his role as a mogul to perfection.

Hennie and I have no open conflict. I soon pick up that he has been making films for some time, but am totally unaware of his astonishing ignorance. Hennie is not a cinematographer. He is just a guy who owns an Arriflex. Hennie has no knowledge of photography in any professional sense. His method is to point the camera in the direction of the action and let it roll. Framing, tilting, widening, narrowing a shot – none of these are in his vocabulary. I get that he is not from the School of Cinema Nerds like me. That he is not the movie buff, the pretentious self-pedigreed cinema intellectual who bandies names like Fellini, Antonioni, Chabrol and Truffaut, a true aficionado. New wave, *Cinema Verite*, expressionism, *Battleship Potemkin* – anything vaguely cinematic is lost on him. I wonder whether he can name even one director.

Hennie is Mr Saturday-Night Movie. *Skop, skiet en donner*. Cowboys *en kroeks. Braai en brandewyn*. A *lekker-lag fliek*. But the art of everything is lifting a cliché to a higher peg. *Timer Joe 3* may just aspire to be a *Pink Panther*ish comedy, but it deserves to be shot and cut like *Citizen Kane*.

CHAPTER 56

The King of Comedy
(1982)

A terrible, wannabe stand-up comedian played by Robert De Niro seeks fame by first stalking and then kidnapping a celebrity funnyman, Jerry Lewis, just about playing himself. De Niro surprises as the funny, embarrassing stalker. The King of Comedy is pitched as possibly Martin Scorsese and Robert De Niro's finest collaboration. A masterpiece of biting satire. Underappreciated at the time of release, even more relevant now, it deals with our media-crazed society obsessed with celebrities. The movie was a commercial and critical failure labelled The Flop of the Year by Entertainment Tonight.

We have the Beaconsfield kitchen for just the morning. We have to shoot all the *Timer Joe* kitchen scenes in double-quick time. The club is where the good and bad guys cross paths and the plot begins to bind. It is Day 3 of the shoot, after the chase, which leads into the kitchen. Here, Frank hides the diamonds in some ice trays, puts them in the freezer, leaves a message in a tape player and runs off. Later, elsewhere, we will film him running to a phone booth to make an important phone call, where he gets shot. Sadly, after that, we have no further use for Frank.

We need to start promptly.

Enter Jabulani Masondo, known as Jabu-Jabu or Jay-Jay, our star.

He arrives at Central City Films and is immediately mobbed by the cast. Everyone clamours for a moment of his attention. Jay-Jay wants to give time to every fan. His celebrity crowds out any chance of intimacy. There is a lot of ceremonial handshaking and excited chatter, and though we are properly introduced he passes me by with just a nod, then on to the next handshake.

The formalities over, we rush in different vehicles across town to Beaconsfield Club in Victory Park to our set. This is where Jabu, as a cheeky waiter working in the club, makes his first appearance. Everything depends on the performance of our lead, and in a moment the character comes alive. Jay-Jay understands the script better than I have written it.

All he needs is an outline of the scene and he fills in the rest, which saves us a lot of time. He enters the kitchen and owns it. The staff, other than Jabu's boss, work at Beaconsfield. We have brought with us foodstuffs, which they can be seen preparing. Beaconsfield is a kosher venue and our oversight has the chefs working with nothing, in other words, pretending to prepare food that isn't there, exactly as the staff in the heist scene have to polish diamonds without polishers or diamonds. It makes for a lot of puzzled looks. But, hey, who other than *schmucks* like me look that closely? It is Jay-Jay who grabs our attention as this background stuff flashes by unnoticed.

Jay-Jay's boss hates him for always creating mischief. In the kitchen stands the boss's new radio-tape player, the size of a briefcase, which contains the tape that explains where the diamonds are hidden. The boss has given strict orders that no one is to touch this prized property.

The action reads: Jay-Jay comes in, sees the music player, turns it on and begins to dance. That is the outline. Jay-Jay creates business as he goes, grabbing props and improvising. He brings the thing alive. Enter the enraged boss who grabs a carving knife and chases him around a table, threatening to kill him.

The blade is razor sharp and the actor wielding it tries to keep his grimace, wave the knife, stab while really trying not to cause injury. He doesn't convince. It is here that Jay-Jay displays his trouper colours. He distracts us from the other player's shortcomings and brings it together. Unrehearsed, he creates a choreography even as he endangers himself while maintaining a stream of gibberish. We have brought no first-aid kit. We flinch as we watch. Jay-Jay is fully aware of the limitations of his partner and keeps the thing going, and we get it in one take. He pulls focus on himself as he picks up various items of food, sweeps within the arc of the knife to impale the items one by one on the blade, and then dance to safety. It is harrowing to watch and feels like it is all about to go horribly wrong.

At the end, the knife looks like a kebab on which are speared an entire salami, a lettuce, some rolls, a tomato and a carrot. He succeeds, finally, in making the weapon look ridiculous and harmless.

Jay-Jay understands the secret of all magic: misdirection. He holds the scene together. He understands film. It is his own eye that looks back at him through the camera. He is in perfect harmony with the medium and the task at hand. His job is to crowd every second with memorable nonsense. He takes a weak moment of scripting and forces it to work. It gets as good as it possibly can.

Everyone fades from the screen when Jabulani Masondo steps up. Even without the carving knife limiting him, the boss is never going to be called an actor, but Jay-Jay makes him look like one. Jay-Jay assures that *Timer Joe* remains a hit.

Timer Joe 1 and *2* are apparently criticised for their absence of plot and that is why I have been engaged. Plot is not a major talent of mine. How do I ever sell this script?

Moe understands the value of his asset perfectly. Forget Blake Edwards, or Woody Allen, or whatever comic reference with which you come burdened. Jay-Jay will have none of it anyway. Just get out of the way and let him do his thing. *Timer Joe* doesn't need plot – it just needs Jay-Jay.

Moe is Jay-Jay's biggest fan. He should be. According to Moe, 15 million people flock to see Jabulani Masondo, Jabu-Jabu, Jay-Jay, *Timer Joe*, or whatever name he chooses to go by. Fans rush to see Elvis in any *schlock* his manager Colonel Parker forces him into doing, like *Fun in Acapulco*, *Girl Happy* and *Blue Hawaii*. He may be the King, but he has a boss. Oh, how the mighty one has fallen. Now they queue to see Jay-Jay Masondo. If the figures that Moe quotes me are to be believed, that many fans are not wrong.

Moe stands at my side, beaming, as we watch a comic star go through his paces. He elbows me in an I-told-you-so gesture. 'Isn't he just the best comic ever?'

A history of comedy
Part 3

CHAPTER 57

Take a Chance
(1970–1985)

Michael Meyer meets me outside Broadcast House on Commissioner, between Troye and Delvers streets. It is less than a block from Dad's factory on the corner of Troye and Market. As one enters Fedlers Printing and Stationery (Pty) Ltd, the SABC monolith winks over the rooftop to 172 Market Street, from where I stand at the factory entrance. If I had a catty, a real one, with a strong *mik* and good elastic, I could knock out its windows.

Owning a catty and knocking out windows is a wishful thought. Mot has often promised to make me a catty, but some protective filial instinct has prevented him from ever delivering on his promise. We are not allowed weapons at home. I have heard Mot beg for a Daisy pellet gun. I never ask. I'm the baby, and if my big brother is not allowed one, I am certainly not going to be either. Everyone in Mayfair knows of Ockie Getz, who shot his sister's eye out with a pellet gun. I don't know of any Jewish boy in Mayfair other than Ockie who has a pellet gun. Our mothers have seen to that. Ockie's sister and Dad are the only people in Mayfair who have glass eyes. The fact is, I never see a pellet gun until we move to Greenside and get to shoot one. But there it is, advertised in every comic book I ever read, tempting every boy to want and own a Daisy Red Ryder BB gun. Dad says that a real man doesn't own a gun. I know that Red Ryder is a comic character, but the gun is real. Charles Atlas flashes his muscles in every comic with this promise, 'In just seven days I can make you a man!' I bet he owns a pellet gun.

When I am six, Mot takes me to Broadcast House to a recording of the programme *Calling All Youth*. It is a radio quiz show that we know well, hosted by Percy Baneshik, who will ultimately start me on my career as a political cartoonist. Entrance is free but one has to arrive early to be assured of a seat. We are nearly an hour early, first to line up. As a precaution, we are dressed appropriately in sports jackets and ties, our hair parted straight and plastered with Mot's own pomade. I am in awe of seeing a radio personality in the flesh.

I am picked out of the crowd to become this afternoon's gong-master. I am called onto the podium and made to stand near a gong, which is miniature of the opening credit to the J Arthur Rank movies of the forties and fifties, where a Charles Atlas impersonator holds a giant sledgehammer. My gong is about the size of a waiter's tray and stands on a small table to the side of the quizmaster's. This is my first time standing in front of an audience and it is terrifying. I must have been chosen for my attention to wardrobe, thanks to Mot. It is the Windsor knot and my *yarmulke* of Brylcreem and Vitalis that almost glows that make me stand out of the crowd. Strange how we would dress for radio back then and appear so casually on television now.

Gong-master is something to rack up as one of my failures in life. My heart races and my head reels when it is announced, 'Our gong-master today is David Fedler.' The universe knows who I am now, or so it feels. I tremble and my head buzzes, and I have to be prompted repeatedly to hit the gong when required. And as I will later witness Furtive Frank freeze on camera, I am struck with performance panic. Or rather, the opposite. An inability to perform. I miss all my cues, and the prompting from the side become loud stage whispers. 'Now! Now! The gong!' I try to compensate for my error and hit it twice, which in the lexicon of this show has an entirely different meaning. One is right. Two, wrong . . . or is that three?

Percy, of course, has no memory of that awful afternoon. He probably has a calendar full of awful gong *klutzes*. A lot of water has passed under the bridge when we next renew our association. I am twenty-three years old. He needs a cartoonist to illustrate the column he writes every week for the *Rand Daily Mail*. In quick time, he leaves the *Mail* to become the arts editor of a new Argus newspaper called the *Sunday Chronicle*, and which needs a young cartoonist. I spend the next fifty years working for that group.

Waiting to meet Michael outside Broadcast House thirty years later opens the sluice gate of memory. I feel a twinge of anxiety as if even now I will be denied access, too late in the queue, no longer grease on my scalp, no tie. I am here to attend a recording of a different radio show.

Visitors are not permitted to attend this recording. It is a very private affair. The show is called *Take a Chance*. Well, it is called that when the show first starts, but it evolves with other names: *Take Another Chance, Won't You Have a Little Cake?* and lastly *The Rooty Toot Toot Show*. Today, I am to attend the penultimate recording of this series. It is a day of mourning. I have come to know Michael through a number of sources, the chief being Robert Kirby, the *enfant terrible* of acerbic satire. No one can cut them down like Robert Kirby, who is fearless in the face of repressive apartheid censorship. I am a fan of *Take a Chance*, as I am of *The Goon Show*, which is the highest praise I can offer. It is that good, on top of which it is purely South African. Michael and Robert are soulmates, and that both elect to commission me is the greatest compliment. I must be doing something right. Like all great artists, Michael has everything but money. He is the show's writer, and his sole collaborator is Darryl Jooste, who I have yet to meet. Michael asks me, rather sadly, that with the show closing and money being what it is, can I go easy on my fee? The universal lament of the arts.

'I'll do it for free if I can come to a recording.'

Deal.

Michael is a little late and hurries to get to the recording studio. 'Listen,' he tells me on the trot. 'You must understand that there is only Darryl and me in the studio at any recording. We don't allow anyone in there.' It's a privacy thing. I get it. 'You have to understand, Darryl is shy. I mean abnormally shy.' I get it. I intend to listen, not talk. 'I mean he's not good with people. It is painful.' Michael is like an overprotective mother shielding a child with a social impediment.

I promise to say not a word.

The size of the studio is a surprise. My early memory of a studio is of an auditorium, a vast space, but here, there is only a table and three chairs laid out. Darryl Jooste is inside, already seated at the table. We are introduced and immediately, his eyes are playing catch-me-if-you-can with mine. He is tense and uneasy. Even the handshake comes at great cost, as if he is a terrified germophobe. What I am expecting is that the two voice magicians have rehearsed their script beforehand and know their lines, but something else begins to happen. Michael has a few pages of notes. He is officially the scriptwriter, except there is no script, just some vague guidelines. Darryl listens intently to Michael's short brief and then just like that, they are off. No rehearsal. They just swing into it.

The room is suddenly filled with made-up people – Wouter Marais, Miems Meiring, Charles Teller, Philemon Khumalo, Colin Jubilee, and more. They switch effortlessly from one voice to another and in one sketch there are four people having tea. It is Darryl Jooste who is the surprise. In front of the microphone, he is Clark Kent suddenly becoming Superman. All inhibitions fall away. Each character lives and breathes. I am with magical mad hatters, in the company of genius.

There are few left who will share my passion for these extraordinary comics simply because they have slipped under history's shabby carpet, like yesterday's lint and cigarette ash. Trevor Noah would stand in reverence. I have a CD I treasure, a gift from Michael Meyer called *Totally Ridiculous*. My illustration graces the cover. My favourite is a sketch where Michael plays an old apartheid censor reading through Hamlet's soliloquy and scratching out phrases with what can only be an old-fashioned dipping pen (remember those?), the typical weapon of the minor bureaucrat, a row of rubber stamps like a firing squad at the ready at his anally retained station. He reads out every syllable with dark suspicion: 'To suffer the slings and arrows of outrageous fortune, or to take arms against a sea of troubles. Mm, violence hey? (*Skritch! Skritch!*) And by opposing end them? Violence again? When are they going to learn not to push their luck?' (*Skritch! Skritch!*) It gets more ridiculous as each line is carefully scrutinised. 'When he himself might his quietus make with a bare bodkin? A bare bodkin? A bodkin is all right, *maar* a bare bodkin?' (*Skritch! Skritch!*)

Genius! Genius! Genius! I am privileged to have been a witness.

CHAPTER 58

O Brother, Where Art Thou?
(2000)

'The old man tells me you're making a film.'

There are no preceding pleasantries when my big brother phones to ask me what the hell mad scheme I am involved in now. I know that the old man has had an almighty *huck* about how I am so bad at business, perhaps, in his estimation, even worse than Mot.

'Is that what the old man told you?'

When they are not fighting at the factory over which machine Mot wants to buy that Dad has vetoed, they discuss everything else. They stand side by side at the stone, the big metal table putting together settings for printing until Dad retires. Dad and Mot are 'comps' – compositors to the uninitiated.

'You're going into the film business? Are you fucken mad?'

'I'm not going into the film business. I'm writing a script.'

Mot will not be stopped. He is only beginning with a telling off, something he has done since we shared a bedroom. The fact that he is beginning with a skewed fact is not a hindrance. He has to tell me where I am going wrong.

Secretly, Mot loves all the 'wrong' things I do. It goes counter to everything Dad thinks. It was he who urges me to go out on my own when everyone else sees me headed for a massive fall. He reserves 'fucken' for important issues on which I need guidance. It's a hangover from childhood, a big brother showing his seniority by using this banned word. Everything that is banned belongs in the adult world.

'Tell them all to go to hell. What do you want to get involved with these people?' I half expect him to mention nightclub-johnnies and *laydik-gayers*.

'You listen to me. There's a lot of work out there. I've got friends in business. They need logos. Caricatures? I'll get you hundreds.'

But I am doing everything that has cramped Mot's life. His dream still is to go into radio and electrics, anything with things that switch on and off. But he is trapped in the cage of the family business. He understands the machines and sees where the new technologies are going. Fedlers needs to move with the times, but Dad stops him at every turn, manacling him to the past.

'You can't run a factory on a Cropper. The British Thompson is crap. We need a Heidelberg,' Mot argues.

Dad has a fit.

'A German machine in my shop? Never. Why do you curse me with such a son? All he knows is how to spend money and who does he want to give it to? The *Deutsch*!'

And comes the day, Fedlers has a Heidelberg, but still Dad hangs onto Mot's heels and won't let him move.

Technology runs away with it all and they are finally lucky to get out.

'You're not putting money into a film?' Mot asks me.

'No.'

'Bloody right. Film is kaput. It's all going to video.'

CHAPTER 59

The Graduate
(1967)

The American dream is there for the taking. The graduate Benjamin Braddock (Dustin Hoffman) is poised to inherit. An elder offers this sage advice to success: 'One word – plastics.' But Ben is troubled, uneasy about this prescribed future in upper-middle-class suburbia. This is the sixties and the youth are in revolt. It is a crooked path through his affair with Mrs Robinson (Ann Bancroft), a friend of his parents, to finally running off with her daughter on her wedding day. Underscored by the quiet, rebellious music of Simon & Garfunkel, it is the sounds of silence that drive this important film.

Mot and I lie in our beds on opposite sides of the room, in the dark, looking for meaning on the ceiling. It has been a terrible evening. Tonight, Dad has been told the results of my first-year architecture results. They are not very good. It is some record. I have failed five out of six subjects. All I passed was History of Art. There has to be a message in there somewhere for Dad. He wouldn't allow me to study fine arts, so we have reaped the whirlwind. I have been The Last Hope Kid, Dad's final chance of ever having a capped-and-gowned photograph to boast on a mantelpiece. The ghost of my grandfather, who I have never known, has been summoned this evening, all the way down from the Steppes of Russia, to witness the calamity. I have been assured that, though I may be lying secure in a bed, tucked in with opportunities undreamed of, the old man sits in paradise like a mourner tonight. Even in Eden, it's sackcloth and ashes, I am assured.

For once, the weight of disappointment has finally come down to crush me instead of Mot. We are truly brothers tonight, bonded in failure.

It is a long way from Mayfair and Greenside, living in a flat in Parkview. Thank God Mom has not lived to witness my disgrace. Dad has been careful not to mention her in front of Fanya, the second Mrs Fedler, in his eulogy to dashed hopes. But I can rest assured that she is up there with Zayde as they sit down beside the rivers of Babylon and weep.

From where I am lying, the future is as dark as the ceiling. I don't need Dad to spell it out for me.

'It's tickets for you, *boykie*. You'll end up in the *blerrie* factory just like me.' Mot's voice cuts the thick silence.

It is the very end of 1958 and only ten years since we lived in paradise in Mayfair. That is about four thousand days since Mr Reese, the headmaster of John Ware Primary, pronounced on Mot's chances as a scholar. Which he estimated at nil. We have lost so much in that short time. Mom was really ill for four years until she died, and we had to mourn for a year. Count five bad years. One thousand eight hundred and twenty-five days. Count the two years since Dad married Fanya. Seven hundred and thirty days. Not great years. No one's fault. Especially not hers. Subtract the bad years from the total and you get about a thousand days. What's left is about three years of not-bad times.

We stare at the ceiling, knowing we're both wide awake.

'You think you're going to work for Walt Disney?' he says finally. 'Just because you like to read books, you think you'll end up doing what you want? Fat *blerrie* chance. It's the *blerrie* factory for you, *boykie*. You think animation is easy? You know how they do that stuff? Julian told me.'

If Julian told him, what follows is *din torah*. It's the word from Sinai. It is fact.

'You know how many pictures they have to draw for one second of film? Twenty-four. That's one thousand four hundred and forty drawings for just one minute. You think it's all just a few drawings? Rubbish. Twenty-four frames per second. You understand what that is? One thousand four hundred and forty drawings for just one minute. You'll be in the *meishev zkeinim* (old-age home) by the time you've drawn an hour.'

The Jewish Old-age Home in Doornfontein is not a place I ever want to go to again. I have been there exactly once. We went to see old man Adelson there once and it was eerie seeing so many really old people shuffling about.

'It's not a string of different fancy pictures,' Mot is hammering the point. 'The same drawing, virtually the same, just with an adjustment. It's a slog. It's real work. Draw someone scratching his nose? The whole thing, backgrounds, everything. One thousand four hundred and forty times. Can you see yourself doing that? You? Mr Impatience? Not in a million years. It's like the old man says. You never finish anything.'

It smarts. I'll prove them both wrong.

The next day, I am trying to do exactly that. I sit with a pile of paper, determined to have finished an animated sequence of someone scratching his nose. I bail out at about drawing number twelve. This wishing upon a star is rubbish. Maybe, after all, I don't want to work for Walt Disney.

CHAPTER 60

The Entertainer
(1960)

A very ordinary music hall comedian tries desperately to survive. Written by John Osborne and starring Laurence Olivier.

Jabu is a director's dream. As I watch him, my heart sinks. Given the restrictions of a lousy script, he milks it. It is not that I think that *Timer Joe 3* is going to be a failure, but precisely the opposite. Our star is a seasoned clown. This small man fills every scene he is asked to play. He can play everything, from furtive to anxious. He understands precisely what I want of him and rises high above any of my expectations.

In the nightclub scenes – all shot in one day, thanks to the time he saves us all – he plays a waiter hovering between incompetence and genius. He trips holding a full tray of food and drink that goes flying off; but he quickly recovers and, in a spectacular display of juggling, catches all the food items one by one, back as they were, and goes on to serve a table. It is his timing that captures it all. He is the epitome of consummate ease – he is a born entertainer. Dealing with another patron who complains that the bread that has been served him is brown, where he specifically ordered white, presents no problem to Jabu. Returning to the kitchen, he finds a can of white paint, sprays the bread and returns it to the customer, who takes a bite. We expect the man to choke, but in this *Tom and Jerry* world of my movie, the diner smiles, satisfied.

But none of it satisfies me. It is not Jabu's but my own performance that is lacking. I feel as if I have failed yet again. What I have created is no more than a cartoon, something that belongs in a supporting programme of my childhood matinée days. I'm a big boy now, and I don't want to be just a supporting programme or, still, end up in the factory. I want to be a main feature. I want to be part of the history of South African comedy.

CHAPTER 61

Stop the World: I Want to Get Off
(1966)

An allegorical musical about an Everyman called Little Chap.
Memorable for one song, 'What Kind of Fool Am I?'

When I go to town with Mom holding her hand, we stop at prescribed spots where there sits a beggar. She hands me her shopping bag with this instruction, 'Dovid, you're a big boy now. Hold my parcel and don't drop – there's eggs inside.' I clutch the bag tightly for fear of being downgraded to baby status should I drop it, while she patiently rummages in her purse.

'How are you this week, missus?' asks the old lady sitting on the cold pavement, her hand cupped for a few pence.

'No better, no worse. Life goes on. And how are you?'

'Ha! My arthritis is very bad.'

'You shouldn't sit on the cold concrete. Get a box.'

'Yes, missus. Thank you and God bless.'

'And get a box,' says Mom as we move off.

There are many such stations along the way and Mom stops at every one. The transaction is repeated with similar conversations, though we are late in meeting her friends at John Orr's for tea. After each one comes the instruction, 'Dovid, you never pass an open hand.'

>   I beg of you make me a promise,
>   To be honest and sincere at all times.
>   Let justice be your guiding light
>   And be caring of your fellow man.

This is part of a poem she writes for my *bar mitzvah*. Everything is logged in her diary. The beggars, the exploitation of mine workers, the general unfairness, all recorded in verse. Mom has barely been to school, but she has been an aspiring poet since early childhood.

When we finally arrive at John Orr's she is greeted warmly by every lady in turn and it doesn't take long before she has them laughing.

'Oy, Chaya, you are a tonic,' says Mrs Dembovsky, 'a real comedienne. Better even than Molly Picon. Now read us a poem.'

She just has the knack of making people feel better.

Our house is a counselling home. Many neighbours come to seek advice. Even Mrs de Bruyn from across the road who is having trouble with her son Billy seeks Mom's counsel.

It is not her words that remain with me as much as the deeds. The stopping to rummage in her bag for a few coppers is a ritual and tea at John Orr's can just wait. She is always polite, never in a hurry, always addresses everyone as an equal. By these small deeds she hopes to reform the world and I am part of that master plan. She will take second place to no one.

Mom meets Dad head-on in argument, a perfect match, though he displays the louder temper. I remember Mot's description of Dad coming to George's aid with those two *frusks*. Block by block, both parents assemble the Lego of my ego. I must stand against injustice and give it voice. It is inevitable that I become a political cartoonist. It is destined.

It has taken me fifty years to reach that insight, which makes me a slow learner indeed. Piece by piece, they patiently build me. Always talk straight and tell the truth. And take action when it is called for. '*A frusk in ponim*', a slap in the face, if that's what it takes. Force. There is a right and there is a wrong. It is wrong that needs always to be addressed. It is my mother whom I now see as a force to be reckoned with. She is the driver in so much that my parents strive for. It is she who urges Dad to come to South Africa and seek out a better life. Mom also wants to change the world with her writing, as does Dad with his. And everything is logged, written with the Parker 51 pen Mot gives her when he makes a big score of pens for his *bar mitzvah*. He has no use for it.

Chaya's parents are poor. His name is Noach and his wife is Dvorah. I am named after both. She is the youngest of five children. She worships her four brothers and adores her sister. Hers is a soul immediately on fire, in love with her world. She wanders down the narrow, cobbled streets, the market square, the smell of fresh apples, the peal of church bell rings her heart. She revels in the magic of this place. Her energy is boundless. If there is a wall, it has to be climbed to see what's on the other side. Falling off is nothing. A scraped elbow, a bruised knee. It's wondrous. Everything is a new experience. The river freezes from its deep green to winter white and she is the first to run down and skate, bang her head. Repeatedly. What sort of behaviour is this for a respectable girl? I imagine it as a play for voices, like something out of Dylan Thomas's *Under Milk Wood*, the first poetry that I and my daughter Joanne share:

Voice 1: What will the neighbours say? What will the neighbours say?
Voice 2: Barred from writing exams at school.
Voice 3: A *shande*. A scandal
Voice 1: What's to become of her? Her mother, in a state.
Voice 2: Who can blame her?
Voice 3: Poor, poor woman.
Voice 1: Hired a tutor.
Voice 2: Taught her Russian.
Voice 3: Latin also.
Voice1: Did she learn?
Voice 2: No, not a thing.
Voice 3: There she goes falling.
Voices in unison: Out of a tree.
Mother: Chayele, Chayele, grow up!
Voices in unison: What will become of you Chayele, Chayele?

Poverty inhibits her ambitions. There is nothing for it but to learn a trade. There is no time for a proper education. Her parents never have one. Though barely literate, my maternal grandmother teaches her verses and songs and instantly a poet is born.

She has a few lessons in Latin and Russian but at the age of thirteen she is sent off to the city, the *shtot* of Riga to learn to be a seamstress. Sitting behind a sewing machine, working under intolerable conditions, she feels like she's stitching her own shroud. She is all for the October Revolution. She writes, 'The fervour of the Revolution appealed to me as I was one of the exploited.' And come the Revolution in the early days of 1917, and the weight seemed to lift for the first time. Hers is not a spirit that will be crushed. There has to be more to life than this. When her apprenticeship is over, she returns to her beloved Žagarė, a confirmed socialist. But there is greater hardship to follow. A world war begins when she is barely fifteen. All the Jews are expelled from their homes, their beloved *shtetl*, put on cattle trucks, and travel for months to be dumped in far-off places. Their crime: the Tsar fears that because their languages are similar, they might collaborate with the Germans, should they occupy the town. What little they have, they lose. After the war they are allowed to return. On another arduous trip of weeks herded like cattle, her father suffers frostbite and, having lost all he has, now loses all his toes. Chaya has no opportunity to improve her lot. The Fedlers are not much better off. It is only after the war when they return to their broken town that Mom and Dad first meet.

She seeks company that is like-minded and joins a Zionist socialist club whose number is filled with would-be poets and writers. She joins these intense young men and women in staging Yiddish plays, writing charades, skits and spoofs, and reading their own poetry, and Chaya blooms. She writes songs, and plays. She is adored for her sharp wit and is fondly dubbed *Der Wietsling*, The Wit.

She is committed now to becoming a poet. Perhaps not great, but a poet nonetheless. She loves this language, Yiddish, and how easily it adapts to verse. She will be published and she will be read. Such are her ambitions.

Chaya cannot compete with this intellectual group in terms of their backgrounds and education, but they all fall under her spell. She is multitalented, able to take up a mandolin and pick out a tune. She has a passion for learning and is a fast learner. Everyone admires her writings. She is particularly taken with one member of this culture group. He is a great organiser. If anything needs doing it is delegated to Chona Fedler. This serious young man is surprisingly not lacking in a sense of humour. He runs the library for the club and recommends books for her to read. In casual conversation, bit by bit, she learns of his background

This Chona Fedler, though he has attended nothing but *cheder*, has taught himself to read Russian by reading his younger sister Eta's primers. He has read Lermontov, Gogol, Turgenev, Krylov's Fables, Nekrasov, Tzechov, Gorki, Tolstoi and of course Dostoyevsky. All of the great Russian masters. In translation he has also read Victor Hugo and Mark Twain, has paid for private lessons, and knows arithmetic, science, history, geography. His hunger is insatiable. It makes him irresistible. He is a compositor working in a print shop who has plans for a great Yiddish newspaper of which he will be the editor and in which he will promote writers and poets. Now, with the war behind them, the future appears like the sunrise on a glorious day. Chona cannot help but throw glances in her direction. It is difficult to do with one glass eye and not appear to be obvious. His good eye strains to take her all in, and he is met by a look of undisguised interest and warmth.

It is convention for a man to make the first advances but Chaya Michelson has never been conventional. Their romance is headed for a rocky road indeed. My maternal grandfather, Noach, is by no means a *mechutan* for my paternal grandfather, Yitzchak Abba Fedler, a Torah and Talmud scholar. There is no equivalent of *mechutan* in English that summarises the relationship of fathers-in-law. It's a Jewish thing. A *machateneste*, the female of the species, is of no consequence really unless she is from a wealthy family. No such luck for my grandmother, and less so for my mother.

A boy with a good Torah background could marry well. It is all detailed in *Fiddler on the Roof*.

So my parents begin as star-crossed lovers. Not quite Romeo and Juliet, for the antipathy to the match is purely one-sided. It is my grandfather, Yitzchak Abba, who opposes it. Also, he claims particular ownership of this son. They are bound as if by the *akedah*, the sacrifice that Abraham was going to make of Isaac. Yitzchak has rescued his son from blindness and Death itself. This son is the apple of his eye, his scholar. With the meanest of opportunity his Chona is turning into a *talmid chochem* – a wise student. With the right match, a wealthy father-in-law to back him, he will yet become a great rabbi, a teacher. Oh, yes indeed, Yitzchak Abba has big plans for his son.

At one of the group's socials Chona receives a secret note one evening – a *sekretke*. It allows a certain discretion and spares public humiliation if the one you fancy does not reply. You write your note, place it in an envelope and write the name of the intended on it. It is considered forward for a young woman to write such a note, and although this is a group of Moderns, who enjoy a *papaross*, a smoke, Chona cannot believe that someone has sent him this secret note. He reads and feels almost dizzy. His heart pounds. Unbelievable. It is from her! They begin a correspondence expressing unbearable longing. They are instantly in love. Deeply and passionately and forever. And diligently, it is logged.

SPRING IV
March 1923
Spring that year was beautiful
Joyfully they shared it
She found him interesting
He was ever so complimentary
All too soon Summer arrived
bringing hot scorching days in its wake
Both hearts harboured secrets
seeking a path to their love
It was she plucked up courage
and confessed 'I love you.'
He was totally taken aback
To hear such a declaration
How could she be so brazen?
Confessing to emotions
burning deep in her heart
Propriety will surely frown upon this
This is not the way it should be done.
Society must progress and explore
New unchartered paths
For disapproval and hypocrisy
No longer is their place
Let live,
Love and enjoy
Freedom

Being my mother's son, I imagine a sketch, or a first scene in a movie like I write for *Haak Vrystaat*. Inspired by my mother, edited by my father.

FADE INTO MOVIE:
Titles over a backdrop falling leaves BLETTER FALL. Subtitle: Falling leaves – Fall. Daylight.

EXT.C.U: Leaves falling in slow motion all in sepia. Track back wide shot. A forest in autumn. SFX: Feet trampling on fallen leaves, quiet laughter as young couple emerge as we change to colour. She holds a sprig of wildflowers and traces a loving hand on every tree as she passes. He is formally dressed in a tight dark suit, waistcoat and tie. His arms are folded at his back, uncertain what to do. She wears a light-coloured dress and stockings. It is the early 1920s. It is a first date. She is relaxed as he is nervous. They speak Yiddish.

CHAYA: Really? You were surprised that a girl should make the first move? (*She brushes his face cheekily with her bouquet. He is taken aback, unsure of how to proceed.*)

CHONA: (*He reaches into his inside pocket to remove an envelope from which he carefully extracts a small piece of paper.*) I have carried it since you sent it to me.

CHAYA: Let me see it. What was it I wrote? (*He hands her the note, she reads out loud but slowly like someone with difficulty stumbling over difficult words.*)

    Friend Feidler

    Here is my address and if you wish you may write to me to this address

    Žagarė, Dvaros g-ve No. 30 Ch. Michelson

    PS – Remember Sunday 8th April 1923. (*She laughs, teasing.*) I can't remember writing that.

CHONA: Miss Michelson. (*He is not yet comfortable addressing her by first name.*) Why me?

CHAYA: Why not you?

CHONA: Look at me. Look where I lost an eye. Look at my skin, pitted like a lemon from the smallpox. What do you see in me? Take a good look. You are beautiful as I am ugly. What do you see?

CHAYA: Opportunity.

CHONA: Huh! If only I had the opportunity. (*Thinks.*) Where, when did you see opportunity in me?

CHAYA: That evening at our club.

CHONA: What club?

CHAYA: The socialist. You, our librarian. (*She boldly takes his hand.*) You stood proud. And you shook hands.

CHONA: With whom?

CHAYA: With Sidney Hillman and thanked him for, what was it? Three hundred books he gave us?

CHONA: It was two hundred books. And what books.

CHAYA: There you go, always the editor. So, *nu*, two hundred. I stand corrected and I appoint you my editor – for life. You thanked him on our behalf. Someone took a photograph and standing shoulder to shoulder you could have been brothers and I thought, There's my opportunity.

CHONA: Miss Michelson, Chaya. (*The first time he speaks her name.*) You are so clever, witty. Everyone admires your verses. Your satire, your writing. You could do so much better than me.

CHAYA: Look at me, Chona, I am a poor girl from a very poor home. The poorest probably in all Žagarė. I am a seamstress working to support my mother and father. They can barely read, let alone write. What prospects are there for a girl like me? If I am lucky, some old widower will take me as a second wife. (*She shudders.*) God forbid. Such are my opportunities. Who will have me?

CHONA: With all my heart. I will

CHAYA: Why Mr Fedler (*teasing*), are you proposing to me?

CHONA: And what are my prospects? The Revolution ruined all my chances. Opportunity has passed me by. I too work to support an ageing father. What will become of me?

(*They sit against the trunk of a large oak tree. She puts down her bouquet and reaches over to adjust his tie and brush her fingers over his hair.*)

CHAYA: You will have every opportunity. You will become a Sidney Hillman.

CHONA: (*laughs*) A Sidney Hillman? Never.

CUT.

CHAPTER 62

The Men
(1950)

Marlon Brando in his debut role as a paraplegic struggling to come to terms with his disability.

Mom's drawing my attention to beggars is the first sociopolitical lesson of my life. The voices of protest in my own *shtad* Johannesburg begin while I am still in short pants. Mandela is involved in anticolonial and African nationalist politics when he joins the ANC in 1943. I am three years old. He co-founds the Youth League in 1944. When Nadine Gordimer tells of *A World of Strangers* in 1958, I am still a stranger in the strange land of grown-ups. My political *bar mitzvah*, the occasion when a boy assumes the mantle of a man, happens at sixteen when I read John Steinbeck's *The Grapes of Wrath* and later, when I am twenty-one, encounter *The Blood Knot* – a play by Athol Fugard about two brothers, one African and one white, who live together in a crumbling area of Port Elizabeth and who juggle with the hypocrisy of our great racial divide. Scratch Afrikaner history and you learn that the mother of Simon van der Stel, a father of the white Afrikaner nation, was Indian and from Mauritius. Athol Fugard will not allow us to ignore apartheid's ugly presence. On stage at the YMCA Theatre, at the bottom end of Braamfontein, Fugard and Zakes Mokae as the brothers drop this depth charge.

The torch of justice begins its slow burn in me. It has yet to burn bright. But it is finally alight. I feel a pride in the legacy left by a long line of fighters for human rights that go back to the only origins of which I am certain. It goes back to a modest town, a *shtetl* called Žagarė, known for its wisdom. As a Jewish Humphrey Bogart might have said, 'Of all the lousy *shtelach* in all the Pale, all the wise guys come from Žagarė.'

Each *shtetl* breeds particular traits. If you come from Shkudvil, you are modest in your attire, like the Amish or Quakers. Mrs Joffe, who is my first Hebrew teacher, and her sister Mrs Kantor wear only one style of dress ever – navy blue or brown with buttons to the neck. Those who come from Anixt are only interested in appearance, and Chelm is legendary for its naiveté and stupidity. But Žagarė is known for its thinkers who long for real freedom and a better life for all. *'Chachmei'* refers mainly to its men but the torch of liberty burns almost brighter in the daughters of Žagarė.

But it begins with a man.

Sidney Hillman is born in Žagarė, Lithuania, on 23 March 1887. Sidney's maternal grandfather is a small-scale merchant; his paternal grandfather is a rabbi known for his piety and lack of concern for material possessions. Hillman's father is a poor merchant, who neglects his business for reading and prayer. He is a less-than-ambitious person. Sidney seems destined to follow his father and grandfather. By the age of thirteen, he has memorised several volumes of the Talmud and is sent to a *yeshiva* in Vilijampolė, known as the 'mother of *yeshivas* in Slabodka', a small town across the river from the city of Kovno, to study further. His parents hope he will follow his grandfather and become a rabbi.

Sidney proves to be a *talmid chochem*, living up to the reputation of Chachmei Žagarė. He is possessed of an ever-open mind and strays from the confines of the restrictive *yeshiva* ideals. Being so near to a major city he is first attracted, then corrupted, by the company he keeps. He becomes a truant who mixes with a new crowd bent on changing the world. He is an instant convert to the ideas of Karl Marx, and the writings of John Stuart Mill and Herbert Spencer, who preach a new political economy. In quick time he becomes a fervent Bundist – a member of The Bund, a revolutionary socialist union of Jewish workers set against Tsarist rule. At seventeen he leads the first May Day march ever, through the streets of Kovno. He is arrested and sits in prison for several months. Like Nelson Mandela, his university of revolutionary social theory is enlarged by his encounter with his jailers and his fellow prisoners.

But the Tsarist repression becomes brutal. Police raids and organised pogroms force the socialists underground and they start to leave the country. In October 1906, travelling under a false passport through Germany, Sidney Hillman makes his way to Manchester, England, where he joins his uncle, a prosperous furniture dealer. He already has two brothers living there.

Prosperity does not agree with him and in 1907, aged twenty, Hillman leaves for America, struggles in New York, then heads for Chicago where he finds work in the garment industry as an apprentice garment cutter. The appalling working conditions in the sweatshop and its lack of rights make it a place crying out for a voice. These rumblings need leadership and direction. Who better than a *talmid chochem* steeped in Bundist ideals to lead? In 1910 he leads a spontaneous strike by a handful of women workers, gathering more people to their cause, which swells to a city-wide strike of 45 000 garment workers. He is twenty-three years old.

It is inevitable that he heads the Amalgamated Clothing Workers of America, the most powerful union in the country, which steers him to the highest offices of power. He becomes a supporter of Franklin Delano Roosevelt and finally one of his most trusted and valued aides. The most popular president in the history of the country has issues of great import that need constant attention. FDR leans heavily on his aide. His clear-thinking Talmudic mind cuts to the heart of problems and when yet another issue that needs immediate attention lands on the desk of the president, he passes it on with this instruction: 'Run it by Sid.' Hillman is part of his brains trust, trying to lift America out of the Great Depression. His okay makes it kosher. Hillman supports Roosevelt's New Deal from the outset. And his star rises even higher. FDR names him to the Labor Advisory Board of the National Recovery Administration in 1933 and to the National Industrial Recovery Board in 1934. He is key to the drafting of the National Labor Relations Act and in winning enactment of the Fair Labor Standards Act. Hillman is naturally an opponent of Nazi Germany and a supporter of US aid to England and France, crucial to the eventual defeat of Hitler. Wise indeed. Roosevelt appoints Hillman to the National Defense Advisory Committee in 1940 and names him associate director of the Office of Production Management. When FDR creates the War Production Board in 1942, he appoints Hillman as the head of its labour division.

CHAPTER 63

Little Women
(2019)

Various films have been made of Louisa May Alcott's account of the coming of age of four sisters in the aftermath of the American Civil War. The best is the latest cited here, directed by Greta Gerwig.

What of the women of Žagarė? Are there any to cite, other than my mother?

There is one, the daughter of an immigrant watchmaker from Žagarė, an escapee from Tsarist oppression who has come to settle in South Africa near Springs. His name is Isidore Gordimer. His daughter's name is Nadine, born on 20 November 1923.

It is not necessary to track her entire career. She is a giant of South African literature. She not only writes but sets out to do right. She is an activist, joins the ANC, has books banned, devotes herself to the poverty and discrimination against African people, founds a crèche for black children and is forever in contention with censorship. She hides ANC leaders in her own home to aid their escape, facing dire consequences, declares that the proudest day of her life is when she testifies at the 1986 Delmas Treason Trial on behalf of twenty-two South African anti-apartheid activists.

She helps Nelson Mandela draft his Rivonia Trial speech, the last paragraph of which includes many of her own actions and sentiments.

'During my lifetime I have dedicated myself to this struggle of the African people. I have fought against white domination, and I have fought against black domination. I have cherished the ideal of a democratic and free society in which all persons live together in harmony and with equal opportunities. It is an ideal which I hope to live for and to achieve. But if needs be, it is an ideal for which I am prepared to die.'

The last note about this immigrant from Žagarė's daughter is that in 1991 she receives the Nobel Prize for Literature, recognised as a woman who, through her magnificent, epic writing, has been of very great benefit to humanity.

In her last years, she declares herself to be an atheist but adds: 'I think I have a basically religious temperament, perhaps even a profoundly religious one.'

Perhaps a remnant of the *shtetl* remains within her?

Rose Zwi is anxious about the speech she has to deliver. She is well prepared, rehearsed and ready. It is an occasion of some pomp and ceremony and speeches, at which she is guest of honour and is to unveil a plaque commemorating the massacre of some three thousand Jews in the town square in which she now stands. The massacre included men, women and children, some of whom were taken to Naryshkin Park to be mowed down and buried in a mass grave there. The park was once bequeathed by Count Naryshkin to the town and had, over centuries, been a place of leisure, for picnics and for lovers to court and steal private moments. Now it is a graveyard.

The previous speakers have covered most of the ground that Rose plans so purposefully to tread. But now she loses confidence and does not want to come across as repetitious and ultimately boring. This is the single moment of her entire life where she needs to be heard. She trashes most of what she has to say and remembers just the last two things that need saying. Rose's father Gershon's entire family die in the killing in the town square of Žagarė and Naryshkin Park, and Rose wants them remembered.

'... As I stand before this plaque, I am overwhelmed by the thought that my parents and I may have lain in the mass grave together with my father's family had they not left Žagarė in the 1920s. I never knew my father's family, but I mourn them to this day ...

'Remember us, their unquiet spirits seem to call from the grave. As though one could ever forget. They do not ask for vengeance, only remembrance. They will always be remembered. And in the language we would have had in common, I say: MIR ZEINEN DOH. We are here.'

'*Mir zeinen doh*' is the anthem of Holocaust survivors sung at memorial services.

Rose Joffe is born in 1928 after the Joffes make an abortive attempt at emigration to Mexico but quickly run from there for fear of the anti-Semitic sentiments they encounter in Oaxaca. Once in a lifetime is enough. They pack for Johannesburg. Not only do they come to The Burg, but they settle in the suburb of Mayfair, just a few houses away from the Fedlers, and I become intimate with her family. Gershon arrives a broken man. He feels responsible for abandoning his family, who are slain. It is a guilt with which he never comes to terms.

At the age of four I remember looking at Rose Joffe with lustful eyes. She was by far the prettiest of my sister's friends. Rae and Rose go through to matric together and there is a photo of them as prefects at Commercial High, standing centre at the back, beaming, giggling. There is a more deeply rooted connection that brings us that close. Her father Gershon and her mother Sheva suffer the same expulsion and eventual return to Žagarė. They are members of the same clubs as my parents and are participants in the plays and poetry readings that are staged. There is a photograph of the whole group holding a banner advertising some play. Gershon, as well as my mother are there. Chona should be too but for some reason is absent.

It seems that Chaya and Rose share a special relationship. The one recognises the artist in the other. The age gap is immaterial. This story illustrates the point and I repeat it as Rose once told it to me.

'Once my parents went to family in Springs and left me behind. I was most upset. So I went to your mother and said, "Give me the train fare to go to Springs." (Perhaps it was Benoni.) I must have been four or five years old.

'Your mom asked, "Do you mean to go by yourself to the Mayfair station, get on the train and buy a ticket? And do you know where to get off?"

'"Yes!" I answered.'

My mother handed over the shilling or two and Rose, all on her own, went to join her family in Springs. When she and her family returned, Rose's outraged mother Sheva came to deliver a *mapole*, a dressing down, to Mom. 'How could you trust such a small child to find her way? How could you be so irresponsible?'

Today, such a story is unthinkable, with predators of the worst kind prowling everywhere.

But back then, it was a time of trust. Would Mom have handed the money to another four-year-old? I doubt it. Mom was anything but irresponsible. But what Mom saw was the young Chaya, the climber of high walls, the skater, the adventurer, the true artist, afraid of nothing and capable of everything.

Rose has been chosen as guest of honour and keynote speaker because of her book *Last Walk in Naryshkin Park*, which has enjoyed wide success. It wins the Asia Pacific Publishers' Association Award and is shortlisted for the New South Wales Premier's Literary Awards – General History prize.

Like Nadine Gordimer, she is an anti-racism activist and a member of the South African civil rights organisation Black Sash until she moves with her husband and family to Australia in 1988.

Unlike my sister, who finishes high school with shorthand and typing as her main skills, suiting her to office work, Rose goes to the University of the Witwatersrand and graduates with an honour's degree in English literature in 1967. She is employed as an editor at Raven Press, who publish her debut novel, *Another Year in Africa*, which wins South Africa's Olive Schreiner Prize in 1982. The expression 'Nog a yor in Afrika' is one often quoted by our parents. In 1995 it is published in Australia by Spinifex Press when it is listed among the Australians' best books of the year. Rose's next novel *Safe Houses* wins Australian Human Rights award for fiction in 1994. She concentrates on historical novels and short stories. But the book that she considers her life's work is *Last Walk in Naryshkin Park*, which is published in 1997. This is a close-up, in-depth study of the history of the Jews of Lithuania, but in particular of Žagarė. Her research is extensive, impeccable and intensely personal.

Brave Rose makes the pilgrimage to Žagarė as she once made her way to – was it perhaps Brakpan? She peels back the curtain of time. Her research brings her back to Johannesburg, desperate for some detail or tidbit about the *shtetl*. Mom and Dad have been active with the Zagarer Society that assists *landsleit* who have been struggling since before the war. Dad is the treasurer. Rose phones my sister to make a date to meet Mom. Rose says, 'Chaya would have told me about Žagarė, warts and all.' 'Don't worry,' says Rae ' I know other *landsleit* who have clear memories of Žagarė. My father wrote a memoir before he died. Come for tea.'

'Me and the other woman?' asks Rose.

She recalls the joke our families share. Many years before, Mom drops in to pay Sheva a visit. 'Shevke,' she says, 'I'm hot and tired and dying for a cup of tea.' She drinks the cup and, revived, holds it up. 'I feel like another woman and now the other woman would like a cup of tea.'

Rose dies on 22 October 2018 and Rae passes on 22 November 2017. There is so much more I would like to ask. Now all I have are Dad's memoir *Shalechet, Last Walk in Naryshkin Park* and Mom's poems.

Rae speaks Yiddish before she learns English. Dad insists that she attend the *Yiddishe Volkshul* and she can read and write in the beloved tongue before she starts her public-school education. She starts school like an immigrant child, at times having difficulty with a second language. Rae never regrets that she can write a fluent letter in Yiddish but often asks, 'What did I need it for?'

And the spirit that is Žagarė, like a fallen leaf, comes to rest upon on Rae with the answer. In the last four years of her life (she lives to be eighty-nine) she devotes herself to translating Mom's poems, to preserve them for the family and grandchildren. She prints but a few copies, which she distributes among us. It is called *Falling Leaves*. My sister makes no attempt to doctor the verses in any way and what is reproduced here is the painful word-for-word translation. In English the poems lose rhythm and at times comes out like Yoda-speak. Thus, they are preserved.

The thread of this dreamcloth connects the past to the now. *The Dreamcloth* is the name of my daughter Joanne's first novel and its themes are exactly that. And the thread of wisdom still passes from some ancestors back in a forgotten past. Joanne is born in 1967, and becomes internationally known as the author of ten books that are translated into many languages and sell close to 750 000 copies worldwide, mostly in Germany. She is an activist from the time she can speak. She is awarded a Fulbright scholarship to study law at Yale, becomes a law lecturer and a volunteer legal counsellor at People Opposing Women Abuse (POWA) before setting up and running a legal advocacy centre to end violence against women. It is one too many acts of violence too close to home that has her move her family to Australia. She is appointed by the then minister of justice to sit on a project committee of the Law Commission to re-sign new domestic violence legislation. I introduce her to Rose Zwi on a visit to Sydney. Joanne starts her own publishing house, Joanne

Fedler Media, and mentors mainly women writers, assisting them to publication.

The torch passes yet again to Joanne's daughter Jesse, whose ambition it is to be a writer, poet, playwright, novelist and musician. She is accepted to do an artist's residency at Chateau d'Orquevaux in France in April 2020.

That's a long way from Žagarė.

From whence these Fedlers on the roof?

Roes unveils the plaque. It reads:

'For hundreds of years Žagarė had been home to a vibrant Jewish community. Žagarė's Market Place had many Jewish shops and was a centre of commerce for the merchants from here and a range of other towns. Many of their shops surrounded this square. Žagarė was also famous for its many Hebrew scholars, the 'Learned of Žagarė'. German military occupiers and their Lithuanian collaborators brought the region's Jewish men, women and children to this square on 2 October 1941. Shooting and killing of the whole Jewish community of Žagarė began here and continued in the forests nearby. About 3 000 Jewish Citizens were killed.'

Rose's tears are Chaya's.

Rose might have quoted a poem by mother.

Neither Mom nor I have harboured any illusions as to the quality of her writing. It does not compare to an Avrom Reyzen, the most popular Yiddish poet, who assumes the posture of an average person. Mom does not assume an identity. It is her identity. She writes to her audience, women of her station with little schooling. She gives this silent majority voice. Her recurring themes, like theirs, are the legacy of a *shtetl* destroyed, Life, Hope, Grief and Death. Of her own writing, she says,

> Mother Tongue
> A friend came calling
> with flowers in her outstretched hands
> She asked me of the reason I write
> No offence is thus intended
> should the language lack perfection
> and the prose and lines found wanting

> The grammar too, may limp along
> but the words expressed in rhyme
> is the language taught to me by my Mother
> not wrapped up as gifts did they come to me
> Just some personal reflections
> from The School of Life
> Need alone has been my mentor
> drawn from experience
> and hardship endured.

Nearing death, she may not achieve the precision of a Dylan Thomas. She does not rage against the dying of the light but has the same clarity.

> SUN DO NOT SET
> I stand midway
> far from the goal
> The sun wants to set
> And abandon me halfway
> Much there is still to complete
> A long way still from the finish
> Sun, please do not sink
> Do not threaten
> Just light up my way

And for her epitaph, she ends with:

> There was a woman quite ordinary
> No different from any other
> From a yearning did she expire
> To be a writer was her fervent desire

The women of Žagarė yet sing the anthem.

CHAPTER 64

Watchmen
(2009)

First a much-praised graphic novel, then an uneven movie, and now an intriguing television series. The premise is superheroes being ordinary people without comic superpowers.

Robert Kirby is a thorn in the side of Jimmy Kruger, our Minister of Justice and chief censor. This Kirby needs to be permanently banned. He and other troublemakers are springing up like poisonous mushrooms everywhere. Jimmy Kruger, 'The Just', cannot rest. He has to be ever vigilant. Lo, he who keepeth our moral rectitude neither slumbers nor sleeps. Under his watch, Steve Biko gets his unjust desserts.

Our Jimmy says of his death, *'Dit laat my koud'* – it leaveth me cold. Jimmy is the guardian of our virtue, appointed by our uber-leader, John Balthazar Vorster. He oversees what we may look at, listen to and say. This Kirby is an agent of the Hate South Africa campaign. He and the cursed English Press are undermining everything this country stands for. We are sworn to preserve our leader's wishes to build a South Africa on what he calls *kleurevolke*, nations according to colour and ethnicity, a government based on the model of Nazi Germany. Vorster wants to Christianise, civilise and sanitise black beliefs. 'Everyone must convert. We will later deal with Islam and show them the right way. Everyone must be more like us. This constant undermining of the grand plan by the English press must be stopped. These bloody satirists that are springing up everywhere like weeds are leading us to chaos. First to go must be this Kirby and his *Early Morning Show* on the English service of the SABC.'

The *Early Morning Show* features comedy as we have never heard it before. It is brand new, exciting and achingly funny, and is a problem for the watchmen. Above all, we must retain our standards for the good of everyone.

Radio has always been for entertainment and those in charge don't know what's hit them. The same goes for theatre and film. Suddenly they have to watch what the people are watching. 'We must excise the devil in our midst before he turns red like all the communist, thespian, lesbian, moffie, artsy-fartsy terrorists. On screen black men and white women are kissing and vice versa. It is shocking to think who is coming to dinner. How can this be stopped? We are for the good of the people but not of or by the people. It's like bloody Hollywood. McCarthy was right. Kick them out. Blacklist them. Add this Kirby to our white blacklist.'

In the golden days of Joburg in the sixties and seventies, before the fortress walls, the barbed, electrified, Stalag encirclement of suburban life, it is no trouble to drive directly into the driveway of 60 The Braids Road, find an open front door, and make oneself at home.

Being a double-storey house, the family is often all upstairs in their rooms. We will, on occasion, hear a Scott Joplin Rag, a sonata or some honky-tonk being played by a maestro on our piano. Thus does Robert Kirby announce his presence in our home. We are that close.

It is more than flattering that this brilliant satirist seeks me out to collaborate for a show in 1975. Six years earlier, *The Star* commissions me to draw two political cartoons a week. I am to share the pages with Abe Berry, a seasoned veteran. By the time Robert Kirby invites me to do the graphics for a show called *Eight Birds*, seven years later, I have become something of a veteran myself, with a following and fans.

I am a match for his biting tongue with my more tongue-in cheek-approach. We are a good balance. This association sharpens my wits and my pen strokes begin to show a deep-seated anger. The Kraken is finally wide awake. I produce a series of send-ups of famous paintings, which I name Hyperkitsch. I build a punchbag of John Vorster's face. I paint massive pictures on primed Masonite board, spoofs of famous paintings. They are elaborate cartoons like anything I might produce for the paper on any given day. The one idea of which I am most proud is a parody of Gainsborough's *The Blue Boy*. The title derives from the costume of the wearer. A domestic worker, a Zulu man, carries a feather duster and wears the humiliating short-sleeved, short-pants uniform of servility of the time. The picture is called *White Boy*. I am being raised to a different standard of political comment. I take a swipe at Connie Mulder, our Minister of Information. All are a protest against this iniquity called apartheid. Working alongside Robert is like being an assistant to a surgeon whose speciality is amputation. I get close enough to his personal wrangle with the censors. I understand something of Nadine Gordimer's frays. Robert cuts to the underbelly of these authorities who constantly hound him. He uses his wit as a scalpel trying to behead this Hydra, this monster of many heads. I realise that what I am learning is not new, but just more sophisticated lessons already instilled by Mom and Dad. When there is a wrong, Kirby is quick to pounce on it with his acerbic wit. His writing is a broadsword that he carries over to journalism, into the public domain.

Mom's platform is a kitchen table, writing a piece about the people on whose backs this country has been built. She hopes that the little-read South African *Yiddishe Tseitung* might be publish it. Her political activism has been doused by years in which she and Dad have been cowed into the daily routine of survival. Her own family are now the centre of her ambitions and hopes. But injustice still rouses her.

> Clad only in threadbare rags
> You harmonise your songs
> The hardship endured is ignored
> And songs ring out with joy

Chaya has empathy. Robert Kirby has none. The time demands a louder, more strident voice.

My second Hyperkitsch painting is a send-up of the Mona Lisa with Connie Mulder in drag. Connie is most famous for a scandal called Muldergate, exposed by two *Rand Daily Mail* journalists, Mervyn Rees and Chris Day. The reporters document the Vorster government's attempts to sway international and local public opinion about them and so begin their own propaganda war. They claim that the English press works to spread only bad news about South Africa and distort the good.

There is an ongoing Hate South Africa crusade, and so begins their own propaganda war. It starts in 1973 when Vorster agrees to Mulder's plan to shift about R64 million from the defence budget in order to finance the venture. But Muldergate spoils Mulder's chances of becoming Vorster's successor.

This is the prey that has Robert salivating like a pit bull. He loves to ravage politicians. His satire is acid thrown in your face.

Connie becomes our Minister of Bantu Administration and Development and changes the name of the department to Plural Relations and Development. The homelands are to be called self-governing entities, and Africans to be referred to as Africans, not Bantu.

It's the plural part that is funny. Maybe he can't spell equal? Crocodile tears stream from the corner of one of Mulder's eyes in my painting, from a minute hole drilled and rigged from behind, a swipe at Vladimir Tretchikoff's *Weeping Rose*. Tretchi, as he becomes known locally – originally a Russian import but now a local and international commercial success – is probably the world's most commercially successful painter. Prints of his works are in demand everywhere. There is no greater craftsman of kitsch than him.

That every joke offends somebody down the line is the principle by which Kirby stands. 'Humour that didn't plunge the knife into somebody's ribs is pale, vapid and weak,' he preaches.

Our collaboration earns me a visit from an undercover Special Branch agent. I have him at 'hello'. Posing as a fan, he gently probes into my associations.

'What about Robert Kirby?' oozes from under his blanket of blarney.

'Oh! I barely know him,' I lie.

Even Robert's friends come out with stab wounds. No one calls him Bob. It is difficult to get close to the man and not end up in a fight. He is the Grim Reaper, scything through anything in his path to a laugh. You may love him, but he is hard to like. Robert Kirby is most comfortable in the presence of his enemies. His cup runneth over with vitriol. *Trebor Ybrik vs The Rest*, a title of one of his books, tells precisely which way Robert marches. Trebor, as someone writes of him, is just angry.

His epitaph could well be Trebor Ybrik vs The Rest in Peace.

CHAPTER 65

Gone with the Winds

Gone with the Wind (1939) was one of the all-time international blockbusters. It was based on the novel by Margaret Mitchell and was about the fractured romance of Rhett Butler and Scarlett O'Hara, played by Clark Gable and Vivien Leigh, against the backdrop of the American Civil War. A movie about which to give a damn.

'Ever since he got back from London working for the *blerrie* BBC, he's been stirring *kak*. We know all that's been going on over there since that *Beyond the Fringe* in the early sixties. It has really changed everything. These damned university students should know their place and not write these seditious revues. This Jonathan Miller, *'n Jood*, this Dudley Moore and Alan Bennett have stirred up a hornet's nest. It has even reached America and that other *Jood*, Zimmerman, who calls himself Dylan, is singing that the times they are a-changing. Nothing is sacred.'

Harold Macmillan knows it. He can't stop it spreading there. He talks of The Winds of Change. They are farting in the face of our conservatism. They are mocking the church and our devotion. No one is safe. Nothing is sacred. Then there is the cursed Monty Python, probably another *Jood*, making fun of our Saviour. *Life of Brian*? 'We must have the death of Brian!'

And what has happened to the cartoonists? 'Call that drawing? They are slashing images on paper. Where is the tranquil quill of the engraver?'

Nothing is confidential any more. Now it is all in *Private Eye*.

'And this Kirby thinks he can come back here from the BBC and start the *kak*? *Nooit!*'

CHAPTER 66

Censor Sensibility

Sense and Sensibility (1995), a novel by Jane Austen and well adapted to a movie by Emma Thompson and directed by Ang Lee.

The *Early Morning Programme* is so successful that the SABC shuts it down after two years. The story dished out is that there are complaints from advertisers that it is drawing listeners away from the rival, commercial station Springbok Radio. Yea, Bokke!

The *Early Morning Programme* is too clear a window on to the skewedness of the beloved country for it to be allowed to flourish. The show attracts other intellectual talents. Walter Mony, who is a violinist from Winnipeg and becomes chair of music at the University of the Witwatersrand in Johannesburg, is one player in the show. No doubt it is their music that brings that pair together. The show includes comic talents like Hal Orlandini, Annabel Linder, Linda Stewart and the occasional participation of Cyril Green, a real-life shoe salesman, sometime piano-player, comic and choirboy.

As the FBI hounds Lenny Bruce for using language that Eddie Murphy, Chris Rock and Quentin Tarantino now use so glibly, so too are The Vorster Gang after Kirby.

Our chief censor sends him notice, demanding that he remove certain four-letter words from a play he has written. The notice, of course, lists the offensive words. This is Robert's kind of fight. He lays a criminal charge against the censor for sending obscene material through the mail.

But the Special Branch will not let up. This scathing satire makes them uneasy. Their harassment of him is played in the shadows, unlike their open persecution of Winnie Madikizela-Mandela. There is no likelihood of him being taken to John Vorster Square where he might jump out of a window or be beaten to death like Steve Biko in a cell, and have it covered up by the reasons and excuses that were given by the apartheid police for killing people in prison.

What to do about this Kirby? If only he were a communist, then we could do a real number on him like Ruth First and Albie Sachs.

Kirby's play, *Gentlemen* – which stars Kirby's good friend Michael Mayer and features the first onstage kiss by two men in South Africa – affords our guardians in the government the opportunity to launch the fake news that Ybrik is homosexual, a devastating charge at the time. Michael Mayer, yet another troublemaker who needs to be monitored, is cited as his lover. Somehow, Kirby acquires a copy of his police file. His roar is not of anger but of uncontained laughter.

And the surveillance begins. Very swiftly, the authorities are watching the antics of all these 'Hate South Africa fifth columnists', their filthy columns in the papers and the outrage of what appears in the theatre. Is that not too for entertainment? These liberal rebels, Des and Dawn Lindberg, are allowing black people onto a 'white' stage. The Mulder millions feed the cannons of censorship. And with dispatch, Kirby, Pieter-Dirk Uys, the Lindbergs and journalists of good conscience render it silly.

'I believe that we can do without censorship. I do not believe that censorship saves us from anarchy. It serves very little apart from itself. There has been no noticeable decline in pornography as a result of censorship,' says Kirby.

Pieter-Dirk Uys carries it beyond the fringe of the sixties into the next century. As Evita Bezuidenhout tries to adapt or die, he/she declares, 'Whoever thought we whites would get away with apartheid? Nothing happened to us. No Nuremberg Trials. None of us was hung like Saddam Hussein for crimes against humanity. And even now, with the parole of Eugene de Kock, we do not release him in Soweto on a Saturday afternoon!'

De Kock is a security policeman sentenced for unspeakable acts of murder of black opponents.

Kirby does little to cover his back where the axe must inevitably fall.

'I don't think much about the SABC. After all, they don't think that much about me . . . But I do think their graphics on the news are marvellous. We're doing a thing on them in the show. You know what I mean.

The hunger strikes are symbolised by a loaf of bread crossed out. That sort of thing.'

The government's 'I Love South Africa' campaign continues its own tortuous route.

'Lest we be called unfair, look what we are giving to black culture. We have the subsidies for black films. Black films for black people. We want no Alan Paton *kak-stirring* trouble.'

* * *

Jabulani Masondo makes the most of the *Timer Joe* jokes. My heart sinks as we go forward.

'Isn't this the best comedy you've ever seen?' Moe asks me once again.

What I would do for one authentic Zulu gag.

CHAPTER 67

The Choirboys
(1977)

'Joseph Wambaugh wrote a dirty, tasteless, vulgar book, which I think I've managed to capture. And that's what the film is: an ode to vulgarity,' says its director Robert Aldrich. It delights in gay-bashing and race-baiting.

On the bus going to high school, this younger kid, whose first day this is, throws me a cock-eyed look that makes me smile. For some unremembered reason, I take his name to be Oz, and for the most part of the year, when we pass each other in the playground, we greet each other.

'Howzit, Ozzie?'

'*Gans gutt*, Fez.' I'm glad that he knows some Yiddish.

At our next encounter, he replies, 'Over and easy, Fez,' the one after, 'Toasted *und* crisp, Fez,' followed by 'Sunny side up, Fez.' Has he just got it wrong? Some of classmates call me Feds, so it's probably a mistake. The cock-eyed grin leaves me wondering.

It is only the following year, when we both join the choir of the Greenside Shul, that I learn his real name, Cyril Green. His Fez is a response to my Oz.

We leave school to pursue our lives and careers, and we become adults with children. I am, as ever, addicted to comics, and someone introduces me to the dizzying world of Marvel Comics. I read my first X-Men, Spider-Man and Thor, and instantly have new gods. Stan Lee and Jack Kirby bring a new intelligence to the reading. The work, like *Mad* magazine, does not take itself seriously. Everything is written in a grandiloquent manner. But the artwork is seriously great. Thor reads like Shakespeare on dope. The fun begins on the title page – wonderfully worded by Stan Lee and dramatically drawn by Jack Kirby. Incredibly inked by so-and-so-and-so-on. No one draws action like Jack Kirby. There are pages dedicated to just one drawing that explodes off the page. Comic characters burst out of the old restrictive panelled boxes, inviting us in. New sound effects are created. Gone is the simple *BANG! CRASH! SOCK!*

POW! Now there is *PTCHOO! GRRMBLLLK!* and *VAROOOM*. Where, oh where, do I get my own Marvels? Only one store imports them, which is how I come to be beneath the Savoy cinema in Butch Berman's bookshop every month.

By chance, I discover Green's Shoe Store just one block up and begin to make a regular visit to Cyril. He now favours his father's bold moustache, which makes him look Mexican. I encounter him at the odd wedding where he is the stand-in at the piano for the eccentric band leader, Archie Silansky, famous for taking out his dentures and resting them on the top of the piano so he can really get into 'Hava Nagila' and 'Embraceable You'. Cyril is a musician who never has a music lesson. He is the easy Ozzie of my schooldays. My monthly trips to Butch Berman's every month now include an obligatory stopover at Green's – only twice ever for shoes. Like my must-have Marvels, I must hear a new joke from Cyril Green.

I have no idea of how he comes to be acquainted with Robert Kirby, but there is no doubt that somewhere the master satirist enjoys the privilege of listening to another master, which is how Cyril Green comes to do gigs on radio on Kirby's *Early Morning Programme*, standing in for no one.

Cyril graduates to television, as a comedian, and is remembered by a generation of baby boomers who grew up with a television programme called *Biltong and Potroast*, which catapults a couple of comic careers into the public heart and eye of white South Africa.

The show presents the most skewed idea of diversity and highlights an understated feature of apartheid at the time. In this 1975 definition of the South African social order, we are categorised into just two groups – both white. There is not a hint of colour anywhere. In this mindset, there are those who eat biltong, a staple of the Voortrekkers, carrying with it an almost religious significance – not quite the wafer of Catholic confession, but closer to *matzo*, the Jewish bread of affliction. We may all love biltong, but never forget from whence it came. Biltong defines Afrikanerdom. Pot roast is a lazy generic that does not quite define the diversity of English culture. Fish and chips may be nearer the mark.

Biltong and Potroast fails at the outset, for nowhere is there a black or Indian comedian included, and the representative of the jerky team employs two, and sometimes four, Jews – Cyril Green, Len Davis, Cy

Saks and Mel Miller. There is not an authentic biltong brother among them. It desperately needs an Afrikaans raconteur, like Jan Spies, Fanus Rautenbach or PG du Plessis. Those, however, only speak Afrikaans (on television, that is) and will have nothing to do with anything that prefers English as a first language. All these greats are locked in the Vorster laager, *kleurevolke*. Do the Biltong team tell authentic South African jokes? Not really. Mel Miller does, sort of. But he is a Jew playing out of character. Cyril Green tells Jewish jokes, while Len Davis tells Portuguese jokes in an accent that has everyone referring to cabbage as 'cabarge'.

There is no better teller of a Jewish joke than Cyril Green anywhere. That includes Mel Brooks, or Jackie Mason, or whoever is in the top ten.

The key to Jewish joke-telling is to make it a layered sandwich, a pastrami on rye, tiers of meat separated by a pickle, relish, another pickle, pastrami again. It's like an episode of *Seinfeld* or *Curb Your Enthusiasm*, which returns again and again to the nuance of just one word.

The trick of the Yiddish gag is taking time. Who but the Jews could have wandered in a desert the size of a Texas ranch backyard for forty years? What's to rush? Life is short enough. Slow down. Make it last. Take a lesson from the Red Sea pedestrians, Simon and Garfunkel. Sit down. Don't move so fast. Have a cup of tea, a bagel and lox, a piece of cake.

Cyril Green layers that sandwich like a Carnegie Delicatessen special. He is a master funnyman since he was a little boy on a bus, always just a gag away from the Hall.

The surprising thing is that, in general, I know few Jews of my generation who can really do justice to a good *viets*. One has to have real knowledge of Yiddish to get it right. The fault is like a bad cook who adds too much seasoning. Most thicken or lean out the accent to sounding German or Afrikaans. The true accent eludes most *goyim* – gentiles. Jews may say 'gentile' with impunity, but *goy* is *verboten*. One may say black, but not *schwartz*. There is a yellow star appended to the Yiddish language.

Only one non-Jewish person of my acquaintance can pitch a perfect Jewish joke.

There can be none more not-Jewish than Robert Kirby. The Lenny Bruce benchmark of goyishness is the Kennedys. Robert Kirby is mine.

Robert's mentor in Rhythm and Jews is a real-life shoe salesmen and piano player, comic and choirboy I once called Oz.

CHAPTER 68

People Will Talk
(1951)

An intelligent talky film about a doctor who tends to treat patients philosophically, and who runs into resistance from a jealous colleague. It is a gentle, wacky comedy with a big heart and is a dig at the House Un-American Activities committee and the McCarthy witch-hunt.

We crave something authentic, be it a sound or taste. Our pasta has to be at a trattoria where everything is cooked by someone called Mama who speaks nothing but Italian. Opera has to be sung in Italian – if we can forgive Mozart for *Die Fledermaus*. We want our cafés to be French, our tavernas, our cantinas, to be the real thing. If it's a beer fest, even a Jew would want it to be German.

There is a joke that defines heaven and hell.

Heaven: The police are British. The cooks are French. The engineers are German. The administrators are Swiss. The lovers are Italian.

Hell: The police are German. The cooks are British. The engineers are Italian. The administrators are French. The lovers are Swiss.

Racial stereotypes define us in broad strokes. To say that strict discipline is a common German characteristic, as Latins are passionate, seems an acceptable generalisation.

Back in the sixties, Lufthansa employed the famous Bill Bernbach (another hymie) to advertise the airline. (Note that I take the lesson of TS Eliot's custom of penning any reference to my race in lower case.) I know my place.

This is how the ad reads.

Headline: At times you may be annoyed by the fanatical thoroughness of the Germans, but not at a time like this. The picture part of the ad is just these words, no fancy graphics:

FASTEN YOUR SEATBELTS. *BITTE ANSCHNALLEN.*

It all looks sparse and extremely Aryan. Brilliant art direction. Then comes the body copy and the genius of Bill Bernbach, that reads:

'If you've known many Germans, you know how precise they are. Sometimes it's not a terribly endearing quality. Not even for other Germans. (Germans are always complaining about how German other Germans are.)

'But keep this quality in mind just before take-off on a Lufthansa jet. Think about the irritating Germans who worked on your plane. And as you settle back into the comfort of your plush seat, an amazing thing happens.

'You're comfortable.'

Only a *yiddishe kop* could have come up with that one. It does wonders for Lufthansa.

The joke is told at a deliberate plod, the antithesis of its subject's urgency. The ad is a gentle but elaborate Jewish joke. The copy reads like something out of *Seinfeld*, not *Mein Kampf*.

'Even Germans complain about how German other Germans are' is pure Yiddish humour.

Have I gone on too long? Layered it all too much? How was all that – too Jewish?

CHAPTER 69

The Green Shoes

The Red Shoes is a 1948 British drama film written, directed and produced by the team of Michael Powell and Emeric Pressburger, known collectively as The Archers. It is about a ballerina who wears shoes that won't allow her to stop dancing and who finally makes an Anna Karenina jump in front of a train. It was voted the ninth greatest British film of all time by the British Film Institute. In 2017, a poll of 150 actors, directors, writers, producers and critics for TimeOut *magazine saw it ranked the fifth-best British film ever. Filmmakers such as Brian De Palma and Martin Scorsese have named it one of their all-time favourite films. Is all of the above but scared this eight-year-old shitless.*

Cyril has a shoe and a joke for every occasion, even a shoe story. Time and timing are the core of this carefully paced narrative.

A man steps out of a shoemaker's shop, having left a pair for resoling. As he steps out, the air is suddenly full of sirens, armed police. He is arrested, bundled into a Black Maria, thrown into a cell as he enters a Kafkaesque nightmare. He never learns the crime of which he is accused, goes to trial and then to prison for thirty years, and steps out as confused as when he first went in. He comes back to his city like Rip Van Winkle, a stranger in a strange land. Everywhere there are skyscrapers. Everything familiar has been demolished. He wanders about, lost, and spots something he recognises tucked beneath a massive flyover. It is the shoe-repair shop. At last, something to which he can relate. He reaches into a pocket and finds the ticket stub given to him so long ago, the link to the past he so desperately needs. He enters the shop and, of course, the cobbler is the same Jewish *shuster* he recalls from thirty years back. He hands over his ticket, and the old man goes to the back of the store. There is the sound of boxes being moved, shoes falling, grunts from the old man who finally returns empty-handed.

'Tell me, these shoes, they were a pair two-tone brown suede?' he asks.

'Yes! Yes!' The man is overjoyed.

'They'll be ready Thursday.'

I have told the story here in two hundred words. Cyril makes that ten minutes in the telling. My sides ache as I chuckle all the way back to Victory House, across town on the corners of Harrison and Commissioner.

Someone, please tell me an authentic Zulu joke.

CHAPTER 70

The Party
(1968)

Blake Edwards directs Peter Sellers in a movie worthy of Jacques Tati, the French Chaplin. Hilarious moments with Sellers, an Indian émigré in la-la land.

Apart from the names of magazines, the words 'penthouse' and 'playboy' hold no real meaning for me until I first step onto the roof of Winchester Mansions on the corner of Rissik and Jeppe streets. My old neighbour Craig Wood, the photographer, has moved on from Victory House and found this unique living and working space. It is a bachelor pad that, in its prime, probably has few rivals. Winchester is the tallest building in the vicinity and is far from any prying eyes. One is immediately tempted to throw off one's clothes and plunge naked into the small swimming pool that leads straight off the main living space, knowing no inquisitive eye will disturb the peace. It must be a pretty unique space in the heart of the city. Craig discloses that he often strolls about naked, from his eyrie peering down like an eagle at the rat race below. What was, was.

The penthouse is not as run down as the Norma Desmond grand palace of Sunset Boulevard, but like some benign, inanimate object with a will, like something out of a more pleasant Stephen King story, this nest screams, 'Party! Party!'

Winchester Mansions is diagonally across from the Criterion, the poshest restaurant in the town. It is a perfect eatery at which to entertain and impress a lady friend, and from which later to cross the road for a midnight skinny-dip. In one quick insight, I understand both 'penthouse' and 'playboy'.

Alongside the pool is an awning that once, I imagine, sheltered naked revellers at many a Roman-like orgy. It is difficult to imagine the space as the habitat of a celibate monk. No, we are definitely in playboy-penthouse territory.

In Victory House, I miss meeting Xaviera Hollander, whose autobiography *The Happy Hooker* would make a Henry Miller blush. She goes on to write an agony (or is that ecstasy?) column for *Penthouse* magazine, which is not about real estate. I always seem to miss all the action. Penthouses and playboys just pass me by.

I wonder at first if it is just my repressed self that executes these torrid thoughts. This is my third visit to the pad, but it is a first for both the cast and crew. As we step onto the roof, both Moe and Hennie expel sounds that echo the whistles of old wolves. There must be something in my theory of the space exercising a kind of *Phantom of the Opera* spell over a first visitor. We are here to work, but something whispers urgently, 'Party! Party! Party!'

'*Jislaaik!*' exclaims Hennie.

Moe's response is slower but more revealing. As he looks around, his gum hanging like a snake's tongue from his surprised pout, his eyes widen as he declares, 'Today is my birthday.'

But as much as the tempter calls, we are here to work. We have a set to dress and a lot of scenes to shoot. It is an easy task to set up and convert the awning into an intimate nightclub set. Craig has walled it, so all it needs is to be dressed with half a dozen tables, some chairs, crockery, cutlery, glasses, salt and pepper shakers, table lamps, a mirrored disco ball, some intimate lighting, music posters on the walls and, for real atmosphere, a smoke machine. Craig is a great asset at dressing sets, a master at small-nail-and-hammer carpentry, and a gaffer-tape wizard.

This is a first experience at dressing a set for me. When it is all ready, the place is virtually screaming 'Party!'

We stand back to survey all our hard work. The crew has all pitched in to help. There are some new recruits to the *Timer Joe* enterprise. These are the extras who make up the couples at tables. I have nothing to do with their being here and for once I see that maybe we are, after all, a team. The extras are a detail I overlooked, but here they are.

'Have we forgotten anything?' I say to no one in particular as we stand back to admire our handiwork.

'Booze, soft drinks,' says Craig, not even looking up as he applies even more gaffer tape to a flapping wall.

'Are you telling me we have nothing up here to drink?' I am appalled.

We are fourteen floors above the street and the day is warm.

'Who is going to get the drinks?' I ask on the edge of panic.

'It's Moe's birthday, his party,' says Hennie.

Moe does not look keen to go. It is not that he has any problem paying, but once up here one is reluctant to return to earth.

'I'll go,' says Coach.

Moe reaches into his hand-tooled leather bag, brings out a bulging wad of cash and begins peeling off notes to give to Coach.

'What should I get?' asks Coach, watching the pile grow in his palm.

'Better get a few litre Cokes,' says Moe, a dedicated teetotaller.

'A bottle of Klipdrift,' Hennie calls out.

Orders and suggestions pour in from all present, even the extras who, I begin to think, are here for no more than a party. There is a demand for beer. It has to be Carling – no other. Cane Spirit. Mainstay. Captain Morgan.

Coach makes notes.

'And don't forget the champagne,' adds Hennie at the end.

'Spell that,' asks Coach.

'Ag, just write down "birthday". They'll know what you want at Solly Kramer,' says the cameraman.

Coach takes two of the cast with him to go shopping, returns with cases of booze and two delivery men from Solly Kramer to assist with the load. There is Jack Daniels, J&B, 100 Pipers, Oude Meester brandy, Smirnoff vodka, Gilbey's gin, a stone keg of Sedgwick's Old Brown sherry, a few litres of Coke, and three bottles of JC le Roux sparkling wine.

'How did they sell you all this liquor?' Moe asks.

'I just told them "birthday",' Coach shrugs as he hands a handful of coins to the Man.

We are not quite ready to roll.

I have asked that we have a fog machine for atmosphere, not having any knowledge of how one works. Machines are my brother's arena. I have trouble with a torch. But both Craig and Hennie are comfortable with the challenge of what is just a motor that runs off something other than common fuel. I have heard it runs off paraffin oil, like that would seem to add something to the body of my knowledge. Not my department.

None of us has any forewarning of the hazards of the fog machine. Just a casual glance at Google now supplies all the following.

'Most consumer fog machines use fog fluid made of a combination of water and a chemical called glycol, which has been found to be safe in a number of studies and is not considered to be hazardous . . . If you see some sort of fog or smoke rolling at you, and you already have a breathing problem, it's going to get worse. While a fog machine will add to the ambiance of your haunt, if used incorrectly, it can create the added dangers of fire, electrocution and other nasty and potentially disastrous accidents . . . Make sure that the circuit breaker for the outlet you plug your fog machine into can handle the wattage that the fog machine will draw.'

What isn't covered are the perils of using a fog machine on a blistering hot day and that with using liquid paraffin, which today is the fuel of choice, there is the hazard of causing diarrhoea. We find that out too late to take any precautions. We all take in a lot of smoke.

The beers and Cokes begin to disappear even before we get to shoot. Someone finds a runner in the building who dashes to and from Solly Kramer's some blocks away, keeping the flow of fluid constant. Moe's once-ample wad wilts as each trip has to be sponsored. Poor Jabu is dressed in a waiter's full stuffy uniform, wearing both a jacket and bowtie. He is drenched in sweat and has to stop often to take in some fluid. He is the one who makes a dent in the cool drinks which, he is unaware, are being spiked before his cup is passed back to him. The penthouse whispers its siren song.

The club scene fully introduces Jabu to the story. Disco boys and girls undulate beneath the big mirrored orb to disco music as Jabu insinuates his way through to attend to tables. The non-kitchen portions of the whitebread gag have to be filmed separately – the customer complaining and the happy outcome.

Getaway Gus is a major player in the club sequences. Here, he is demanding, aggressive and impossible to please. Waiters are for bullying. The bottles of booze at the tables are meant to be just props but someone, probably me, omits to explain the difference between a *prop* and a *pop* to everyone. Gus downs the best of a bottle of cane spirit on his own and has to eat a bland mix of something that stands in for the poisonous concoction Jabu prepares for him in the kitchen, the preparation of which we have already shot at Beaconsfield.

In real life, the brew that Jabu mixes would give Daisy de Melker pause. Jabu throws everything into a giant cooking pot, from washing powder to oats and turpentine, and mutters like a wicked wizard. There is dry ice in the pot so the smoke rises as if from a cauldron.

It passes our notice that whatever gets put on all the tables is opened and drunk. A whole lot of sampling goes on between takes. Maybe the soul of the penthouse has some evil intent after all? We have to cover the scenes at speed as there is so much to get done. The disco dancers have only been booked for this one afternoon. We are watching the clock and not the monster that is growing invisibly, like something out of a haunting movie.

Craig is having a party of his own, working the smoke machine. My chest closes up and my own breathing becomes laboured, which I take to be just another symptom of stress. I am not at all sure that our club sequence will work.

When Gus pretends to eat the evil concoction, he is given a ham actor's dream dying scene. Not that he is supposed to die but he gets every opportunity to play the throes to death. He rises, stumbles, clutches his belly, spews out what he hasn't swallowed, writhes and falls about. On the disco floor, the dancers take to mimicking each other's moves in a Mexican wave fashion. As one couple introduces a new move, so the others follow. Gus's desperate gasp draws everyone's attention to him, mistaking his clutching of various areas of his body as the moves to follow. Gus brings an unexpected realism to his performance. He sweats, his eyes bulge as his hands move down to grab his broiling gut, his mouth foams (sherbet) and he first oohs, then aahs. His agony is quickly aped by the dancers and has them all oohing and aahing, clutching their throats and stomachs in approval of this cool new step. At some point, I yell, 'Cut,' but Gus is somewhere else. He surprises us all when he ends with a prodigious stream of projectile vomit. He falls over backwards as the dancers clap and whistle approval at the realism of the performance. Gus hears none of it as, without effort, he now plays dead.

We hear another thud and we turn to see Jabu playing the same role. Is he afraid that Gus is upstaging him? There is more applause. Only

Hennie is alert to a problem. He is over our prone star as he undoes his collar and tie, and crouches over like a paramedic. Is mouth to mouth required? Hennie leans over tentatively and quickly sits up.

'Whoa-huh! He's pissed,' he declares through the fog that now engulfs us like a scene out of *Sherlock Holmes*.

The misty aura of Club Timer Joe turns suddenly urgent, like the frantic rush to the lifeboats in one of the *Titanic* movies. In this case, the need is of a toilet, of which there is but one. This is a non-sharing imperative. Winchester Mansions' accommodations are individual apartments, and we are fourteen floors above the street. Thankfully, everyone finally makes it without incident. The main casualty is Craig's supply of toilet paper, and the runner is once more dispatched with urgency. The other casualty is Moe's wallet. For some reason, possibly because we stand back from the action as we shoot and do not get puke drunk, the crew are unaffected.

'Great party!' Furtive Frank says in perfect English.

As we, those who have had our turn at the bog, sit at the pool drinking in breaths of fresh air, like survivors after some grave disaster, I sit alongside Coach.

'Hey, man, that was some *tsorres*,' he chuckles.

I turn in wonder as we begin our first real conversation.

217

CHAPTER 71

Gunfight at the Joburg Drive-in

Gunfight at the O.K. Corral (1957). With two heavyweight stars, Burt Lancaster as Wyatt Earp and Kirk Douglas as Doc Holliday. Good Western based on a famous event. The subject has been filmed a number of times.

'Coach, where did you learn about *tsorres*?'

'My first boss, Joffe. He speaks little English.'

'What'd he do?'

'Outfitting shop, Joubert Park, by the railway station. I started when I am small. My father worked there first. My father is a tailor. Joffe taught my father. My father taught me. Buttonhole, lapels, alterations. Take in waist, make wide – anything. I make my own suits, and even shirts.'

'How long did you work for Joffe?'

Time whistles through his teeth. 'How long? Eish! A long time. Long, long, time. Long, looong time.'

I guess it was for an extended period.

'Where did you live?' I want to hear it all.

'Alexandra.'

I nod.

'You been to Alexandra Township?' he gives me its full title to dispel any doubt.

'Yes. On a Friday night, at the clinic.'

'Alexandra Clinic on a Friday night?' he says in disbelief. The clinic on a Friday, payday, is a warzone.

'My wife's a doctor. I was there one Friday night when she was doing her housemanship. They had to work in Casualty in their last year of study.'

He nods.

'Tough neighbourhood – Alex,' I lamely add.

He thinks it over and smiles. 'Yes, but great place too. Clubs. Shebeens.'

'How about movies?' I ask since this is surely our common ground. 'When you were growing up? You get to see many of those?'

'Movies? No, not so much. Maybe every few months, at a hall.'

I try to imagine a life thus deprived. It was only the year that my mom died that I saw no movies, but thereafter it was a hundred movies or more a year. Six a year or less? I cannot get my head around that. Was that it?

He reads my mind.

'But we also went to the Johannesburg Drive-in. Nearby Alex.'

The drive-in was strictly for whites only.

'They let you drive in?' I ask.

He laughs long and loud at the absurd suggestion.

'Let us in? Never!' He stops to look about him as if the Special Branch were eavesdropping as he takes me into his confidence. He explains that they rode across the veld on Saturday nights, hid their bicycles in the grass, climbed through the fence and crawled under cars.

'You know the Johannesburg Drive-in?' Again, he is sceptical of my knowing the place, as if it were a venue beneath my station, or custom.

The truth is that the drive-in ruins the movie experience for me. I prefer to go to eat after a show. The food and drink are a distraction. In the day, everyone seems to feel the same way. We find ourselves at a road-house like the Doll House on Louis Botha Avenue, or the Casablanca at the bottom of Nugget Hill after having hamburgers and double-thick chocolate malteds. It is a long way yet to the barrel of popcorn and a Coke that is now de rigueur when attending the cinema.

On my first visit to a drive-in, the Johannesburg Drive-in near Alexandra Township, I am eighteen and at university.

That first visit is an illegal one.

'I sneaked in to see *Gunfight at the O.K. Corral*.'

'*Gunfight at the O.K. Corral*? Burt Lancaster, Kirk Douglas? I came back again to see it. I like it very much.'

His look of delight configures as a puzzle. 'Why did you have to sneak?'

'I was young. I was a student. I was drunk.'

All those confessions stream out as one.

It is Rag time, and we first-year architectural students are building our float at Lupini Brothers' premises, a bicycle ride away from the Joburg Drive-in. Italo Lupini, the youngest of the family and a student, has pushed the issue of having our float be a gigantic, fish-tailed car of the fifties. The Lupinis, who make terrazzo, which is used extensively in buildings across the country, are passionate supporters of motor racing and have their own a collection of Alfa Romeos – Scuderia Lupini – which they enter into races. Italo, at nineteen, is the hill-climbing champion of South Africa, whatever that might mean. The vast premises of the terrazzo factory allow us space for the building of our giant. But the enterprise on this evening degenerates into an orgy of drinking and showing off.

'Fuck it! Let's go to the movies,' someone calls out. Italo has a Ford Thunderbird and we all try to pile into that. The troops become divided, since we can't all fit into one car. Some of us even have to pile into the boots of cars, which is how Monty Drucker and I end up in the boot of the Thunderbird on the way to the drive-in. Monty and I sit on the grass, since there is no place inside for us. We hunch over, trying hard like the embattled alcoholic Doc Holliday to sober up.

'Good friends, Wyatt Earp and Doc Holliday. Great movie,' Coach muses.

I turn and look at him with a smile. He may be the first person who gets movies like I do.

CHAPTER 72

Hier's Ons Weer!
(1950)

The follow-up movie to Kom Saam Vanaand.

How long do friendships last? It is close to seventy years since I last saw Raymond Kudsee, and he is still working. Following up on an impulse, I look in the phone book (yes, I still use one of those) and find that Raymond Kudsee is alive and well and living less than ten minutes away in Risidale.

I call. An upbeat voice chirps happily, 'Raymond's Ropes, Raymond speaking. How can I help you?'

We pick up instantly at Abbott and Costello, but he doesn't remember much of that. He has other memories.

When writing my first memoir, *Out of Line*, I invent a name of a mysterious, dangerous figure who hides out on the mine dumps. I call him Blikkie-Sam for I have no recollection of his real name. All I have is a vague, frightened memory of some faceless danger I'd been told about.

I'd asked my brother in Greensboro, North Carolina, if he remembers the name of the guy with the gang who used to hide out on the mine dumps. He's older and should know. The mine dumps? Mot had no memory of anyone like that. Almost the first thing Raymond shares is, 'Hey, remember Thuys and his gang?' And an echo of a deep fear returns.

Thuys and his gang. He lived somewhere in the neighbourhood. How did I forget that? I don't ask myself stuff like that much these days. I cling to my true memories and my own truths but talking to Raymond flings me right back.

'Man, Dov, you remember when you got stuck in quicksand by the Blue Dam? You lost your shoes and socks. Man, I just watched.'

I remember being there with Monty Orkin. Raymond wasn't with us that day. The movies of our mind become our reality. The weird thing is that Raymond talks exactly like my late brother Mot and slips so easily into the Dov-mode, as if that is what he has always called me, instead of Davey.

Raymond, too, had an older brother Claude who died. And an echo of Muti comes back to as Raymond talks of my late brother. He always called him Muti, like Mot was ever difficult to mouth.

All the Lebanese boys called him Muti. Another memory.

In the first moments of talking to Raymond, I understand why I had then chosen him as my best friend. We shared similar dreams.

'Man, I should have stayed with the drawing. I was good, hey?' says Raymond. Now a memory of the two of us sitting with pencil and paper at a table pops out like a friendly genie too long in a bottle.

But this is errand Monday, some weeks since that conversation. I am on my way home from Cresta and, having memorised Raymond's address, I'm taken by an impulse off Beyers Naudé to a road less travelled.

In Verdi Avenue, I find Raymond's home. It has no bell or buzzer and the house itself is frustratingly a far way down the drive.

I hoot. It's a quiet street and I hate hooters. But how else is one to alert anyone? Eventually, a beautiful young man walks cautiously down the driveway to see who it might be so rudely parked across the entrance. One cannot be too careful these days.

It is an indescribable moment for in instant I see the faces of Raymond's two older brothers, the late Claude and the younger Desmond. It is a face straight out of the past. It is Desmond with the same wavy, uncombed cow's lick that I have not laid eyes on in seventy years. I only know Claude's face from the photographs that hung in memoriam outside his bedroom that was always closed. Only once, when Raymond and I were alone in the house with the ghost, did we peep inside to see the white rocking horse, waiting forever for its pale rider.

Had I seen this face in a mall or elsewhere, removed from any association, I half believe I would have known it instantly. But I am too old to be fooled by my own mind games.

It gets even weirder.

When he gets close enough to see my face, he calls out in recognition, 'You're Dov Fedler.'

I am stunned. How is it possible he knows me?

'I saw you on television last night.' Not TV, he uses the full word, 'television', like it's better manners.

Grinning broadly and overjoyed to see me, Regan – for that, I learn, is Raymond's son's name – opens the gate wide and guides me in. There is no awkwardness in us getting to know each other.

Until these moments, I have little knowledge of Raymond's children. He has six, I learnt in our conversation on the phone, and also that he married a woman who is now in a home and has Alzheimer's.

Regan, who is fifty and lives with his dad, tells me he has known about me all his adult life. Until this moment, he thought maybe his dad was spinning a big story about how he was friends with this pretty famous guy. It's clear from his reaction that his joy is that his father has told it true.

Raymond stands waiting at the top of the drive and we embrace. 'You know, Dov, I wondered what happened. I thought you weren't going to call again. We must get together, man – go have coffee.'

'We'll go to Olivia's,' I say. He is surprised that I know the restaurant because it is around the corner for him, but I wonder if Raymond ever leaves the house.

The garden shows the loss of a woman to love and care for it. A withered bush in a planter box sits near the front door, mourning its sorry fate. We step inside.

And though its architecture is somewhat different, I have stepped into No. 16 Eleventh Avenue, Mayfair.

Jesus, now faded but still all-powerful, awaits me. We recognise each other instantly. Everything seems to call out in happy greeting, and a warmth I cannot describe envelops me.

It is as it always was.

Raymond points to the stand that once held a beloved fern that draped over in a cascade as you stepped into the entrance hall of the Mayfair house. It stands empty now, but Jesus still smiles down on it kindly from the opposite wall as he did when times were plentiful. Maybe it will spring back to life.

Easter Friday, after all, is just four days away. Every wall is covered with ancestral history. I take the tour without invitation.

'Ja, I've got a lot of my mom's stuff. We stayed in the house in Mayfair till seventy-seven.' Raymond and Regan follow me down the passage towards the bedrooms as I track each remembered photo on the wall.

We come upon a picture of a group of men. It is a committee of some sorts. Raymond is quick to point out his father proudly.

'My dad was on the first committee of the Lebanese Society, helping immigrants.' I know the story; Dad was on similar bodies as treasurer for both the Mayfair Shul and the Žagarė Benevolent Society.

Suddenly, the image of Claude looks back at me as if we had seen each other just moments ago. But there is no sadness in this encounter. He is where he belongs. Someone to remember, rather than to struggle to forget.

You can't go back home? Not true. It all depends on what you go looking for.

CHAPTER 73

The Greek Tycoon
(1978)

*Thinly disguised portrait of Aristotle Onassis and
his strange marriage to Jacqueline Bouvier Kennedy.
With Anthony Quinn and Jacqueline Bisset.*

The Greek café alongside a cinema is an old tradition. My aunt and uncle own a café across the road from the Regal bioscope in Troyeville. Greeks own cafés, a café being what the Americans call a drugstore, and Portuguese sell fruit and veg. There are many such cafés across the country. It is common parlance to say, 'I'm going to the Greek, get some cold drinks.' Café is instantly implied. Most people are content to follow these prescribed paths to social advancement. Some Jews begin as tailors and go on to create clothing empires.

Taki Xenopolous, the café owner, has big dreams. His is a spirit of great enterprise. He is the father of the supermarket and of late-hour shopping across the country. His bakery becomes a national institution. He begins business as a young immigrant, at the age of nineteen, as the owner of a modest snack bar right next door to the Rex bioscope. In the year we move to Greenside, Taki's shop replaces Feldhun's café for me.

There's a gang of boys who pilfer sweets from Taki. I hate them but they have balls. I know their guilty secret and Taki reads my face as complicit but understands that I cannot snitch. Nevertheless, he watches me like a hawk, even though he trusts me with his comics. I am glad that the shops are too far for Mom to frequent as she did Feldhun's in Mayfair. Mom would make friends with Taki, and there could be a moment where he might let slip that I might be an accessory to stealing sweets. This suggestion would trigger Mom's fear of my suspected delinquency. The fault, of course, are comics and bioscopes.

'You know, Tucker, we try to teach him right from wrong but these days, does a son listen to a mother – a father?'

But Taki has more to do than keep an eye on my possible criminality.

His eye is firmly fixed on the future. The idea of impulse shopping has yet to be born, and Taki Xenopolous is to be one of its fathers.

In the early seventies, he launches a massive bakery, Fontana, in the soon-to-be tallest building in Hillbrow, to be called Highpoint.

He is its prime tenant and probably a partner in its development, and he chairs the body corporate. Highpoint may be up there in its aspiration but hits a low point in getting ready. It remains tantalisingly unfinished, though the shop owners pay rent. Shoppers do not enjoy making their way around building rubble even if this centre promises the sky. The expectant shopkeepers wait in vain for the big rush. To add insult to injury, on top of their monthly rent there is a bill for advertising to attract customers.

There has been no advertising campaign and an angry mob is gathering at Mr Bakery's door with everything but burning torches. Which is why Taki Xenopolous calls me. I am three years into being a political cartoonist, though I have been drawing for *The Star* since 1967. I am barely known, and to be called in by Mr Big himself is an enormous compliment.

When I walk into his office, he greets me, knowing our history, with, 'Feddy, I remember you when you used to come into my shop and steal sweets.'

'Taki, I was the only one who never did. I was terrified of you.'

He laughs, knowing it's the truth.

'You remember when you gave me ninepence the day I was crying outside the bioscope?'

His eyes go wide for a moment as the memory clicks.

'That was you?' He remembers the occasion, not the boy.

We move on to business. He outlines his problem and looks to me to be his Answer Man. I have one at the ready. It is something I learn from my mentor, Stuart Willson, my first boss and life-long friend.

'Nothing can kill a lousy product better than a good advertising campaign.'

Taki gets it instantly. Who knows product better?

'This place is a nightmare. I'll give you a great campaign and it will draw customers. They'll come once and never again. And when the campaign fails, you are going to blame me.'

He nods at the honesty of my answers. I hope that takes me off his list of suspects. He gives me his warmest smile.

My ad campaign pulls the crowds and shoos them away exactly as I predict.

Some thirty-five years later, we begin to meet by chance on Saturday evenings in the foyer of the Hyde Park movie houses. He smiles warmly though his light is dim. I am shocked to be greeted by so frail a figure. It is hard to take in this colossus, reduced to mere human terms. Taki belongs on Olympus, amongst the gods. Surely having conquered everything, having even ascended the Highpoint problem eventually, mere age and illness could not have diminished him so? Yet the fire still burns. He greets me warmly.

'How are you, Feddy?'

'Better than you.' I save us the tedium of social grace. He rewards me with that warm smile. Too late for lies, and an honest joke is a relief. He gives me the short version of his future prospects. There will be no high point.

Every time we meet, he insists on buying me an espresso and will not hear of me paying.

'I remember you. You used to love to come to the bioscope. Me too. But I never had the chance. The café was everything. Now I try to catch up.' He smiles ruefully. Too many movies. Too little time.

We make more small talk, except it drifts into hard truths. I enquire after his life, and in a moment of exquisite intimacy he tells me of his tragedies. In the same year, he endures the loss of both his wife and his son – a man of some thirty-five years. There is no ease to bring to so great a burden. At the end of an awkward pause, he sighs, 'Harder to lose a son.'

* * *

My reconnection with my old friend Raymond at his home is magical. We speak of his first cousin Al Debbo, his mother's brother's son who lives with them for two years at No. 16, and we recall the names of his movies. *Kom Saam Vanaand. Hier's Ons Weer! Alles Sal Regkom!*

Regan sits with us throughout, loving every moment. Raymond catches this.

'Me and Dov? Hey, we were like brothers.'

'Still are,' I add.

'Al? Man, he had talent. I also wanted to do that stuff. Remember he used to sing, *'Hasie, hoekom is jou stert so kort?'*

Raymond is not shy. He sings and moves to the beat.

'Me? I liked to sing. Not that Boeremusiek. "You ain't nothing but a hound dog."' He starts to move again. It's a show.

'I said to Al, let me sing in your show. He says, "If I let you sing, they won't want to hear me." I could have done that. I was in *Alles sal Regkom!*, hey?

'He phones me. He says, "Come, I need you for this film." So, I go off there. Remember when the studio was out there by Lone Hill? I had long hair in those days. So I go into make-up and they're working on the back for a long time, hey? When they finish, they want to walk away.

'"Hey," I say, "when are you going to do the front?"

'They say, "No. Al just wants you from the back."

'In the film, Al talks to this, like, ghost of Elvis. You see the ducktail – that's all. That's me.'

What a perfect Lou Costello moment.

And I remember vividly why Raymond and I were friends in the first place: we were both dreamers who wanted to be Abbott and Costello. He has lost none of that. The magic of this home, in which six kids grew up, shines through the neglect and dust.

Everywhere are the old photographs, the icons, celebrating the past. It is Mrs Kudsee's house as I have always remembered it.

Raymond has celebrated his family life. He enjoys taking me on the tour to yesterday.

His wife's illness has sobered him somewhat. Tough times lie ahead. But the past still brings joy.

I remember Mr Kudsee, always hiding in the shade of the veranda, watching and hearing the happy laughter across the road in the *shul's* forecourt.

And it is here, in this dusty home in Risidale, reaching the end of its cycle, that Claude is no longer a fearsome image, like Thuys and his gang or Daisy de Melker.

He now smiles at me. An impulse in me wants to call out, 'Howzit, my cousin?'

CHAPTER 74

F/X
(1986)

Although it starred Bryan Brown and Brian Dennehy,
special effects were the true star of the film.

Writing, I think only of impressing Moe Mankowitz. The script includes a karate fight, a bullet shattering the window of a telephone booth, and a wild car chase. It is such clichés that make Moe 'The Man' Mankowitz happy. He is glad to attempt anything original, provided it has been tried and tested many times before. That Moe buys my ideas suggests that he has the budget for everything. But most of my ideas have to be scrapped for lack of funds. All of which makes *Timer Joe 3* a very thin action story indeed. Two pages would have sufficed.

A karate fight demands that the actors be trained for a period in martial arts and for it to be choreographed by a specialist. Exit karate fight. To build a false phone booth just for one shot and have glass smash is too complicated. In the movies, they use a sugar glass that allows for stuntmen to fly through saloon windows. Go find sugar glass. As for splashes of blood squirting from bullet wounds, I may just as well specify a piece of moon rock. A car chase is a massive extravagance, if done properly. It requires stunt drivers and cars that may roll, tumble or end up as a heap of mangled metal.

It is impossible for me to let go of everything. There must be something that I can rescue. I look up from my desk and the plastic model of my Dazzle Datsun winks suggestively at me from a shelf and I am back in Scaramouche-thinking mode.

My daughter Carolyn, who is in her matric year, walks in on me playing with a friction toy on my desk. I am vaguely embarrassed. Is it damaging for a child to discover their parent is one too? I am too busy playing with the car to care. If I build up the friction and let go of it, it skids around in a circle. I am already seeing it on film. Oh yes. I knew precisely how to do this. As an adult, a father of three, I secretly visit toy shops and buy stuff with the lie to a disinterested teller that my purchase is for an offspring. I own a Buzz Lightyear articulated figure, and an extensive collection of *Master of the Universe* characters who mingle with Batman, Wolverine, Dinky cars, Mickey Mouse and the Roadrunner.

I know precisely how to bring a car chase to life without stunt drivers or budget. It is time to phone my brother.

Mot is known as the Mayor of Tana Road and is called upon by friends and family to fix and deal with emergency repairs from lamps to car engines. It is a career he would be happy following. We live less than two kilometres apart.

'I need a favour,' I ask, knowing exactly how it goes.

'What the hell do you want?'

I tell him.

'You bloody mad?'

Great, that's a yes. Mot's affirmative is a vehemently expressed negative. 'No' never enters our conversation. My big brother, over whom I now tower, has to hide his easy pushover nature behind a gruff blusteriness. He can't even fake a real temper. He is my proudest fan but would shrink with embarrassment were his real sentiments ever to be exposed.

He is at my house the next night, having come to examine the friction car up close.

'Can you do it?' I ask like Edward Fox as the assassin in *Day of the Jackal*, asking Cyril Cusack if he can build a rifle that appears to be a crutch.

'How the hell am I supposed to get inside? It's one piece of plastic.'

I explain the surgery I have in mind. He is unable to repress his admiration for the idea.

'Just don't ask to use any of my tools.' He scrambles for a frown and fails.

'Don't worry, I have my own,' I tell him proudly.

We are what we learn. Though I am not competent to use most of them, I have picked up my brother's love of gizmos. I am even in possession of ones he does not have, like an angle grinder, a wood planer, a sander and a pop riveter. But the opportunity to rivet never pops up and the gadget lies in its plastic, along with the angle grinder he so covets. Most of my purchases end up as gifts to Mot. Along with my compulsion to buy books and comics is this other magnificent obsession to out-tool my brother. My collection leans more to carpentry. I own three sets of carving chisels.

I would have loved it to be a builder of things small. At VZ, in Stuart Willson's studio, I work alongside Eric Smith, a dedicated puppet-maker. It is in advertising agencies where so many of us begin our apprenticeships. Eric introduces me to the art of making marionettes carved out of a very compliant wood called jelatong. At fourteen, I start making my own world of puppets. I carve them from champagne corks, which I learn to first boil in order to get them to swell to their original cylindrical shape. My carving tools then are Minora razor blades. The figures are carved in parts, which I then glue together and paint with aeroplane dope, a paint like nail polish. They stand, or sit, at six inches.

Charlie Chaplin tips his hat to a quartet that includes Louis Armstrong, who stands alongside Jimmy Durante, for whom I build a piano; Benny Goodman, his clarinet a small dowel, leads the group that includes Gene Krupa sitting at a set of drums, which are made of assorted junk. Jimmy Durante is a comedian known as the Schnozz because his nose is a substantial thing. Gene Krupa is reckoned to be one of the greatest jazz drummers, and once plays for the Benny Goodman Band. I make a figure of Laurence Olivier as Richard III and seat him on a balsa throne. Someone sews him a velvet cape. It is all movies and jazz. They are figurines rather than marionettes.

Through Eric, I now believe the career I want to pursue is puppet-making. Eric, an Afrikaans boy from Pretoria, will eventually find success in Tel Aviv, in his own acclaimed theatre called *Boebot Shel Uric* – The Dolls of Eric. Amongst my first precious purchases of books is one called *Puppets and Puppetry*. Another is about the Czech puppeteer and filmmaker Jiří Trnka, a pioneer in the art of stop-motion animation, an art raised to new heights by Tim Burton in movies such as *The Corpse Bride* and *The Nightmare Before Christmas*. This is a niche into which I would happily crawl, but, like so many of my whims, it passes quickly. It's cartoons, finally, that have my passion.

Special effects attract me more than the idea of working with actors.

Trnka has me wanting to make puppet movies. I have bought fibre-optic lights with the vague idea of incorporating them into something or other. I want to do it all. My bicycle jousting and the making of palm-frond rapiers, burning six guns out of tomato boxes, has me itching to build something. I plan a special effects sequence for the car chase. This is to be some movie with Motty magic.

CHAPTER 75

A Shot in the Dark
(1964)

The Blake Edwards follow-up adventure starring Peter Sellers as the superbly incompetent Inspector Clouseau. Famous for Henry Mancini's Pink Panther theme.

When I tell Moe and Hennie what I plan, Hennie looks like he's about to echo Mot's 'You bloody mad?'

The whole thing is easy to build. It requires three cardboard boxes that stand in as buildings. I spray them concrete grey and I cut windows. The boxes are lit from inside, by my brother, the gaffer, which is movie-speak for electrician. It looks great.

The street and pavements require some detail. The macadam is a sheet of black paper; the pavement, squares of cardboard; and the lamp and electric poles are constructed from the ever-useful dowel rod. The street-light tops are decorated with wire and black string. The lamps require delicate fibre-optic work. Not my problem – my gaffer's. It is all to be shot at night. The night looks kindly upon errors.

It is the car with its headlamps that is the pièce de résistance. I surgically excise the bonnet, using all my own tools. I have graduated to X-Acto knives. As I cut, I am constantly *kibitzed* by my *boet*. I am happy to slip into little-brother mode. We are like two mad-happy surgeons about to perform a Victor Frankenstein transformation. Mot fits the car with a battery and lights. I have not seen him this happy at work since he built radios out of cigar boxes. His tongue works its way on the outside of his lip as he bends to weave the fibre-optic lights into the lamps. Electronics and mechanics are beginning to move beyond his ken. He perfectly understands the world of torch batteries and radio valves, but this new transistor stuff has him baffled. He holds up a wire with a globe and says in wonder, 'How the hell they get it so small?'

Some years after trying to repair something for me, he holds up a small transistor to the light. It looks like a Lego spider. Mot says, 'What the fuck is this?'

The 'F' word is his emphatic word. It is a declaration of defeat. The object is not like a Swiss watch or old clock that he can take apart, study and understand. The transistor remains an enigma. The time of his and his friend Julian's putting together radios from scraps is all but passed. But here is an opportunity for some ingenuity. Side by side, we build the streetlamps. I then pay attention to the facades of the buildings, adding lintels and dressing the windows. In some, I hang a half-drawn curtain. It is these small details that make it authentic. My gaffer brings it all to life, and the darkness welcomes us.

CHAPTER 76

Blow-Up

(1966)

A 1966 mystery thriller directed by Michelangelo Antonioni about a fashion photographer, played by David Hemmings, who believes he has unwittingly captured a murder on film. Great movie. Notable for Vanessa Redgrave appearing topless.

'Letterpress is dead!'

Mot and Dad have been having a real go at it at the table. This is a major blow-up. Never have I known Mot go head to head with Dad and look as if he might win for once.

The remark is one that, if it were a boxing match and this a punch, has Dad reeling, falling back on the ropes. It's a hard blow. He tries to counter.

'There will always be work for compositors.'

Even I, who know nothing, think the return is weak.

Mot gathers steam as he does when he thinks he's on top of an argument. If he were playing poker, he would lose because he has this big tell. His tell is to repeat what has been said and then fall on it in a voracious attack.

'There will always be settings needed? There will always be settings needed? Is that so? Is that a fact?' He pauses to take a breath as he goes for the knockout. 'Bullshit!'

If Mom had lived to hear Mot address the old man like that, it would have killed her. But Dad jumps back to his own defence.

'Such language? From where did you get it? For sure, not from a book.'

Once this would have flattened Mot, but he comes out in a rage neither Dad nor I have ever witnessed. The volcano of his frustration has finally erupted.

'You think you know everything. You think you know printing? Do you know what's going on? It's all going litho. Go ask any of the big firms. Ask Cohen at Palladium. Ask Brill. Everything is going litho. Did I tell you we needed the linotype? Did you bloody listen? No, you always know better. I had to beg. And I told you we needed the Heidelberg. Now we got two. Stand behind the stone and *putske* with lead. That's all you know. It's obsolete. It's all going photographic. You know how they print *Life* magazine? Paper goes in one end, the whole magazine comes out the other side. It's all going to computers. You don't have to stand and cut at the guillotine. It's like the bloody Dark Ages with you. You think you're Gutenberg or Caxton.'

Some of it may be true, but it's skewed. Dad has never been behind the times. He is just cautious. Fedlers has been at the brink of going bust more than once. Mom and Dad started it, and pulled it out of the Depression. The rule has been, 'If it's not broke, don't fix it. Don't incur more debts. Don't make waves. Printing machines don't come cheap.'

Mot is building up to something major. He and Dad are always having a shouting match over something to do with printing, but this is winding up instead of down. My heart races for a reason I cannot yet identify.

'Everyone is switching over to litho. All that junk in the shop, you know what you can do with it? Sell it for scrap. All the small shops are folding. We're working in the Dark Ages.'

'You don't know what you're talking about. What do you know? Such a man. My son the genius. What do you know the first thing about business?'

I watch Mot as he looks about him, blindly talking to himself.

'You know what? Fuck it. I'm finished with this. I hate fucking printing. I always have. I'm gone. I'm out of it.'

The surprise is how softly he says it.

This is his big chance. It is a moment of truth.

I look to Dad and my heart breaks for him. Secretly, he hopes that Mot will finally stand up and leave the nest. But he can't let him go. He needs him too much. Fedlers can't survive without Motty.

Dad has an operatic temper. It is all verbal rage and dramatic gesture. He loves opera, especially *Pagliacci*. There is no smashing of crockery or physical display. It's like an aria, full of dramatics and long-suffering. It is sheer performance, and it works.

The legend is that when I was taken for my first haircut at Sid's barbershop on Central Avenue, just off Church Street, it took five people to hold me down. I was like Samson betrayed. Even now, I feel my teeth sink into Sid's incautious thumb. He will remember me forever. I know how to say no.

Mot is caught and lost in the dramatics, his conviction swept away.

Mot cannot say no. He capitulates before the Dad-storm. His pushback is, in the end, nothing more than window-dressing.

Dad retires in about 1974. Fedlers gets sold in 1987, the year the old man dies. Mot is there to the bitter end. He finds a job selling reconditioned printing machines, forever trapped in printing.

CHAPTER 77

Over the Top
(1987)

*Sylvester Stallone tries to
arm-wrestle his way to the box office.*

There are two cars in the chase. Our heroes are in the lead car, a Golf. For which I have another replica. We have two separate gags to film. 'Gag' is the film term used for stunts. The previous evening, we drive down the alleyways of Hillbrow and Newtown to get footage with the real cars. Tonight, we add the extras.

The chase FX sequence comprises just two parts. There is a gag for the Golf and one for the Datsun. We establish the cars driving at speed. For speed and danger, we use illusion and misdirection. At home, I have a pile of polystyrene, the detritus of TV and microwave purchases with which I intend to experiment in the building of models. My collection of recyclable junk is impressive. We stack it all in a corner of the empty courtyard of a filling station in Newtown and just have my Datsun drive through it as it all explodes into camera. It looks great.

The FX sequence plays like this. The villain's car spins out of control at a T-junction and makes the right-hand turn on the corner to continue the chase. Everything looks great, the cardboard boxes make convincing buildings, and Mot's streetlamps burn bright.

The second gag is the easier. Luki and Connie, in the Golf, are chased into a blind alley. Reaching the far wall, the Golf, like something out of *The Thief of Bagdad* or the scene in *ET* where the bicycles become airborne, does something impossible. It rides up the side of the building. We lay the camera and cardboard buildings on their sides at a tilt, and the Golf does its magic. In the next two shots, it continues to leap over the top of the building to land and crash through a billboard made with a frame of balsa and very thin paper. In Zulu, it reads, 'Drive Safely.' Thus do Luki and Connie elude their pursuers.

This setup is built in the carport at No. 60 The Braids Road, Greenside, on a Thursday night. Mot is there to help Hennie set up lights. There is no need for silence on the set. These are scenes that will have sound effects added. Hennie shoots the sequences in ultra-slow motion, and it is all done in under an hour.

Luki and Constance are there for reaction shots of them in the car. Connie is the designated driver, except she does not know a steering wheel from a cartwheel. She hangs on to it as if it were a snake about to uncurl. Her look of terror is real. Driving a stationary vehicle has its hazards. Two of us shake the car to give it a suggestion of it moving while someone else flashes a torch back and forth across the windscreen to create the illusion of passing vehicles.

The occasion is festive and Dorrine supplies snacks and drinks. My kids are excited at the whole affair. It's like a night at the carnival. Maybe there will be a show of fireworks at the end? The girls are intrigued. Laura, my youngest, looks on in wonder as two of us bounce a stationary vehicle while another waves a torch in the eyes of the passengers. Her eyes are as wide as searchlights. Carolyn, who is the oldest, and Joanne, vaguely understand the process and love the whole buzz.

After the FX sequences, there is a lot of hand-shaking and self-congratulation. Mot, I know, is hoping for it to be a more complicated affair, needing more of his services. But it goes off without a hitch. The car spins perfectly on first take and crashes into a corrugated fence. I could not have written it better.

'So what nonsense you need for tomorrow?' he asks. It is supposed to be a 'big *boet* telling off his *pik* brother', but there is a hopeful note in his asking.

'Nothing,' I sadly tell him.

CHAPTER 78

That's a Wrap

The end of *Timer Joe 3* cannot come soon enough for me. I can't wait to get back to my drawing board. Here is where I truly belong. *Timer Joe 3* fails to live up to any expectations of mine. I hope it isn't going to turn out to be a really bad movie. Even its title echoes the title of the Ed Wood stinker, *Plan 9 from Outer Space*.

The film belongs to Jabu, and he is welcome to it. There is no moment of joy – apart from the special effects – when any part of my vision comes to light as when a drawing comes together in an unexpected way. It is a slog to the very last. I never even get to shout, 'That's a wrap!' after the last shot and be applauded by a grateful cast. No one knows which shot that is anyway.

In the movies, stuff is shot out of sequence. If you keep returning to a location at different times in the movie, you have to shoot everything while you have the location. It is endless tedium, and the fragmented nature of it is wearying and confusing.

It is worse when things get dropped as we shoot. It is a shuffled deck with missing cards. More than half of what I write never makes it to the shoot. Even corners that get cut, get cut. Scenes stop having any sense of continuity. My script is simply abandoned. Will it make any kind of sense? I seriously doubt it.

A lot is trashed because of actors who fail to show up to work. The revisions and rewrites are constant. I lose track of it and am thankful when it is over.

There are no goodbyes or catch-you-laters or regrets. There is no afterparty. Everyone simply fades to black, never to be seen again. There will never be another movie made by me.

Like playing rugby, which is forced on me in high school because of my bulk and from which I withdraw swiftly, I am cured of the movie-making bug. Bulk doth not a rugby player make, nor enthusiasm a moviemaker. One damages my body, the other my ego.

I remain a dedicated spectator of both but I continue to dream of becoming a writer.

I expect to meet with Moe, Hennie, Coach, Jack, Frank, Jabu and all at the premiere.

CHAPTER 79

Cinema Inferno

Cinema Paradiso (1988): A famous movie director comes to the village of his childhood following the death of the old cinema projectionist, with whom he had formed a binding relationship. The viewing of films was once curtailed by the strict Catholic priest who censors any scene in which actors kiss. It is a magical movie.

Circumstances eventually dictate that I go once more to the Savoy. It has been twenty years in which I have avoided going there. The ghost of the past, that hooded figure, yet lurks somewhere in the stalls, keeping watch.

Dorrine, my wife, and I have to go there one late afternoon in the early seventies, when we are both members of the committee for the Society of the Hard of Hearing Child, a society we help establish, along with other members, to preview a film that we are to select for a fundraising premiere. Our previewing is slotted between the midday matinée and the evening show at 8 pm.

I have my regrets about things I will never do or see. My list of nevermores includes never crossing Bezuidenhout Road from my aunt's café to see a matinée at the Regal. I am haunted by other such ghosts of that past. I never do get to the Apollo in Doornfontein, the Scala in Melville, the Roxy in Braamfontein or the Adelphi in Rosettenville, or the other bioscopes whose names or existence I have simply forgotten. I would like to have frequented them all. Not recalling the lost ones feels like a breach of something. I feel duty-bound to remember them all, almost moved to light a candle as for a passed relative. It is the same regret I feel for my parents' photographs, of which I am the last custodian, which are filled with faces, places and histories lost to me. But nix on the Savoy. It is forever jinxed.

Once, demonstrating a modest sense of adventure, I drive with my wife on a stormy night to go see *The Maltese Falcon* in Primrose, Germiston. In a bolder venture later in my thirties, we go to Swaziland to see both

Blazing Saddles and *Lenny*, films that are banned in South Africa. Ah, the days of being a fugitive from the Board of Censors. I am indeed a brave heart.

At the Savoy, we sit, the committee waiting in the foyer for the matinée movie to finish, the afternoon patrons to vacate and the cleaning staff to tidy up. We talk to the manager, Herman Youngelson, who himself looks like a matinée idol, already dressed in his tux for the evening show.

I know the spectre is here somewhere; the back of my neck prickles. I constantly peek over my shoulder.

Grow up, Dov!

We watch the afternoon patrons stream out, blinking blind, their eyes still gummed up with celluloid, and wait for them to dematerialise into the muted afternoon. A troubled usher, wearing a maroon uniform with gold braid and wielding a truncheon of a torch, comes and stage-whispers to his boss.

'There's an old guy that's died in the third row.'

'How do you know he's dead?' asks the manager.

'Come look, boss. You'll see what I mean.'

He turns to gesture with his torch for us to follow. Maybe he feels he needs witnesses? It feels like a scene out of a movie. Herman Youngelson like Rick of *Casablanca*, the usher a clone of Peter Lorre, shifty-eyed and guilty.

We walk in on the cleaning staff who with their scooping pans and brooms are clearing the detritus of the matinée: the spilt popcorn, the cardboard Coke cups, chocolate wrappers, tissues, the empty cigarette packs, the *stompies* from the ashtrays, the chewing gum stuck to headrests, the usual acts of violation that are practised in dark spaces. We are not a caring species.

We come like a jury to stand in an irregular semicircle at the third row from the front. The cleaners never look up to watch any of it. Theirs is to clean and not to reason why.

He sits in an aisle seat as if to make it easier for everyone to move him. He is an old man wearing a sports coat. His eyes are wide open, his head thrown back, and his mouth open and slack. An upper denture has fallen from its mooring and hangs precariously on his lower lip.

You need not be a pathologist to know that he is a very dead old man. He wears one of those hearing aids that has a wire that goes from an earpiece to his inside pocket. How ironic for us, a society for the hard of hearing, for whom that singular thing has such powerful meaning. We don't check to see if that too is dead.

The dead man looks as if some movie director has carefully arranged him to be seated precisely so that the denture would be ready to fall out were we even to breathe on him. That gives rise to an expectation of some sudden impending action, a *Hitchcock* moment when this frozen death scene might erupt into action.

The denture falls dramatically to his lap.

Cut.

'The lady sitting next to him said she heard him croak just before the end. Man, he missed the whole twist,' the usher declares sadly. We are at a loss for words, but Herman, true to the Rick character, gives it cool closure.

'Pity. It's a great movie,' he says.

'We'd better move him to the foyer so you can have your preview,' he says, ending the eulogy.

Thankfully, it is the only time I ever help carry a corpse.

You read and hear of dead weight, but it's academic until you carry it. The denture falls when we touch him. Someone retrieves it and places it in old John Doe's breast pocket.

He looks as if he wants to say, 'Hey, I want my money back. What happens at the end?'

'Surprise. You die, old-timer.'

CHAPTER 80

Double Feature

Mom would be proud of me. I avoid becoming a *laydik-gayer* and a nightclub-johnny, though I try on three separate occasions to learn to play jazz piano. I just don't have it. I am either going to become Thelonious Monk, Oscar Peterson, Ray Charles, or nothing. Nothing prevails. But being a *laydik-gayer* involves another activity. I am warned against ever entering a café bio because only *tzaztkes*, prostitutes, drunkards, perverts and *no-goodniks* are to be found inside.

A café bio is mostly found up a narrow staircase on the first floor of a building that has seen better days. These show movies continuously from morning to late afternoon and are the only cinemas that have double features that run back to back. One need only pay once. It makes for a great dosshouse or a place to spend all day long in the dark doing whatever. A waitress comes around and offers you a drink, some suspicious flavoured cordial served in a glass on a saucer. To have it refilled one need only to turn the glass over in the saucer for her to come around again. Its patrons are mostly vagrants looking for temporary shelter and many free drinks.

Also, in a café bio you can pick up a disease from just sitting down. You are never to go inside and drink one of their colas. That will drug you, kill you, or worse. And who knows what they dilute in that drink that is the colour of a whore's lipstick? And why do they serve you that for free?

Never go into a café bio. If you do, you will pick up lice at the very least.

A café bio is the ultimate visible den of iniquity. And why are they all situated upstairs by the same narrow staircase? It is because at street level, they would spread disease. It is surprising the municipality don't have sandwich boards outside that warn the passing public of the dangers: 'UNCLEAN. HEALTH HAZARD.'

Mom certainly does a job on me. I hurry past these staircases in fear of my life until my late teens, and never venture inside one. But Mot always has the inside information on everything. The seats in these places are hard benches with no padding. Easy to work out why, with Mom's prepping. Bugs breed in upholstery. QED. If you speak to your usher nicely, you probably get more than just a drink.

There are three café bios in the very centre of the city, two across the road from the Johannesburg Post Office. They are the Embassy and the Rivoli. The other is the Royalty in Pritchard Street, in the same street as the Supreme Court, and Mom probably has an explanation for that as well. No doubt it is to do with criminality.

I am twenty-five years old, married, with a daughter who is weeks old, recently but gently fired, between jobs, recovering from a broken neck when I first go up the slippery slope of the staircase of the Embassy Tea Room.

I wonder if, among the patrons, I might find a lawyer.

I am promised a senior position at Forsythe Marketing, and all promises have been broken. I am swindled into becoming my boss's lackey.

Sam Dembo works at Forsythe. And it is Sam Dembo who talks me into going to a karate class and Sam Dembo who manages to drop me off his back and break my neck. I am off work for two weeks after a surgery. It is a fraction of time ahead of the moment that I choose to rebel and confront my boss with her broken promises.

'Do your own fucking layouts,' I think is the phrase I choose for emphasis.

Three days after I return to work, she tells me to take as long as I like but to please find another place of employment.

I spend a week at my desk doing nothing, which is more than disconcerting. I am not one just to sit around. No *laydik-gayer* am I.

A week later, I take to wandering off around the immediate environs of the agency, which is in Loveday off Main. It is two blocks to President Street. For the first time in my life, I pause to read the posters in the darkened entrance to the Embassy Tea Room.

Lonely Are the Brave with Kirk Douglas is showing. It is no time for cowardice.

For three weeks, I become an addict and a regular.

But I never turn over my glass.

CHAPTER 81

Guess Who's Coming?

Guess Who's Coming to Dinner? (1967). A young white woman falls madly in love with an African-American man and brings him home to meet her supposedly liberal parents. Stars Spencer Tracy, Katharine Hepburn, Sidney Poitier and Sandy Dennis.

Day. The film stock is black and white, scratched, tending to sepia. Wide shot. This is the Johannesburg of yesterday. Harrison and Commissioner streets show very little traffic. A few Model-T Fords pass by.
SFX: Rattling of car engines, a klaxon horn sounds. Subtitle Johannesburg 1912. South African Permanent Mutual and Investment Society Building.
POV: Back of an Indian man, aged about forty-five, pausing to look at a card. Searching for an address. C.U. The card reads South African Permanent Mutual and Investment Society Est. 1883.
He pauses at the corner opposite the SAPMIS building. The film subtly changes to muted Technicolor. Camera pans up the side of the imposing five-storey building. He crosses the road. The legend SAPMIS declares itself above the entrance.

Carrying a briefcase, he makes his way purposefully to the entrance in Harrison Street. POV shifts to interior of building as Gandhi enters and we see his face for the first time as he walks towards the lift. The foyer boasts aspidistras and ferns in polished pots of brass and mahogany and the tone is of old-fashioned elegance. Gandhi checks his tie, nervously brushes his hair with his hand as he reaches out to press the button. He looks up through the metal cage and watches as the lift descends. SFX: rattling, whirling sounds and then a final thud as the lift hits ground.
POV: Over Gandhi's shoulder. The lift has two doors. The outer door is wooden with a large pane glass window with a large brass handle to open. The inner i.e. lift door itself is a trellis that has to be opened manually. As Gandhi opens the outer door so too does the inner. Cut

to the hint of a gloved hand shown in gold-braided cuff. We are confronted by a man in white gloves, wearing a maroon uniform, gold braid, epaulettes and cap, the uniform of a liftman of yesteryear. He looks down with distaste as Gandhi attempts to enter the small cage. The gloved hand flashes out. C.U. The hand does not quite touch Gandhi's chest.

Liftman: And where are you going?

Gandhi: Fourth floor please.

He tries to move past the hand, but it remains a barrier. There is a pause. An impasse.

Liftman: I mean where the hell do you think you're going?

Gandhi: I have an appointment. (*Bewildered at the tone.*)

Liftman: I'm not interested in your *blerrie* appointment. I mean what the hell are you doing getting into this lift, *moegoe*?

Gandhi: Going to the fourth floor? (*A question.*)

Liftman: Not in here you don't.

Gandhi: Why ever not?

Liftman: Ha! (*A sneer.*) I tell you why not. Do you know history?

Gandhi: Very well, and the Bible. I was also decorated by the British for my efforts in the Boer War.

The liftman now stands square in, barring the way.

Liftman: Bloody British. I mean Boer history. So, you think that gives you the right to get into my lift? Do you know this was the first building in Johannesburg to have a lift? I fought in the bloody Boer War. I'm decorated with bloody British bullets, *boetie*. This lift is strictly for whites.

He slams the cage door shut and responds to the bell from someone up above. POV: Overhead as the lift ascends. Gandhi stands in a spotlight, looking up as the camera irises down on him.

CUT TO: Victory House in full colour. Same POV as when it first appeared as the SAPMIS building. Subtitle Johannesburg 1983.

A black man stands just as Gandhi did, on the same corner waiting to cross. Hooting minibuses flash by, hooters blare. He waits for the traffic light to change and moves to the entrance. He makes his way across through a wave of pedestrians. Everywhere hooters blare.

He walks into the lobby. We see bits of him but never his face. A hand, his shoes walking. The place is dilapidated, but hints at its former glory.

He presses button to go up. The lift rattles as before. He steps into empty lift and presses the UP button.

CUT TO: Dov in close-up, working. There is a knock at the door. He looks up amazed.

CUT TO: A hand-lettered title within a cartoon thought balloon. THE ZULU THAT CAUSED ALL THE TROUBLE, with isiZulu subtitle. The words switch to title in isiZulu with English subtitle.

Track down to show a cartoon version of Dov sitting scribbling away at speed at his drawing board. Pages fly. He is drawing the Roadrunner. Slightly to the right we see a door drawn in the old UPA cartoon style, as in the classic Gerald McBoing-Boing animated cartoon 1950.

SFX: Knock at door.

Without stopping work, as the pages fly to a paste-up board, to become further titles, the cartoonist calls out 'Enter!' like Walter Matthau bids George Burns in *The Sunshine Boys* (1975). Al Lewis (George Burns) and Willy Clark (Walter Matthau) are two vaudeville comedians who haven't performed together for nearly fifty years and bear an ancient grudge. They are to be in a TV special about the history of comedy.

The titles variously read 'The cartoonist meets Frankenstein', pasted over that is Daisy de Melker. Al Debbo gets pasted over that. Starring: *Laydik-gayers*, Nightclub-johnnies and Bioscope Boys. This is followed by stills from all movies and stars previously mentioned in the text. It turns into a collage that morphs into a still of Dov's surprised face. Action begins as movie.

Dov: Coach???!!!

Cut to still of Coach standing at open door with knuckle in the act of knocking. SFX (*sound of knocking precedes action*). He stands at the door, uncertain. Is he welcome?

Dov: Hey Coach, come in. Come in.

Coach walks in, still uncertain. Cut to his POV from doorway. The camera pans across, zooming into various objects and bric-a-brac that is the studio, finally stopping at Dov looking over drawing board. Cut to

Dov. POV: As Coach steps in timidly.

A silence follows as they assess the situation.

Dov: So, Coach, Howzit? Long time no see.

Coach: Long time.

Dov: What's it, three months?

Coach: Ten weeks.

Dov: So long? (*Thinks*) Ja. It's been a while (*Pause*). Hear anything about Timer Joe?

Coach: No.

Dov: After the shoot I've heard nothing (*Pause*). I wonder what's happened in post-production. I thought they'd call me in for the edit. Not a word. What's the word on the street?

Coach: Coming out maybe next month.

Dov: Next month? What, is it nearly finished? Bastards! (*Shakes head in disbelief.*) Not even the courtesy of a call. What the hell, I'm glad to be out of it, it was a fucking nightmare. (*Goes back to drawing, cross-hatching with anger, muttering.*) Bastards.

Coach moves around Dov to look over his shoulder. The camera follows. Dov is drawing an action sequence of Jet Jungle in pen and ink. Coach watches in silence as Dov ruminates.

Dov: Movies? Who needs them? This is where I belong. This is where I'm happy. Quiet behind a drawing board, in control of everything. (*As he speaks, he punctuates with angry strokes of the pen that become calmer as he thinks it through.*) I write it in a language I know. (*Chuckles as he turns to Coach with broad smile.*) You had a ball with me with all that nonsense about no-one speaking English.

Coach: How do you know? You speak isiZulu?

Dov: There's other languages. (*Dov points to his eyes.*) You all made me believe you didn't understand English. Ha! I was the one who didn't understand anything, am I right? (*Looks Coach in the eye. They hold the look and suddenly begin to laugh out loud.*) You had me.

Coach and Dov laugh again.

Dov: We could make a movie about that. *Revenge of the Black Man.* Sneak in at the drive-in to see it.

Coach explodes with joyous laughter.

Coach: You didn't know what you were doing.

His cheeks streak with tears.

Dov: Remember how that *tsotsi* walked?

Coach: And when everyone needed the toilet up at the dance club. How was that *tsorres*?

Coach slaps his thigh as he looks about the studio and spots the barber's chair.

Coach: You can go back now to haircuts. (*Guffaws. They are unable to speak for laughing. Laughter subsides.*) Why do you have that chair?

Dov: It's where I sit to think.

Coach: About haircuts?

Dov: (*Laughs.*) You're really a funny guy, Coach.

Coach: Really?

Dov: You should write for the movies.

Coach: Really? Me?

Dov: Strue's god.

Coach: I bought a typewriter.

Dov: (*Surprised.*) A what?

Coach: Olympia.

CHAPTER 82

'The Stuff That Dreams Are Made Of.'

The Maltese Falcon (1941). The last line of the movie, spoken by Humphrey Bogart as Sam Shade summing up the false and criminal pursuit of imagined fortune.

There is a cinema in a suburb of Sydney just up the hill from Coogee Beach called the Randwick Ritz, which is a throwback to a time when bioscopes were grand. I imagine there are many such movie houses in places where time hasn't yet eroded memory. It is a lot like the movie house of my imagination, like the famous Roxy in New York, which begins with the birth of sound films. According to the ever-reliable Bill Bryson, he of the impeccable research and amusing turn of phrase, the Roxy is the granddaddy of all movie houses. It can seat 6 200 patrons and is a palace that Ozymandias or Donald Trump would be proud to claim.

My vision of a premiere is of something splendid, hosted in such places, attended only by the royalty of the arts, an audience dressed in white tie and tails, the women outrageously outfitted in gown and jewels. They all await with bated breath the premiere of *Timer Joe Part 3*. They are about to see the movie of movies, written and directed in Technicolor brilliance by Dov Fedler. The entire history of cinema has funnelled down to this one awesome and grand occasion.

In the Royal Circle is Orson Welles, beside him Ed Wood, who sits next to Tim Burton. The entire cast of *The Birth of a Nation* – and the entire casts, including extras, of *Battleship Potemkin* and *The Ten Commandments* – are here tonight. Even Cecil B DeMille is here.

Akira Kurosawa sits with John Sturges whilst the seven gunslingers sit mixed with their seven samurai counterparts. No one tonight will forget Brad Dexter, the least remembered member of *The Magnificent Seven*. Elsewhere, Toshiro Mifune and Clint Eastwood whisper a gritted conversation. Greta Garbo is, of course, alone in her box, exchanging strange glances across the crowded room with Marlene Dietrich, who is next to Angie Dickinson and Betty Grable, discussing personal trainers and leg insurance. Yves Montand and Laurence Harvey share a corned beef sandwich torn in half.

Jane Russell discusses bras with Jayne Mansfield. Edward G Robinson and Joseph Wiseman – Dr No – reminisce about their days in Yiddish theatre, while Lauren Bacall listens intently. Al Capone is right there beside them, giving Marlon Brando, Robert De Niro and Al Pacino acting tips. Humphrey Bogart is getting steadily drunker with John Huston and Jack Nicholson.

Dennis Hopper passes around a cake tin full of snort. Sinatra's clan is, of course, all here, snubbing the Kennedys. But tonight, Sammy Davis Jr, with his arm around Kim Novak, elects to sit with Sidney Poitier and Denzel Washington as if to say, 'Fuck you, Frank!'

'Goodonya, Sam. Play it again!'

Sitting in a gallery of writers, Scott and Zelda are pissed as usual. Arthur Miller broods silent and dark, watching Marilyn, who doesn't give a damn, as she openly makes out with Clark Gable. Raymond Chandler, Dalton Trumbo, Irwin Shaw, Joseph Mankiewicz, Tennessee Williams, Truman Capote, William Faulkner, John Steinbeck and Norman Mailer are all here.

Salvador Dali and Luis Buñuel drag a piano inside.

There is a hush as the lights dim. This is to be the greatest cinematic event ever. All movies from this day forth will be measured by the yardstick of *TJ3*. Forget the other directors, too many to be mentioned, who are all here, to gape and gawk at something beyond the scope of their meagre talents. It is curtain time.

* * *

It is a Monday morning, at about nine thirty, when I get a call.

'Do you know the Starlite bioscope in President Street by *The Star*?'

Moe 'The Man' Mankowitz has never been one for small talk, or even a 'howzit'.

'I do.'

'Can you be there? They're premiering *Timer Joe* at half past eleven.'

He is gone before I can reply.

I am both confused and bewildered. Premiere? The Starlite? Half past eleven? On a Monday morning, the crappiest day of the week? Aren't all premieres night-time affairs? Premiere? Do I need to go out and buy a tie, hire a tux? Is there to be a red carpet? My head buzzes with questions.

The movie is finished? How?

None of it connects. It feels like I'm back on the set, trying to push wrong pieces of a puzzle into place. The Starlite? Even if you are a whitey of my generation and live in Joburg, I bet you have never heard of the Starlite cinema. It is one of Joburg's few black cinemas, modest in size, suggesting just a shopfront. You would walk past it never recognising its dark magic. It doesn't appear to be able to house an audience of any size.

A new thought nags.

As a whitey, will I be allowed inside? Is it not *Slegs Swartes* – 'Blacks Only'?

Does the Starlite even have a curtain?

CHAPTER 83

'My Kind of Town'

Sung by Frank Sinatra at the end of Robin and the 7 Hoods *(1964), celebrating the city of Chicago. A spoof gangster movie.*

Ashley Lazarus, with whom I shoot a number of commercials and producer of the smash hit *e'Lollipop*, tells me a movie should be able to be shot in any city in the world and appear to be in any place else. The anonymity makes the product saleable everywhere. But Johannesburg standing in for the city that never sleeps? Even my wife Dorrine, who is a doctor and no movie buff, has learnt to recognise a New York, Toronto substitute movie. It just doesn't have the same feel. Where's the Brooklyn Bridge or the Chrysler Building? Joburg needs a mine dump.

Maybe it is because Ashley is a Capetonian and hasn't grown up with taking the double-decker tram joyride from Mayfair down Central Avenue, Fordsburg, to the City Hall. It takes about ten minutes and the fare is a tickey, enough to buy a roll of Maynard's Wine Gums. It's better than a ride on the merry-go-round at the Rand Show. Dad likes to tell of the time he could not afford the fare and had to walk home every evening from work.

The trams are all long gone but their ghosts linger in these streets forever. My town stirs deep in memory. I am steeped in it. The trams are replaced now by double-decker buses painted in the same cream and red colours as before.

Alternative locations never quite convince this viewer. Joburg's brickwork is coloured differently from Cape Town's, let alone the Big Apple's. It is the light. Joeys' light is filtered through a thin layer of mine sand, almost like desert. Shooting in close-up is meant to hide the faults and makes for a cramped style of filmmaking. The camera is never allowed to linger or roam, capture the city, as in a Woody Allen, Sidney Lumet, New York, film. Filming Johannesburg has to be expansive, inviting the viewer in. But (sigh!) in the end, Ashley is right. Concrete giants have trampled most of the city and hints of Johannesburg, the mining town, are fast disappearing. Catching a glimpse of corrugated-iron roof painted dust-red and Dutch gable nudges me into yesterday. I loved her when she was fairly young. This is my kind of town.

I am vaguely attracted to the idea of making a film about how it was and what I treasure. As I stroll in any direction of the central city, my memory brims over.

North down Rissik Street, I pass the Plaza cinema where Mot first takes me, when I am six years old, to see my first Tarzan film and later, when I am a teenager, and able to go to a late-night show on my own and catch the last bus home at a quarter to twelve, I watch Orson Welles's *Touch of Evil*, the best movie I have ever seen. The bus terminus is just outside the side exit in Jeppe Street and I ride home on the top deck all alone. The Plaza is known as a bughouse, not a place for a nice Jewish boy, the haunt of *no-goodniks* and ruffians. *Rock Around the Clock* shows there and Les Tennant, a red-headed ducktail known as the King of Rock and Roll for winning a dance competition, leads a riot outside in Rissik Street and the police and fire brigade are called to quell it with firehoses. The newspapers talk of a society lost. But really, all it amounts to is dancing in the street. Oh, to have been there and to have it on film.

I wonder how I would weave these elements into a whole. As I walk east along President Street from my studio in Harrison Street, memories tumble. I am a little boy, just five years old, holding my mother's hand on the way to shop at OK Bazaars, stopping and gaping at the giant mechanical Santa that rolls and laughs at the entrance to Publix. When did Publix disappear? Then, after, to the treat of tea and scones with cream and strawberry jam at John Orr's, where she meets with friends. When we pass the tearoom bioscopes with the narrow stairways that lead up to Sodom and Gomorrah, her grip on my hand tightens. 'Dovid. You never go in there. Promise me.'

'I promise, Mom.'

I am six and there is no need to hold Mom's had. I am a big boy now. We cross Rissik Street to pass the store that displays *velskoene* on the pavement. We have to walk around them. A man steps out of a doorway, snaps a photo and hands Mom a card that she carefully puts in her handbag. Next week, if it's any good, she will collect and pay for it at Happy Snaps, next door to the *velskoene*. When she gets home, she will carefully paste it into the old family album she brought from across the world. If the photo is no good, the next time we pass and the man steps out from behind the shoes to take a snap, Mom will snap back: 'Why you took such a terrible picture of my Dovid?' Of course, it never happens that way, but my film has to have some comedy.

Mom, the shoes, the photographer, the café bios and Publix are long gone. Everywhere, memories embrace me. This is Joburg and no place is like it.

When I am eight, I take the tram that goes through to Malvern and Bez Valley to visit Auntie Molly and Uncle Harry in their café on Bezuidenhout Street, Troyeville, across the road from the Regal Bioscope, where I get off. I am not allowed to cross the road, but I can read what's now showing on the poster plastered outside – *Miracle on 34th Street*. The poster features Santa Claus hugging a young girl. Their names are Edmund Gwenn and Natalie Wood. The movie is late coming to the suburbs and the Santa looks a lot like the one I saw at Publix. I am familiar with Edmund Gwenn from *Hills of Home*, a Lassie film to which Mom and Dad take me at the Metro in town. Mom and Dad think Lassie films are not to be missed but are never convinced to own a dog, no matter how clever. It is way past Christmas and my movie miracles are at the Regal, which I am forbidden ever to enter. It's a bughouse, worse even than the Plaza. Only gangsters live in Troyeville, apart from my aunt and uncle and my cousin Sike. I love the café for the penny Nestlés and milkshakes that are free. The café features a milk bar and a display rack of comics. Behind the counter are the sweets, cigarettes, boxes of Black Magic. Later, Dad will fetch me, when he comes from work. I remember all the other cafés that I have frequented with such fondness, like the one at the bus terminus in Loveday Street from Emmarentia, my alternative bus route from Greenside when I am in my teens. I sit at the milk bar on a rotating bar stool and watch a man make and serve me a toasted cheese-and-tomato sandwich.

I discover Plotty's by chance only when I am an adult sharing a studio with John Meyer. It becomes our daily haunt. Plotty's is two blocks away from Victory House, located between Loveday and Harrison in Pritchard Street. John, who is half-Irish, half-Afrikaans and hails from Klerksdorp, has an instant love affair with hot beef on rye. Mr Plotkin is an expansive host with a twinkling sense of humour. He deserves a movie of his own. Plotty's trade depends heavily on bus drivers and conductors and is the secret haunt of lawyers and accountants whose offices are mainly south, in Loveday Street where it continues over the City Hall that squats between. They come in tight-lipped, maintaining one of Joburg's best-kept secrets. There is no better place to eat. The café is a long room divided by a counter on the left as one goes in.

At the door sits Mrs Plotkin, manning the till. She suffers from Parkinson's disease and one has to be patient as she shakily deals with the bill. At front are displayed, as in my aunt and uncle's café, arrays of sweets. But there is more to have. There are kitschy ornamental cruets for mustard and ketchup that look like hamburgers and hot dogs, and elegant porcelain ladies in exaggerated poses of swooning and dancing, which are sometimes lamps. All to be had. This is the impulse-buying end of the establishment. Alas, they have no plaster flying ducks diminishing in size for the real collector. Behind the counter at the front, behind the till and Mrs Plotkin, are the cigarettes, pipe tobacco, pipes, pipe cleaner, boxes of Lion matches, Ronson cigarette lighters, lighter fluid – whatever one needs or craves. This blends into the short-order food section equipped with fryers and toasters manned by three cooks. There is a row of bar stools facing the counter, standard for such eateries. It is Keith Maisels, a lawyer, who introduces me the joy that is Plotty's.

From the entrance on the right to the back are a number of booths with plump, red-leather padded seats, seating four diners over a particleboard table of a mottled white-and-red veneer edged with metal. Durable and built to last forever. At the back wall, behind which is the kitchen, there is a payphone in constant use by the drivers and conductors. I hear that Plotty lends them money. I surmise that the front-of-shop display is there mostly for these guys, to buy last-minute presents for their wives for an anniversary almost forgotten. I bet these are sold on tick while Mrs Plotkin keeps a painful tally of the debts. Mr Plotkin is a born comic.

When John and I are installed in a booth and we have exchanged our hellos, he says, 'Dov? Maybe some chopped liver made with my own hands, on rye freshly baked? I was up all night. John, can I maybe tempt you with a fried sole, caught fresh from the Zoo Lake this morning with my own hands? No? The hot beef is as good as yesterday. But brought from my home kitchen this morning?'

Plotty is a busy guy and must get little sleep. I bring all my colleagues and friends to this amazing eatery. I am close to Marshall and Kate Lee, two journalists. Marshall and I do a book together called *The Flower Bunch*. He writes and I draw. Kate is a model and editor and writes for the supplement to the *Rand Daily Mail* called 'Eve'. Marshall hails from Durban and Kate is London-born and -bred. Neither has ever experienced a kosher deli. They come into this Licorice Allsorts dive surrounded by men in blue uniforms talking loudly and men in suits conversing quietly and confidentially. Plotty comes over, always happy to welcome new customers. He rubs his hands, ready to serve, and asks, 'What can I get you?'

The Lees are uneasy. I admit, the place looks like a dive. They look to me to bail them out. I take command and do the Plotkin sales pitch.

'Three hot beef on rye – you won't be sorry.'

Plotty comes quickly with the order, delivers it with a flourish and then goes to attend elsewhere. We look at our plates piled high and the aroma of hot beef tantalises. It comes served with coleslaw and sliced pickled cucumber. Jewish boy heaven. Marshall and I tuck in but Kate, a Joanna Lumley-type beauty, studies her plate with unease.

'What's the matter?' I ask as my saliva glands go into overdrive.

'Does this bread have caraway seeds?' she asks.

I wave to Mr Plotkin and immediately have his attention. He comes over, the picture of concern.

'Dov, something is wrong?'

'Mr Plotkin, does this bread have caraway seeds?' I ask, like I would know a caraway from a bird.

'Of course. What is rye bread without caraway seeds?'

Kate looks up from her plate, her sky-blue eyes fixed on Plotty.

'I don't eat caraway seeds,' she says quietly.

Mr Plotkin lets out a big sigh and folds his hands over his apron. He looks Kate up, then down, then up again and, having studied her like a student studies a model at art school before he starts to draw, says, 'For you, [a pause], I'll take out the caraway seeds.'

Kate is back in London somewhere, Marshall is gone, and alas so is Plotty's. Memories linger there. Diagonally across the road from Plotty's is SA Arts and Crafts where I buy nibs and India ink. A block away in Kerk is Yardleys, where I go in my teens to buy glue and aeroplane dope for my figurines. I go with Mot who buys another model-plane kit that he plans to construct with Sike, who is a master of balsa and tissue paper. Yardleys is where I buy my first Joseph Rogers penknife. Gone. Heading back to the studio, on the corner of Loveday and President streets, is Hyde Brothers, from whom I once buy a jacket. All gone. At the corner of Harrison and President facing west is what I call The East. It is a short stretch of President Street beyond the library and museum. Every centimetre is crammed with delight. My movie must start or end here.

Every other day I walk over to *The Star* to deliver drawings for some supplement or other. It is all of two city blocks from Victory House. I amble through the Library Gardens, which stirs a gentle reminiscence of the days when I am eleven and have a card that entitles me to take out two books I must to return in two weeks. Walking up those grand steps into this imposing structure always gives me a sense of such privilege. There, too, is the Afrikaner Museum, with a Voortrekker wagon on display. Look but don't touch. The day my cards are swopped from the Children's Library Card to an adult one is a day of pride, like having won some award at school.

Behind the library is the Gateway to the East. On the right is the Argus building, the offices of *The Star*. On the opposite corner is the Bank of Lisbon monolith, a building Sike designed. Beyond that, Little India beckons. Here is where my movie begins or ends.

Day. The camera tracks slowly down the channel created by two massive buildings as we enter the alleyway. The crazy city just across Sauer magically disappears. We are past the gritted, uncompromising concrete, the hectic panicked tick-tock of the heavy-treading deadlines, lorries and trucks that constantly pour from *The Star* building with bales of newspaper that come out in a constant stream. There is the morning edition, then the afternoon, and then the late. The sound of the never-ceasing press drowns out every other sound, then we pass quickly beyond the fuss and thunder. We move in slow motion to blunder, to stumble and tumble into the humble jumble of the beckoning bargains.

First, we pass what appears to be an abandoned building with billboards of films long forgotten on the left. Next door, on the corner, is a small, busy café serving impatient customers. We cross Kort Street as we move in ultra-slow motion. Welcome to Little India. Here something exotic and magical is always on offer, like Aladdin's lamp, a bottle with a genie inside, and we don't really care if it is made in Taiwan. Is this a genuine flying carpet? Is that a really a morning in a bowl of night? We look deep into the third eyes, a dab of paint above on the brow, promising a third off silk, embroidery and tapestry hand-sewn in monasteries, ashrams, spun by Mahatmas, fable and fabric, weave and wonder, all are here. Voices echo over each other in whispered contest. 'Please, sir, how may we help you?' 'A bargain.' 'Two for one.' 'I give you good discount.' The sound blurs as we move into the bright fabrics everywhere.

Music over. 'Stranger in Paradise' from the musical *Kismet*. Borrowed din from Borodin, as *Time* magazine once called it. It is the original classical Polovtsian Dances played on balalaikas we hear. The colour is enhanced Technicolor as we intercut with scenes from *The Thief of Bagdad* of the cheeky Sabu running through the marketplace, all slowed down. We cut back to women in colourful saris and others mysterious behind black burkas. The building on the right is painted a bright aquamarine and across the road all is shaded by an awning that stretches to Diagonal Street. The shaded part is subdued, in sharp contrast to its heavy-peddling neighbours across the street. We are swept to a slower, gentler rhythm. Diagonal Street marks the end of the enchanted alley, less than a hundred metres. It all ends at the corner facing the Diamond Building, a giant inverted blue mason's chisel made of reflecting glass designed to trample our dreams. But we quickly go into reverse and move up instead of down the street. We go back to the café on the corner and pan up to a sign. It reads 'Starlite Café'. We move into the street and pan to the silent, derelict building. We see that it is not quite abandoned as a few men step out. We zoom back to read a large, well-worn sign above. Starlite Cinema.

CUT.

Even in writing this, I have almost slipped right past the Starlite.

Of all the bughouses in all the suburbs, in all the towns, my premiere has to be here?

Where else?

CHAPTER 84

Starlite Memories

Stardust Memories (1980). A semi-autobiographical film, a box-office flop by Woody Allen.

There is no red carpet waiting outside the Starlite. It is just Moe and Hennie lounging in their usual casuals. I am relieved that I gave up the idea of a tie for the occasion. I have no idea what awaits me inside. Is the press going to be there? Maybe Barry Ronge or Peter Feldman waiting outside, pad and pen at the ready for a snap interview before they run back across the road and make sure that the news is really hot off the press?

There is to be no award ceremony, no acceptance speeches, pleas to save the whale, the rhino, the economy, the poor, the hungry, longing to be free, no interviews, no photos to sign for adoring fans wanting a moment with the creator. There is absolutely nothing to disturb the order of this very ordinary morning.

Moe, Hennie and I exchange greetings. It has been some time since we saw each other last. Even as they see me, they step inside. I check my watch. It is ten minutes to curtain time. There are no tickets waiting for us at the cashier. I find myself standing in a loose line of black men who shamble in, without much purpose or order, but in a casual nonchalance. None demonstrate any surprise at seeing a white man in this strictly black venue.

I find myself paying for my own ticket. Stupidly, I ask the cashier, 'Are these seats reserved or can one sit anywhere?'

This must be the dumbest question she has heard in her many years of service. What is a white man doing here in the first place? She pauses for the briefest moment to look me over.

'You can sit everywhere.'

Moe and Louis, already inside, have kept a seat for me. We sit in the back row of what is a small hall. Another movie is just finishing. The lights in here are anything but dim.

What hits me in a wave is the total informality of it all. This is a café bio at street level. The movies here are continuous.

You pay, you stay for the day. Have it your own way.

There is no anticipation or contemplation of what came before or what comes next. The movie is incidental. People walk in and out in a constant stream. The show is no more than a backdrop, a kind of visual muzak, to which no attention is paid whatsoever. This is a place to socialise. A place to put up your feet. Literally.

Everywhere I see *laydik-gayers*.

But this crowd does not go about hands in pockets by choice. These are the unemployed whose week begins with the search for work. Here is where they gather to pick up possible leads on a job. To use the old-fashioned polite Dickensian reference to the jobseeker, they are seeking 'a situation'. It is like a bus depot where people are just waiting for something better to come along. Everywhere sit men with their feet up over the edge of the row in front. Others stand up and call loudly to friends seated elsewhere, their silhouettes like cut-outs on the screen. Some have their backs to the screen, and they occupy two seats, the top of one on which to sit, and the seat of the one behind as a footrest, as they talk with friends seated further back. The conversations are loud. Nowhere is the convention of the hushed whisper employed.

There is no shushing, no do-you-mind-we're-trying-to-watch-a-movie-here.

The air is thick with cigarette smoke and the unmistakable aroma of weed.

Elsewhere, others use the seat next to them as a picnic table as they share some Russians and chips, from Pops McGee's, no doubt. None of the ancient conventions and rituals of the great white movie houses applies here.

Gone is the ceremony of dimming the lights. There is no curtain to go up. The lights remain at an even dimness throughout. There is little darkness in here.

I look over to Moe and Hennie. This is not a new experience for them. They are very laid back. I realise they have been here before – at least twice. Hennie is probably a regular.

How does it work in here? Like a café bio? Is there a free drink? Is there a popcorn machine? I might have missed it as I came in.

It is obvious that the Starlite is not exactly the Roxy, the Ritz or the Metro. Did *The Best Days of Our Lives* ever show here, I wonder? Is there to be no fanfare whatsoever? Will a manager in a tuxedo and bowtie perhaps suddenly appear in a spotlight in front of the screen to announce this important event?

But this is not going to be any kind of occasion whatsoever.

Eleven thirty on a Monday morning.

What was I expecting? This is Monday mourning, the binge of the weekend lost to the sobriety of deadlines and schedules. Heigh-ho! It's back to work we go.

I spot someone in a uniform, arms folded, fast asleep, sitting in a corner using the wall as a pillow. Is this to be my audience?

CHAPTER 85

The Greatest Show on Earth
(1952)

Betty Hutton and Cornel Wilde are trapeze artists competing for the centre ring in the Ringling Bros and Barnum & Bailey's circuses. Charlton Heston stars as the circus manager.

The first thing that strikes me is the music score and that we go straight into the action. Zoom away from the signage – The International Diamond Co. – to reveal the security guard, Popeye, in his uniform and cap.

Enter Furtive Frank. The music score is a short loop that quickly becomes an irritant. It is active and frenetic and tries to marry to the action. But instead of being carried into the fantasy, I am remembering every detail of the slog to get things in place.

Popeye's wardrobe, his nightstick, are only there due to my hard work.

As I watch, so the props list grows. There is a metal security box that is handcuffed to the wrist of a courier. The case is a portable metal filing cabinet, something I purchase at the beginning of my freelance career and that now just adds more junk to the space I call my studio at home.

Also, I am seeing how the movie has been cut and, so far, it all works rather well.

Every moment takes me to the shoot. But it is all surprisingly good, though Getaway Gus, drumming away at the steering wheel of my car, still looks pissed off.

There is a shift towards silence in the audience as the dialogue comes on and more attention is paid to what is being said on the big screen. The titles come in after the first flurry of action with a song called 'Timer Joe', the lyrics of which are in English. 'Jabu and Connie are back in *Timer Joe*. Whoa! Whoa!' There has been a lot going on in post-production. I am impressed.

From the back, we can gauge the laughs, the oohs and aahs that hopefully our offering will evoke. And suddenly, I realise we are in a room full of critics.

How will they accept our offering?

The title drawings appear. I remember labouring lovingly over each one. I watch everything with a sense of displacement, an inability to see the whole, as it was intended. It feels like watching home movies, something with which one is totally familiar.

Just reading the opening shot, which is just some signage, has its story. What is on the cutting floor but never actually shot is me calling out, 'Hey! Where's the signage? Didn't anyone get a sign made?'

I remember my frantic call to my mate Cliff Webb.

'Does anyone have any Prestik? How are we going to stick that to the door? Where the hell is the nearest CNA?'

And so my viewing of it all goes. I am standing in the stockyard calling Frank to give up the running and walk back. I am back in the Oriental Plaza chasing down a knife.

Every moment triggers another memory. And when Jabu comes on, I am swept away by the genius he brings to everything. The audience knows and loves him. There are peals of delighted laughter and loud, shouted comments at the screen and across the room as the critics confer in their own way.

The special effects sequence, which is supposed to evoke a big laugh, brings the room to a stunned silence. The illusion is lost as the audience takes the car running up the side of a building to skip over undamaged as a testament to Volkswagen and their superior automotive engineering skills.

Jabu turns the business of switching on a radio into a lesson in the art of making a prop a comedy partner. He is like Fred Astaire with a coat rack, Gene Kelly with an umbrella.

The audience hoots and whistles. I know I am projecting, but it feels as if, around me, the place comes alive with an energy that lifts me with something hopeful.

Does Jabulani Masondo end up bitter like Al Debbo? Bitter about the bastards Mankowitz and Basson, who get rich on his back? I wonder again how much he was paid.

Beside me, Moe chomps more vigorously on his gum as the laughter grows. Perhaps he is counting box-office receipts.

As I leave the Starlite, I turn back for one last look at the screen.

Was that really a movie I made up there? The traffic backs up at the exit. I catch a Kodak moment as I see Coach standing, talking excitedly to a bunch of guys somewhere near the front of the house, the seats we would fight over in my childhood – as close to the action as possible.

Our eyes lock, and he shows me a hand signal that needs no translation.

It is just a thumbs up.

THE END

ACKNOWLEDGEMENTS

I began *Starlite Memories* over a decade ago when my reputation was of someone who never completes anything. My bottom drawer is filled with unfulfilled promises, and this manuscript could easily have become yet another one.

After a near-death experience in 2019, I knew I had to finish this book.

Every book needs a captivating first line and that I had. But the rest was chaos. I needed help.

My middle daughter Joanne is an internationally bestselling author and publisher who mentors writers. She took me on as one of her students. She taught me that good writing is editing. She was also committed to publishing it – as long as it was 'good,' and not out of *rachmonis* (pity).

After years of stern mentoring and rewriting, she told me, 'Dad, this book is good, but it needs an editor. Leave it to me.'

And that is how the brilliant Karin Schimke came into my life. Karin edited the manuscript with such precision and care. I followed her suggestions to the letter. Her overwhelming enthusiasm for the book prompted her to share it with a publisher at Tafelberg, where Erika Oosthuizen agreed to publish it.

I wondered in the dark days of Covid whether I would live to hold *Starlite Memories* in my hand.

I did and I have. It is a book I am immensely proud of.

It takes a village to raise a child. It takes women to rear them. Thanks to all my mothers - Joanne, Karin, Erika, Kristen and Jean from Tafelberg.

Enjoy our baby.

Dov Fedler, Johannesburg 2020

DOV FEDLER is one of South Africa's most beloved and pre-eminent political cartoonists. In 2016, he retired after a career of 50 years drawing for *The Star*, one of the country's leading daily newspapers.

He is also a sculptor, artist and author of his memoir *Out of Line* (2015) and *If You Can Write, You Can Draw* (Joanne Fedler Media, 2019). In 2015 he was honoured with the *Jewish Report*'s Art, Sport, Science and Culture award.

These days he spends his time writing and rewatching his favourite old movies.

www.ingramcontent.com/pod-product-compliance
Lightning Source LLC
Chambersburg PA
CBHW011316080526
44588CB00020B/2727